London

in Dickens' Day

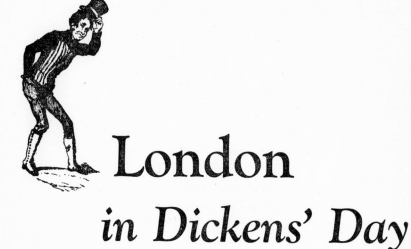

London
in Dickens' Day

edited by

Jacob Korg
University of Washington

Prentice-Hall, Inc.
Englewood Cliffs, N. J.

1960

The illustrations in this book are reprinted from *Phiz: Illustrations from the Novels of Charles Dickens* by Albert Johannsen by permission of The University of Chicago Press. © 1956 by The University of Chicago. Published 1956. Composed and printed by The University of Chicago Press, Chicago, Illinois, U.S.A.

PRINTED IN THE UNITED STATES OF AMERICA

54013

Contents

Introduction

THE LONDON that appears in Dickens' work is so characteristic of the novels themselves that it is likely to seem purely imaginary to the modern reader, a queer realm created by the novelist as a stage for his characters. These eye-witness reports about the life and customs of nineteenth-century London provide some facts to go with Dickens' fiction. Intended primarily to serve as sources for controlled research projects, either alone or in conjunction with one or more of Dickens' novels, they have the incidental value of showing that Dickens' accounts of London are, in the main, true to the life they portray. In addition, they offer the reader an opportunity to see something of the fictional imagination at work by enabling him to compare parts of Dickens' evocative and symbolic world with reportorial accounts of the raw material from which it was drawn.

While it has a special relevance to Dickens' novels, this collection is also designed to be used independently as a self-contained source of material on the largest, busiest and most intensely civilized city of the nineteenth century. Incredibly vast, complicated, and wealthy, London represented both the failures and the successes of nineteenth-century European civilization at their most extreme. It underwent many changes, of course, during the period spanned by these selections, which closely approximates the period of Dickens' career as a novelist. The first of these selections, one of Dickens' earliest compositions, was published about 1835, and the last appeared in 1872, two years after his death. Between those dates the diameter of the circle which formed a rough boundary for London grew from less than four to more than six miles, the city's population increased from two million to three and a half million, and many physical improvements accompanied this growth. On the whole, however, the development of these forty years consolidated instead of altering existing conditions. In spite of political and social reforms, the conditions of daily life in London, as in England generally, changed slowly, and in degree rather than in kind.

This continuity in the face of gradual change makes it possible to think of Dickens' London as a single unit, not static by any means, but recognizably the same throughout his writing career. In 1835, for example, it was a city of narrow streets and low houses with a few broad thoroughfares like Regent Street and Oxford Street; it retained the same character in 1872. In 1872, as in 1835, the West End of the city was the fashionable and residential quarter, while the Eastern part, called the City of London, or just "the City," was the commercial district. St. Giles', Clerkenwell, Whitechapel and many other areas which were slums in 1835 were still slums in 1872. Gas lighting for streets and large public buildings was well established by 1835; by 1872 it was the usual method of illumination and was being used in homes. The Londoners of 1835 travelled by carriages and horse-drawn omnibuses; in 1872 they were using improved versions of the same conveyances in greater numbers, and creating worse traffic jams with them. In 1872 the very rich and the very poor parts of the population lived in essentially the same quarters of the city they had inhabited in 1835, led the same sort of lives, carried on the same sort of occupations, and followed the same social customs, though their numbers had, of course, grown much larger.

The distinctive character of London was felt by Londoners and foreigners alike, but because of the city's size and diversity, no writer claimed to be able to formulate it accurately. These selections, obviously, cannot make that claim either. They leave much untold. But they do enable the student to develop coherent and reliable information about a few of the aspects of life in the London that Dickens knew. They focus upon such topics as social customs, transportation, manners, and crime and its correction, providing facts which the student can relate to each other to form a vivid general impression of his own.

For example, the selections contain many references to the ways in which Londoners bought and sold goods. Retail institutions ranged from the open market at Covent Garden described by Saunders and Platt through the humble neighborhood shops described by Boz to the handsome clothing and drapers' establishments which appear in Dodd's account, the latter staffed, no doubt, by the class of superior shop-assistant so vividly described by Wey. Similarly, the student will encounter many related facts in the material about crime, its prevention and its punishment. The boy pickpockets of the kind whose training is described by Mayhew appear in court in the article "London Sparrows" from *Household Words*, and we learn, from a casual warning given by a shopkeeper to Taine as he wandered through Shadwell, that they were a constant menace. The numerous facts and observations about the position of women in Victorian society suggest a third research topic. Wey, in reporting the freedom enjoyed by the English girls, makes it easy to understand why they should have the natural, athletic bearing observed by Taine, and why they should be willing to face hard lives by following their husbands to India or marrying on modest incomes; but the same facts also suggest some reasons for the high proportion of criminals among women, as reported by Knight.

While the student does not have to know Dickens' work to make use of this book, any one of the novels containing London scenes will provide a valuable research supplement to it. For example, the reader who knows Dickens will recognize in the wine warehouses mentioned by Taine as a part of London's busy waterfront the originals of such places as the firm of Murdstone and Grinby, where little David Copperfield worked. He will find in Max Schlesinger's comment about the Englishman's habitual indifference to the comforts of the place where he does business an explanation for the picturesque disorder of the offices of Spenlow and Jorkins in *David Copperfield*, Mr. Dombey in *Dombey and Son,* and Jaggers in *Great Expectations.* G. Dodd's survey of the eating-places characteristic of London covers the classes of restaurants which include the "Slap-Bang" where Guppy, Jobling, and Smallweed dine in the twentieth chapter of *Bleak House,* and the pudding-shops where David Copperfield buys his dinners as a London waif. A visit to the theater-circus known as Astley's occurs in Chapter 39 of *The Old Curiosity Shop;* Dickens described this place earlier, in one of the *Sketches by Boz* reprinted here, from a somewhat different point of view. Mayhew's description of the pickpockets' school exactly parallels the methods employed in Fagin's den in *Oliver Twist;* Taine's description of Shadwell supports Dickens' description of Tom-All-Alone's in *Bleak House;* and J. C. Platt's report on the prisons of the time, with its statistical information, is relevant to the prison experiences of Pickwick, Micawber and Dorrit.

Perhaps even more significant than the factual reports of Dickensian scenes are the comments about the character and psychology of the sorts of people who appear in his books. Schlesinger's comparison of the London thief with the Italian bandit sheds light on the character of Bill Sikes in *Oliver Twist.* The comfortably omniscient detective who solves the burglary in "The Modern Science of Thief-Taking" is obviously a real-life counterpart of Inspector Bucket in *Bleak House.* Emerson's report that the English family is exceptionally self-contained and Taine's conversation with the Englishman who professes to value domesticity provide points of departure for Dickens' caricature of the Pecksniffs in *Martin Chuzzlewit,* just as Taine's account of the rigidity of household rules in comfortable families suggests a basis for the exaggerated figures of Mr. Dombey and Mr. Murdstone.

As the work of responsible and perceptive men trying to relay their impressions accurately, these reports bring us as close to the truth of a past time as we can come. But this does not mean that they are coldly factual. On the contrary, the reader will notice that they contain many interpretations and evaluations, both overt and implied, which reflect personal judgment, national taste, prejudice, or even ignorance. The opinions of a Frenchman like Taine about the coldness of English family life cannot be taken at face value. Allowances must be made for the attitudes the observer brings with him. It is fair to say that an opinion tells as much about the writer as it does about the facts he is evaluating. Some readers will find that the opinions expressed in these readings are as interesting as the facts in them, and may wish to treat them as research topics. The important thing is to remember that here, as in all research sources, facts and opinions have different values and must be carefully distinguished from each other.

NOTE. The selections have been reprinted in chronological order, without regard to their subjects. Most of them are excerpts, and breaks made in a continuous text, either before, after, or in the middle of the selection, are indicated by ellipsis marks. The pagination of the originals has been indicated by putting the page number in brackets *before* the first word of the material found on that page. Hence, [4] occurring in the middle of a text means that the material following it is found on page 4 of the original.

CURRENCY VALUES. During this part of the nineteenth century, the British pound was worth about $4.68 and the French franc about $.20 in modern American dollars. Purchasing power was, of course, much greater for all three currencies during the nineteenth century.

from

Sketches by Boz: *Illustrative of Every-Day Life and Every-Day People*

Charles Dickens

THE PSEUDONYM "Boz" which Dickens signed to his early work was a comic mispronunciation of Moses, the pet name of one of his younger brothers. The *Sketches by Boz* were written between 1833 and 1835, while Dickens was working as a reporter, and were published in various periodicals. Born in Portsmouth in 1812, Dickens was the son of a minor government official who moved his family to London, where he ran up large debts. As a child, Dickens was educated at home, and allowed to roam the London streets which later became material for his novels. His family became so impoverished that the boy had to work in a warehouse for six months, and his father spent some time in debtors' prison, taking his family there to live with him, as was the custom, so that for a time Dickens' home was his father's cell. Later the family became relatively prosperous, and Dickens was able to go to a good school for a few years. After working as a law clerk and learning shorthand, Dickens became a reporter, taking down Parliamentary proceedings for later publication. His journalistic work was a natural outlet for his curiosity and love of observation, and it often took him on long trips to places where exciting political campaigns were occurring. It was during this time that he wrote the *Sketches by Boz*, which were published in book form in 1836 with illustrations by George

Cruikshank and Hablôt K. Browne. This first book was successful, and soon after its publication Dickens began work on *Pickwick Papers,* the first of the long series of novels which are among the most popular works of fiction ever written. *Sketches by Boz* has many of the qualities found in Dickens' later work. They are witty, incisive, and accurate as portrayals of actual conditions.

The Works of Charles Dickens, vol. XXVI.
New York: Charles Scribner's Sons, 1911.

Chapter I, The Streets—Morning.

[55] The appearance presented by the streets of London an hour before sunrise, on a summer's morning, is most striking even to the few whose unfortunate pursuits of pleasure, or scarcely less unfortunate pursuits of business, cause them to be well acquainted with the scene. There is an air of cold, solitary desolation about the noiseless streets which we are accustomed to see thronged at other times by a busy, eager crowd, and over the quiet, closely-shut buildings, which throughout the day are swarming with life and bustle, that is very impressive.

The last drunken man, who shall find his way home before sunlight, has just staggered heavily along, roaring out the burden of the drinking song of the previous night: the last houseless vagrant whom penury and police have left in the streets, has coiled up his chilly limbs in some paved corner, to dream of food and warmth. The drunken, the dissipated, and the wretched have disappeared; the more sober and orderly part of the population have not yet awakened to the labours of the day, and the stillness of death is over the streets; its very hue seems to be imparted to them, cold and lifeless as they look in the grey, sombre light of daybreak. [56] The coach-stands in the larger thoroughfares are deserted: the night-houses are closed; and the chosen promenades of profligate misery are empty.

An occasional policeman may alone be seen at the street corners, listlessly gazing on the deserted prospect before him; and now and then a rakish-looking cat runs stealthily across the road and descends his own area with as much caution and slyness—bounding first on the water-butt, then on the dust-hole, and then alighting on the flag-stones—as if he were conscious that his character depended on his gallantry of the preceding night escaping public observation. A partially opened bedroom-window here and there, bespeaks the heat of the weather, and the uneasy slumbers of its occupant; and the dim scanty flicker of the rushlight,* through the window-blind, denotes the cham-

* A candle made of the stem of one of various plants dipped in grease. It gave a dim light and was used for temporary lighting.

ber of watching or sickness. With these few exceptions, the streets present no signs of life, nor the houses of habitation.

An hour wears away; the spires of the churches and roofs of the principal buildings are faintly tinged with the light of the rising sun; and the streets, by almost imperceptible degrees, begin to resume their bustle and animation. Marketcarts roll slowly along: the sleepy waggoner impatiently urging on his tired horses, or vainly endeavouring to awaken the boy, who, luxuriously stretched on the top of the fruitbaskets, forgets, in happy oblivion, his long-cherished curiosity to behold the wonders of London.

Rough, sleepy-looking animals of strange appearance, something between ostlers and hackney-coachmen,* begin to take down the shutters of early public-houses; and little deal † tables, with the ordinary preparations for a street breakfast, make their appearance at the customary stations. Numbers of men and women (principally the latter), carrying upon their heads heavy baskets of fruit, toil down the park side of Piccadilly, on their way to Covent-garden, and, following each other in rapid succession, form a long straggling line from thence to the turn of the road at Knightsbridge.

[57] Here and there, a bricklayer's labourer, with the day's dinner tied up in a handkerchief, walks briskly to his work, and occasionally a little knot of three or four schoolboys on a stolen bathing expedition rattle merrily over the pavement, their boisterous mirth contrasting forcibly with the demeanour of the little sweep,‡ who, having knocked and rung till his arm aches, and being interdicted by a merciful legislature from endangering his lungs by calling out, sits patiently down on the door-step, until the housemaid may happen to awake.

Covent-garden market, and the avenues leading to it, are thronged with carts of all sorts, sizes, and descriptions, from the heavy lumbering waggon, with its four stout horses, to the jingling costermonger's§ cart, with its consumptive donkey. The pavement is already strewed with decayed cabbage-leaves, broken hay-bands, and all the indescribable litter of a vegetable market; men are shouting, carts backing, horses neighing, boys fighting, basket-women talking, piemen expatiating on the excellence of their pastry, and donkeys braying. These and a hundred other sounds form a compound discordant enough to a Londoner's ears, and remarkably disagreeable to those of country gentlemen who are sleeping at the Hummums‖ for the first time.

Another hour passes way, and the day begins in good earnest. The servant of all work, who, under the plea of sleeping very soundly, has utterly dis-

---

* Ostlers were men who took care of horses. Hackney coachmen were drivers of hired carriages.

† Fir or pine cut into planks at least seven inches wide and three inches thick.

‡ A chimney-sweep—a boy who climbed into chimneys to clean them.

§ A costermonger is a peddler who sells fruit and vegetables in the streets.

‖ Hummums, the name of an old Turkish Bath in Covent Garden, later became attached to an inn that stood on the same site.

regarded "Missis's" ringing for half an hour previously, is warned by Master
(whom Missis has sent up in his drapery to the landing-place for that purpose), that it's half-past six, whereupon she awakes all of a sudden, with
well-feigned astonishment, and goes down-stairs very sulkily, wishing, while
she strikes a light, that the principle of spontaneous combustion would extend itself to coals and kitchen range. When the fire is lighted, she opens
the street-door to take in the milk, when, by the most singular coincidence
in the world, she discovers that the servant next door has just taken in her
milk too, and that Mr. Todd's young man over the way, is, by an [58]
equally extraordinary chance, taking down his master's shutters. The inevitable consequence is, that she just steps, milk-jug in hand, as far as next
door, just to say "good morning" to Betsy Clark, and that Mr. Todd's young
man just steps over the way to say "good morning" to both of 'em; and as
the aforesaid Mr. Todd's young man is almost as good-looking and fascinat-
ing as the baker himself, the conversation quickly becomes very interesting,
and probably would become more so, if Betsy Clark's Missis, who always will
be a-followin' her about, didn't give an angry tap at her bedroom window, on
which Mr. Todd's young man tries to whistle coolly, as he goes back to his
shop much faster than he came from it; and the two girls run back to their
respective places, and shut their street-doors with surprising softness, each of
them poking their heads out of the front parlour window, a minute afterwards, however, ostensibly with the view of looking at the mail which just
then passes by, but really for the purpose of catching another glimpse of Mr.
Todd's young man, who being fond of mails, but more of females, takes a
short look at the mails, and a long look at the girls, much to the satisfaction
of all parties concerned.

The mail itself goes on to the coach-office in due course, and the passengers
who are going out by the early coach, stare with astonishment at the passengers who are coming in by the early coach, who look blue and dismal, and
are evidently under the influence of that odd feeling produced by travelling,
which makes the events of yesterday morning seem as if they had happened
at least six months ago, and induces people to wonder with considerable
gravity whether the friends and relations they took leave of a fortnight before, have altered much since they have left them. The coach-office is all
alive, and the coaches which are just going out, are surrounded by the usual
crowd of Jews and nondescripts, who seem to consider, Heaven knows why,
that it is quite impossible any man can mount a coach without requiring at
least sixpenny-worth of oranges, a penknife, a pocket-book, a last year's [59]
annual, a pencil-case, a piece of sponge, and a small series of caricatures.

Half an hour more, and the sun darts his bright rays cheerfully down the
still half-empty streets, and shines with sufficient force to rouse the dismal
laziness of the apprentice, who pauses every other minute from his task of
sweeping out the shop and watering the pavement in front of it, to tell another apprentice similarly employed, how hot it will be today, or to stand
with his right hand shading his eyes, and his left resting on the broom, gazing

at the "Wonder," or the "Tally-ho," or the "Nimrod," or some other fast
coach, till it is out of sight, when he re-enters the shop, envying the passengers
on the outside of the fast coach, and thinking of the old red brick house
"down in the country," where he went to school: the miseries of the milk and
water, and thick bread and scrapings, fading into nothing before the pleasant
recollection of the green field the boys used to play in, and the green pond
he was caned for presuming to fall into, and other schoolboy associations.

Cabs, with trunks and band-boxes between the drivers' legs and outside
the apron, rattle briskly up and down the streets on their way to the coach-
offices or steam-packet wharfs; and the cab-drivers and hackney-coachmen
who are on the stand polish up the ornamental part of their dingy vehicles
—the former wondering how people can prefer "them wild beast cariwans of
homnibuses, to a riglar cab with a fast trotter," and the latter admiring how
people can trust their necks into one of "them crazy cabs, when they can
have a 'spectable 'ackney cotche with a pair of 'orses as von't run away
with no vun;" a consolation unquestionably founded on fact, seeing that a
hackney-coach horse never was known to run at all, "except," as the smart
cabman in front of the rank observes, "except one, and *he* run back'ards."

The shops are now completely opened, and apprentices and shopmen are
busily engaged in cleaning and decking the windows for the day. The bakers'
shops in town are filled [60] with servants and children waiting for the drawing of the first batch of rolls—an operation which was performed a full hour
ago in the suburbs; for the early clerk population of Somers and Camden
towns, Islington, and Pentonville, are fast pouring into the city, or directing
their steps towards Chancery-lane and the Inns of Court. Middle-aged men,
whose salaries have by no means increased in the same proportion as their
families, plod steadily along, apparently with no object in view but the
counting-house; knowing by sight almost everybody they meet or overtake,
for they have seen them every morning (Sundays excepted) during the last
twenty years, but speaking to no one. If they do happen to overtake a personal acquaintance, they just exchange a hurried salutation, and keep walking on either by his side, or in front of him, as his rate of walking may
chance to be. As to stopping to shake hands, or to take the friend's arm, they
seem to think that as it is not included in their salary, they have no right to
do it. Small office lads in large hats, who are made men before they are boys,
hurry along in pairs, with their first coat carefully brushed, and the white
trousers of last Sunday plentifully besmeared with dust and ink. It evidently
requires a considerable mental struggle to avoid investing part of the day's
dinner-money in the purchase of the stale tarts so temptingly exposed in
dusty tins at the pastry-cooks' doors; but a consciousness of their own importance and the receipt of seven shillings a-week, with the prospect of an
early rise to eight, comes to their aid, and they accordingly put their hats a
little more on one side, and look under the bonnets of all the milliners' and
staymakers' apprentices they meet—poor girls!—the hardest worked, the
worst paid, and too often, the worst used class of the community.

Eleven o'clock, and a new set of people fill the streets. The goods in the shop-windows are invitingly arranged; the shopmen in their white necker-chiefs and spruce coats, look as if they couldn't clean a window if their lives depended on [61] it; the carts have disappeared from Covent-garden; the waggoners have returned, and the costermongers repaired to their ordinary "beats" in the suburbs; clerks are at their offices, and gigs, cabs, omnibuses, and saddle-horses, are conveying their masters to the same destination. The streets are thronged with a vast concourse of people, gay and shabby, rich and poor, idle and industrious; and we come to the heat, bustle, and activity of Noon.

Chapter II, The Streets—Night.

[62] But the streets of London, to be beheld in the very height of their glory, should be seen on a dark, dull, murky winter's night, when there is just enough damp gently stealing down to make the pavement greasy, without cleansing it of any of its impurities; and when the heavy lazy mist, which hangs over every object, makes the gas-lamps look brighter, and the bril-liantly-lighted shops more splendid, from the contrast they present to the darkness around. All the people who are at home on such a night as this, seem disposed to make themselves as snug and comfortable as possible; and the passengers in the streets have excellent reason to envy the fortunate individuals who are seated by their own firesides. . . .

[64] Flat-fish, oyster, and fruit vendors linger hopelessly in the kennel, in vain endeavouring to attract customers; and the ragged boys who usually disport themselves about the streets, stand crouched in little knots in some projecting doorway, or under the canvas blind of a cheesemonger's, where great flaring gas-lights, unshaded by any glass, display huge piles of bright red and pale yellow cheeses, mingled with little fivepenny dabs of dingy bacon, various tubs of weekly Dorset, and cloudy rolls of "best fresh."

Here they amuse themselves with theatrical converse, arising out of their last half-price visit to the Victoria gallery, admire the terrific combat, which is nightly encored, and expatiate on the inimitable manner in which Bill Thompson can "come the double monkey," or go through the mysterious involutions of a sailor's hornpipe.

It is nearly eleven o'clock, and the cold thin rain which has been drizzling so long, is beginning to pour down in good earnest; the baked-potato man has departed—the kidney-pie man has just walked away with his warehouse on his arm—the cheesemonger has drawn in his blind, and the boys have dis-persed. The constant clicking of pattens on the [65] slippy and uneven pave-ment, and the rustling of umbrellas, as the wind blows against the shop-windows, bear testimony to the inclemency of the night; and the policeman, with his oilskin cape buttoned closely round him, seems as he holds his hat on his head, and turns round to avoid the gust of wind and rain which drives against him at the street-corner, to be very far from congratulating himself on the prospect before him.

The little chandler's shop* with the cracked bell behind the door, whose melancholy tinkling has been regulated by the demand for quarterns of sugar and half-ounces of coffee, is shutting up. The crowds which have been passing to and fro during the whole day, are rapidly dwindling away; and the noise of shouting and quarreling which issues from the public-houses, is almost the only sound that breaks the melancholy stillness of the night.

There was another, but it has ceased. That wretched woman with the infant in her arms, round whose meagre form the remnant of her own scanty shawl is carefully wrapped, has been attempting to sing some popular ballad, in the hope of wringing a few pence from the compassionate passer-by. A brutal laugh at her weak voice is all she has gained. The tears fall thick and fast down her own pale face; the child is cold and hungry, and its low half-stifled wailing adds to the misery of its wretched mother, as she moans aloud, and sinks despairingly down, on a cold damp door-step.

Singing! How few of those who pass such a miserable creature as this, think of the anguish of heart, the sinking of soul and spirit, which the very effort of singing produces. Bitter mockery! Disease, neglect, and starvation, faintly articulating the words of the joyous ditty, that has enlivened your hours of feasting and merriment, God knows how often! It is no subject of jeering. The weak tremulous voice tells a fearful tale of want and famishing; and the feeble singer of this roaring song may turn away, only to die of cold and hunger.

[66] One o'clock! Parties returning from the different theatres foot it through the muddy streets; cabs, hackney-coaches, carriages, and theatre omnibuses, roll swiftly by; watermen† with dim dirty lanterns in their hands, and large brass plates upon their breasts, who have been shouting and rushing about for the last two hours, retire to their watering-houses, to solace themselves with the creature comforts of pipes and purl; the half-price pit and box frequenters of the theatres throng to the different houses of refreshment; and chops, kidneys, rabbits, oysters, stout, cigars, and "goes" ‡ innumerable, are served up amidst a noise and confusion of smoking, running, knife-clattering, and waiter-chattering, perfectly indescribable.

The more musical portion of the play-going community betake themselves to some harmonic meeting. As a matter of curiosity let us follow them thither for a few moments.

In a lofty room of spacious dimensions, are seated some eighty or a hundred guests knocking little pewter measures on the tables, and hammering away, with the handles of their knives, as if they were so many trunk-makers. They are applauding a glee, which has just been executed by the three "professional gentlemen" at the top of the centre table, one of whom is in the chair—the

---

* A shop where candles and other household supplies were sold.
† Men who supplied the horses at the hackney-stands with water.
‡ A slang term meaning servings of food or drink.

little pompous man with the bald head just emerging from the collar of his green coat. The others are seated on either side of him—the stout man with the small voice, and the thin-faced dark man in black. The little man in the chair is a most amusing personage,—*such* condescending grandeur, and *such* a voice!

"Bass!" as the young gentleman near us with the blue stock forcibly remarks to his companion, "bass! I b'lieve you; he can go down lower than any man: so low sometimes that you can't hear him." And so he does. To hear him growling away, gradually lower and lower down, till he can't get back again, is the most delightful thing in the world, and it is quite impossible to witness unmoved the impressive [67] solemnity with which he pours forth his soul in "My 'art's in the 'ighlands," or "The brave old Hoak." The stout man is also addicted to sentimentality, and warbles "Fly, fly from the world, my Bessy, with me," or some such song, with lady-like sweetness, and in the most seductive tones imaginable.

"Pray give your orders, gen'l'm'n—pray give your orders,"—says the pale-faced man with the red head; and demands for "goes" of gin and "goes" of brandy, and pints of stout, and cigars of peculiar mildness, are vociferously made from all parts of the room. The "professional gentlemen" are in the very height of their glory, and bestow condescending nods, or even a word or two of recognition, on the better-known frequenters of the room, in the most bland and patronising manner possible.

That little round-faced man, with the small brown surtout,* white stockings and shoes, is in the comic line; the mixed air of self-denial, and mental consciousness of his own powers, with which he acknowledges the call of the chair, is particularly gratifying. "Gen'l'men," says the little pompous man, accompanying the word with a knock of the president's hammer on the table— "Gen'l'men, allow me to claim your attention—our friend, Mr. Smuggins, will oblige."—"Bravo!" shout the company; and Smuggins, after a considerable quantity of coughing by way of symphony, and a most facetious sniff or two, which afford general delight, sings a comic song, with a fal-de-ral—tol-de-ral chorus at the end of every verse, much longer than the verse itself. It is received with unbounded applause, and after some aspiring genius has volunteered a recitation, and failed dismally therein, the little pompous man gives another knock, and says "Gen'l'men, we will attempt a glee, if you please." This announcement calls forth tumultuous applause, and the more energetic spirits express the unqualified approbation it affords them, by knocking one or two stout glasses off their legs—a humorous device; but one which frequently occasions some slight altercation [68] when the form of paying the damage is proposed to be gone through by the waiter.

Scenes like these are continued until three or four o'clock in the morning; and even when they close, fresh ones open to the inquisitive novice. But as a description of all of them, however slight, would require a volume, the con-

* An overcoat.

tents of which, however instructive, would be by no means pleasing, we make our bow, and drop the curtain.

CHAPTER V, Seven Dials.*

. . . [82] The stranger who finds himself in "The Dials" for the first time, and stands Belzoni-like,† at the entrance of seven obscure passages, uncertain which to take, will see enough around him to keep his curiosity and attention awake for no inconsiderable time. From the irregular square into which he has plunged, the streets and courts dart in all directions, until they are lost in the unwholesome vapour which hangs over the house-tops, and renders the dirty perspective uncertain and confined; and lounging at every corner, as if they came there to take a few gasps of such fresh air as has found its way so far, but is too much exhausted already, to be enabled to force itself into the narrow alleys around, are groups of people, whose appearance and dwellings would fill any mind but a regular Londoner's with astonishment.

On one side, a little crowd has collected round a couple of ladies, who having imbibed the contents of various "three-outs" ‡ of gin and bitters in the course of the morning, have at length differed on some point of domestic arrangement, and are on the eve of settling the quarrel satisfactorily, by an appeal to blows, greatly to the interest of other ladies who live in the same house, and tenements adjoining, and who are all partisans on one side or other.

"Vy don't you pitch into her, Sarah?" exclaims one half-dressed matron, by way of encouragement. "Vy don't you? if *my* 'usband had treated her with a drain last night, unbeknown to me, I'd tear her precious eyes out—a wixen!"

"What's the matter, ma'am?" inquires another old woman, who has just bustled up to the spot.

"Matter!" replies the first speaker, talking *at* the obnoxious combatant, "matter! Here's poor dear Mrs. Sulliwin, as has five blessed children of her own, can't go out a charing for one arternoon, but what hussies must be a comin', and 'ticing avay her oun' 'usband, as she's been married to twelve year [83] come next Easter Monday, for I see the certificate ven I vas a drinkin' a cup o' tea vith her, only the werry last blessed Ven'sday as ever was sent. I 'appen'd to say promiscuously, 'Mrs. Sulliwin,' says I——"

"What do you mean by hussies?" interrupts a champion of the other party, who has evinced a strong inclination throughout to get up a branch fight on

* A London neighborhood, so called because it lay around a place where seven streets intersected, and where a pillar topped by a clock with seven dials once stood. It was a notorious slum neighborhood in Dickens' time.
† Belzoni was a strong man at Astley's circus.
‡ A three-out glass held a third of a quartern; a quartern is one-fourth of a pint.

her own account ("Hooroar," ejaculates a pot-boy* in parenthesis, "put the kye-bosk on her,† Mary!"), "What do you mean by hussies?" reiterates the champion.

"Niver mind," replies the opposition expressively, "niver mind; *you* go home, and, ven you're quite sober, mend your stockings."

This somewhat personal allusion, not only to the lady's habits of intemperance, but also to the state of her wardrobe, rouses her utmost ire, and she accordingly complies with the urgent request of the bystanders to "pitch in," with considerable alacrity. The scuffle became general, and terminates, in minor play-bill phraseology, with "arrival of the policemen, interior of the station-house, and impressive *dénouement*."

In addition to the numerous groups who are idling about the gin-shops and squabbling in the centre of the road, every post in the open space has its occupant, who leans against it for hours, with listless perseverance. It is odd enough that one class of men in London appear to have no enjoyment beyond leaning against posts. We never saw a regular bricklayer's labourer take any other recreation, fighting excepted. Pass through St. Giles's in the evening of a week-day, there they are in their fustian dresses, spotted with brick-dust and whitewash, leaning against posts. Walk through Seven Dials on Sunday morning; there they are again, drab or light corduroy trousers, Blucher boots, blue coats, and great yellow waistcoats, leaning against posts. The idea of a man dressing himself in his best clothes, to lean against a post all day!

The peculiar character of these streets, and the close resemblance each one bears to its neighbour, by no means [84] tends to decrease the bewilderment in which the unexperienced wayfarer through "the Dials" finds himself involved. He traverses streets of dirty, straggling houses, with now and then an unexpected court composed of buildings as ill-proportioned and deformed as the half-naked children that wallow in the kennels. Here and there, a little dark chandler's shop, with a cracked bell hung up behind the door to announce the entrance of a customer, or betray the presence of some young gentleman in whom a passion for shop tills has developed itself at an early age: others, as if for support, against some handsome lofty building, which usurps the place of a low dingy public-house; long rows of broken and patched windows expose plants that may have flourished when "the Dials" were built, in vessels as dirty as "the Dials" themselves; and shops for the purchase of rags, bones, old iron, and kitchen-stuff, vie in cleanliness with the bird-fanciers and rabbit-dealers, which one might fancy so many arks, but for the irresistible conviction that no bird in its proper senses, who was permitted to leave one of them, would ever come back again. Brokers' shops, which would seem to have been established by humane individuals, as refuges for destitute bugs, interspersed with announcements of day-schools, penny theatres, petition-writers, mangles, and music for balls or routs, complete the "still life" of the subject; and dirty men, filthy women, squalid children,

---

* A boy hired to serve the patrons of a tavern, and to carry drinks to outside customers.
† "Put the kibosh on" is a slang expression, still in use, which means to spoil or bewilder.

fluttering shuttlecocks, noisy battledores, reeking pipes, bad fruit, more than doubtful oysters, attenuated cats, depressed dogs, and anatomical fowls, are its cheerful accompaniments.

If the external appearance of the houses, or a glance at their inhabitants, present but few attractions, a closer acquaintance with either is little calculated to alter one's first impression. Every room has its separate tenant, and every tenant is, by the same mysterious dispensation which causes a country curate to "increase and multiply" most marvellously, generally the head of a numerous family.

The man in the shop, perhaps, is in the baked "jemmy" * [85] line, or the fire-wood and hearth-stone line, or any other line which requires a floating capital of eighteen-pence or thereabouts: and he and his family live in the shop, and the small back parlour behind it. Then there is an Irish labourer and *his* family in the back kitchen, and a jobbing man—carpet-beater and so forth—with *his* family in the front one. In the front one-pair,† there's another man with another wife and family, and in the back one-pair, there's "a young 'oman as takes in tambour-work, and dresses quite genteel," who talks a good deal about "my friend," and can't "a-bear anything low." The second floor front, and the rest of the lodgers, are just a second edition of the people below, except a shabby-genteel man in the back attic, who has his half-pint of coffee every morning from the coffee-shop next door but one, which boasts a little front den called a coffee-room, with a fireplace, over which is an inscription, politely requesting that, "to prevent mistakes," customers will "please to pay on delivery." The shabby-genteel man is an object of some mystery, but as he leads a life of seclusion, and never was known to buy anything beyond an occasional pen, except half-pints of coffee, penny loaves, and ha-porths of ink, his fellow-lodgers very naturally suppose him to be an author; and rumours are current in the Dials, that he writes poems for Mr. Warren.‡

Now anybody who passed through the Dials on a hot summer's evening, and saw the different women of the house gossiping on the steps, would be apt to think that all was harmony among them, and that a more primitive set of people than the native Diallers could not be imagined. Alas! the man in the shop ill-treats his family; the carpet-beater extends his professional pursuits to his wife; the one-pair front has an undying feud with the two-pair front, in consequence of the two-pair front persisting in dancing over his (the one-pair front's) head, when he and his family have retired for the night; the two-pair back *will* interfere with the front kitchen's children; the Irishman comes home [86] drunk every other night, and attacks everybody; and the one-pair back screams at everything. Animosities spring up between floor

---

* A baked sheep's head.
† This terminology is used to indicate the location of apartments in a tenement. "Front one-pair" means: "The front apartment up one pair (or flight) of stairs."
‡ Probably Samuel Warren, whose melodramatic sketches, "Passages from the Diary of a Late Physician" appeared anonymously in *Blackwood's Magazine* between 1830 and 1837.

and floor; the very cellar asserts his equality. Mrs. A. "smacks" Mrs. B.'s
child for "making faces." Mrs. B. forthwith throws cold water over Mrs.
A.'s child for "calling names." The husbands are embroiled—the quarrel
becomes general—an assault is the consequence, and a police-officer the result.

CHAPTER XI, Astley's—Family Party at the Play.*

. . . . [122] We like to watch a regular Astley's party in the Easter or
Midsummer holidays—pa and ma, and nine or ten children, varying from
five foot six to two foot eleven: from fourteen years of age to four. We had
just taken our seat in one of the boxes, in the centre of the house, the other
night, when the next was occupied by just such a party as we should have
attempted to describe, had we depicted our *beau idéal* of a group of Astley's
visitors.

First of all, there came three little boys and a little girl, who, in pursuance
of pa's directions, issued in a very audible voice from the box-door, occupied
the front row; then two more little girls were ushered in by a young lady,
evidently the governess. Then came three more little boys, dressed like the
first, in blue jackets and trousers, with lay-down shirt-collars: then a child in
a braided frock and high state of astonishment, with very large round eyes,
opened to their utmost width, was lifted over the seats—a process which
occasioned a considerable display of little pink legs—then came ma and pa,
and then the eldest son, a boy of fourteen years old, who was evidently trying to look as if he did not belong to the family.

The first five minutes were occupied in taking the shawls off the little girls,
and adjusting the bows which ornamented their hair; then it was providentially discovered that one of the little boys was seated behind a pillar and
could not see, so the governess was stuck behind the pillar, and the boy lifted
into her place. Then pa drilled the boys, and directed the stowing away of
their pocket-handkerchiefs, and ma having first nodded and winked to the
governess to pull the girls' frocks a little more off their shoulders, stood up
to review the little troop—an inspection which appeared to terminate much
to her own satisfaction, for she looked with a complacent air at pa, who was
standing up at the further [123] end of the seat. Pa returned the glance, and
blew his nose very emphatically; and the poor governess peeped out from
behind the pillar, and timidly tried to catch ma's eye, with a look expressive
of her high admiration of the whole family. Then two of the little boys who
had been discussing the point whether Astley's was more than twice as large
as Drury Lane,† agreed to refer it to "George" for his decision; at which

* Astley's Royal Amphitheatre, a familiar London institution, was an equestrian circus
which operated in a theater. Its founder was Philip Astley (1742-1814), who had been a
trick rider before becoming a theatrical manager.
† A London theater.

"George," who was no other than the young gentleman before noticed, waxed indignant, and remonstrated in no very gentle terms on the gross impropriety of having his name repeated in so loud a voice at a public place, on which all the children laughed very heartily, and one of the little boys wound up by expressing his opinion, that "George began to think himself quite a man now," whereupon both pa and ma laughed too; and George (who carried a dress cane and was cultivating whiskers) muttered that "William always was encouraged in his impertinence;" and assumed a look of profound contempt, which lasted the whole evening.

The play began, and the interest of the little boys knew no bounds. Pa was clearly interested too, although he very unsuccessfully endeavoured to look as if he wasn't. As for ma, she was perfectly overcome by the drollery of the principal comedian, and laughed till every one of the immense bows on her ample cap trembled, at which the governess peeped out from behind the pillar again, and whenever she could catch ma's eye, put her handkerchief to her mouth, and appeared, as in duty bound, to be in convulsions of laughter also. Then when the man in the splendid armour vowed to rescue the lady or perish in the attempt, the little boys applauded vehemently, especially one little fellow who was apparently on a visit to the family, and had been carrying on a child's flirtation, the whole evening, with a small coquette of twelve years old, who looked like a model of her mamma on a reduced scale; and who, in common with the other little girls (who generally speaking have even more coquettishness about them than much older ones), looked very properly [124] shocked, when the knight's squire kissed the princess's confidential chambermaid.

When the scenes in the circle commenced, the children were more delighted than ever; and the wish to see what was going forward, completely conquering pa's dignity, he stood up in the box, and applauded as loudly as any of them. Between each feat of horsemanship, the governess leant across to ma, and retailed the clever remarks of the children on that which had preceded: and ma, in the openness of her heart, offered the governess an acidulated drop, and the governess, gratified to be taken notice of, retired behind her pillar again with a brighter countenance: and the whole party seemed quite happy, except the exquisite in the back of the box, who, being too grand to take any interest in the children, and too insignificant to be taken notice of by anybody else, occupied himself, from to time, in rubbing the place where the whiskers ought to be, and was completely alone in his glory.

We defy any one who has been to Astley's two or three times, and is consequently capable of appreciating the perseverance with which precisely the same jokes are repeated night after night, and season after season, not to be amused with one part of the performances at least—we mean the scenes in the circle. For ourself, we know that when the hoop, composed of jets of gas, is let down, the curtain drawn up for the convenience of the half-price on their ejectment from the ring, the orange-peel cleared away, and the sawdust shaken, with mathematical precision, into a complete circle, we feel as much enlivened as the youngest child present; and actually join in the laugh which follows the clown's shrill shout of "Here we are!" just for old acquaintance's sake. Nor can we quite divest ourself of our old feeling of reverence for the riding-master, who follows the clown with a long whip in his hand, and bows to the audience with graceful dignity. He is none of your second-rate riding-masters in nankeen dressing-gowns, with brown frogs, but the [125] regular gentleman-attendant on the principal riders, who always wears a military uniform with a table-cloth inside the breast of the coat, in which costume he forcibly reminds one of a fowl trussed for roasting. He is—but why should we attempt to describe that of which no description can convey an adequate idea? Everybody knows the man, and everybody remembers his polished boots, his graceful demeanour, stiff, as some misjudging persons have in their jealousy considered it, and the splendid head of black hair, parted high on the forehead, to impart to the countenance an appearance of deep thought and poetic melancholy. His soft and pleasing voice, too, is in perfect unison with his noble bearing, as he humours the clown by indulging in a little badinage; and the striking recollection of his own dignity, with which he exclaims, "Now, sir, if you please, inquire for Miss Woolford, sir," can never be forgotten. The graceful air, too, with which he introduces Miss Woolford into the arena, and, after assisting her to the saddle, follows her fairy courser round the circle, can never fail to create a deep impression in the bosom of every female servant present.

When Miss Woolford, and the horse, and the orchestra, all stop together to take breath, he urbanely takes part in some such dialogue as the following (commenced by the clown): "I say, sir!"—"Well, sir?" (it's always conducted in the politest manner.)—"Did you ever happen to hear I was in the army, sir?"—"No, sir."—"Oh, yes, sir—I can go through my exercise, sir." —"Indeed, sir!"—"Shall I do it now, sir?"—"If you please, sir; come, sir— make haste" (a cut with the long whip, and "Ha' done now—I don't like it," from the clown). Here the clown throws himself on the ground, and goes through a variety of gymnastic convulsions, doubling himself up, and untying himself again, and making himself look very like a man in the most hopeless extreme of human agony, to the vociferous delight of the gallery, until he is interrupted by a second cut from the long whip, and a request to see "what Miss Woolford's stopping for?" On which, to [126] the inexpressible mirth of the gallery, he exclaims, "Now, Miss Woolford, what can I come for to go, for to fetch, for to bring, for to carry, for to do, for you, ma'am?" On the lady's announcing with a sweet smile that she wants the two flags, they are, with sundry grimaces, procured and handed up; the clown facetiously observing after the performance of the latter ceremony—"He, he, oh! I say, sir, Miss Woolford knows me; she smiled at me." Another cut from the whip, a burst from the orchestra, a start from the horse, and round goes Miss Woolford again on her graceful performance, to the delight of every member of the audience, young or old. The next pause affords an opportunity for similar witticisms, the only additional fun being that of the clown making ludicrous

grimaces at the riding-master every time his back is turned; and finally quit-
ting the circle by jumping over his head, having previously directed his attention another way.

Did any of our readers ever notice the class of people, who hang about the
stage-doors of our minor theatres in the daytime? You will rarely pass one
of these entrances without seeing a group of three or four men conversing
on the pavement, with an indescribable public-house-parlour swagger, and a
kind of conscious air, peculiar to people of this description. They always seem
to think they are exhibiting; the lamps are ever before them. That young
fellow in the faded brown coat, and very full light green trousers, pulls down
the wristbands of his check shirt, as ostentatiously as if it were of the finest
linen, and cocks the white hat of the summer-before-last as knowingly over
his right eye, as if it were a purchase of yesterday. Look at the dirty white
Berlin gloves,* and the cheap silk handkerchief stuck in the bosom of his
threadbare coat. Is it possible to see him for an instant, and not come to the
conclusion that he is the walking gentleman who wears a blue surtout, clean
collar, and white trousers, for half an hour, and then shrinks into his worn-out
scanty clothes: who has to boast night after night of his splendid fortune,
with the painful consciousness of a pound a-week and his [127] boots to find;
to talk of his father's mansion in the country, with a dreary recollection of
his own two-pair back, in the New Cut;† and to be envied and flattered as
the favoured lover of a rich heiress, remembering all the while that the ex-
dancer at home is in the family way, and out of an engagement?

Next to him, perhaps, you will see a thin pale man, with a very long face,
in a suit of shining black, thoughtfully knocking that part of his boot which
once had a heel, with an ash stick. He is the man who does the heavy business,
such as prosy fathers, virtuous servants, curates, landlords, and so forth.

By the way, talking of fathers, we should very much like to see some piece
in which all the dramatis personae were orphans. Fathers are invariably great
nuisances on the stage, and always have to give the hero or heroine a long
explanation of what was done before the curtain rose, usually commencing
with "It is now nineteen years, my dear child, since your blessed mother
(here the old villain's voice falters) confided you to my charge. You were
then an infant," &c., &c. Or else they have to discover, all of a sudden, that
somebody whom they have been in constant communication with, during three
long acts, without the slightest suspicion, is their own child: in which case
they exclaim, "Ah! what do I see? This bracelet! That smile! These docu-
ments! Those eyes! Can I believe my senses?—It must be!—Yes—it is, it is
my child!"—"My father!" exclaims the child; and they fall into each other's
arms, and look over each other's shoulders, and the audience give three
rounds of applause.

To return from this digression, we were about to say, that these are the
sort of people whom you see talking, and attitudinising, outside the stage-

* Gloves knitted of fine dyed wool.
† A lower-class street near Westminster.

doors of our minor theatres. At Astley's they are always more numerous than at any other place. There is generally a groom or two, sitting on the window-sill, and two or three dirty shabby-genteel men in checked neckerchiefs, and sallow linen, lounging about, and carrying, perhaps, under one arm, a pair of stage shoes badly [128] wrapped up in a piece of old newspaper. Some years ago we used to stand looking, open-mouthed, at these men, with a feeling of mysterious curiosity, the very recollection of which provokes a smile at the moment we are writing. We could not believe that the beings of light and elegance, in milk-white tunics, salmon-coloured legs, and blue scarfs, who flitted on sleek cream-coloured horses before our eyes at night, with all the aid of lights, music, and artificial flowers, could be the pale, dissipated-looking creatures we beheld by day.

We can hardly believe it now. Of the lower class of actors we have seen something, and it requires no great exercise of imagination to identify the walking gentleman with the "dirty swell," * the comic singer with the public-house chairman, or the leading tragedian with drunkenness and distress; but these other men are mysterious beings, never seen out of the ring, never beheld but in the costume of gods and sylphs. With the exception of Du-crow,† who can scarcely be classed among them, who ever knew a rider at Astley's, or saw him but on horseback? Can our friend in the military uni-form ever appear in threadbare attire, or descend to the comparatively un-wadded costume of every-day life? Impossible! We cannot—we will not—believe it.

Chapter XVI, Omnibuses.

. . . . [162] Yes, after mature reflection, and considerable experience, we are decidedly of the opinion, that of all known vehicles, from the glass-coach in which we were taken to be christened, to that sombre caravan in which we must one day make our last earthly journey, there is nothing like an omnibus.

We will back the machine in which we make our daily peregrination from the top of Oxford-street to the city, against any "buss" on the road, whether it be for the gaudiness of its exterior, the perfect simplicity of its interior, or the native coolness of its cad.‡ This young gentleman is a singular instance of self-devotion; his somewhat intemperate zeal on behalf of his employers, is constantly getting him into trouble, and occasionally into the house of cor-rection. [163] He is no sooner emancipated, however, than he resumes the

* "Swell" was a slang term in use among the common people. It was a noun, and meant a well-dressed person or dandy.
† Andrew Ducrow (1793-1842) was a famous acrobat and equestrian who performed at Astley's and was one of its owners. Miss Woolford, the performer mentioned earlier in this sketch, was his wife.
‡ The conductor.

duties of his profession with unabated ardour. His principal distinction is his activity. His great boast is, "that he can chuck an old gen'lm'n into the buss, shut him in, and rattle off, afore he knows where it's a-going to"—a feat which he frequently performs, to the infinite amusement of every one but the old gentleman concerned, who, somehow or other, never can see the joke of the thing.

We are not aware that it has ever been precisely ascertained, how many passengers our omnibus will contain. The impression on the cad's mind evidently is, that it is amply sufficient for the accommodation of any number of persons that can be enticed into it. "Any room?" cries a very hot pedestrian. "Plenty o' room, sir," replies the conductor, gradually opening the door, and not disclosing the real state of the case, until the wretched man is on the steps. "Where?" inquires the entrapped individual, with an attempt to back out again. "Either side, sir," rejoins the cad, shoving him in, and slamming the door. "All right, Bill." Retreat is impossible; the new-comer rolls about, till he falls down somewhere, and there he stops.

As we get into the city a little before ten, four or five of our party are regular passengers. We always take them up at the same places, and they generally occupy the same seats; they are always dressed in the same manner, and invariably discuss the same topics—the increasing rapidity of cabs, and the disregard of moral obligations evinced by omnibus men. There is a little testy old man, with a powdered head, who always sits on the right-hand side of the door as you enter, with his hands folded on the top of his umbrella. He is extremely impatient, and sits there for the purpose of keeping a sharp eye on the cad, with whom he generally holds a running dialogue. He is very officious in helping people in and out, and always volunteers to give the cad a poke with his umbrella, when any one wants to alight. He usually recommends ladies to have sixpence ready, to prevent delay; [164] and if anybody puts a window down, that he can reach, he immediately puts it up again.

"Now, what are you stopping for?" says the little man every morning, the moment there is the slightest indication of "pulling up" at the corner of Regent-street, when some such dialogue as the following takes place between him and the cad:

"What are you stopping for?"

Here the cad whistles, and affects not to hear the question.

"I say [a poke], what are you stopping for?"

"For passengers, sir. Ba—nk.—Ty."

"I know you're stopping for passengers; but you've no business to do so. *Why* are you stopping?"

"Vy, sir, that's a difficult question. I think it is because we prefer stopping here to going on."

"Now mind," exclaims the little old man, with great vehemence, "I'll pull you up to-morrow; I've often threatened to do it; now I will."

"Thankee, sir," replies the cad, touching his hat with a mock expression of gratitude;—"werry much obliged to you indeed, sir." Here the young men in the omnibus laugh very heartily, and the old gentleman gets very red in the face, and seems highly exasperated.

The stout gentleman in the white neckcloth, at the other end of the vehicle, looks very prophetic, and says that something must shortly be done with these fellows, or there's no saying where all this will end; and the shabby-genteel man with the green bag, expresses his entire concurrence in the opinion, as he has done regularly every morning for the last six months.

A second omnibus now comes up, and stops immediately behind us. Another old gentleman elevates his cane in the air, and runs with all his might towards our omnibus; we watch his progress with great interest; the door is opened to receive him, he suddenly disappears—he has been spirited away by the opposition. Hereupon the driver of the opposition [165] taunts our people with his having "regularly done 'em out of that old swell," and the voice of the "old swell" is heard, vainly protesting against this unlawful detention. We rattle off, the other omnibus rattles after us, and every time we stop to take a passenger, they stop to take him too; sometimes we get him; some-times they get him; but whoever don't get him, say they ought to have had him, and the cads of the respective vehicles abuse one another accordingly.

As we arrive in the vicinity of Lincoln's-inn-fields, Bedford-row, and other legal haunts, we drop a great many of our original passengers, and take up fresh ones, who meet with a very sulky reception. It is rather remarkable, that the people already in an omnibus, always look at new-comers, as if they entertained some undefined idea that they have no business to come in at all. We are quite persuaded the little old man has some notion of this kind, and that he considers their entry as a sort of negative impertinence.

Conversation is now entirely dropped; each person gazes vacantly through the window in front of him, and everybody thinks that his opposite neighbour is staring at him. If one man gets out at Shoe-lane, and another at the corner of Farringdon-street, the little old gentleman grumbles, and suggests to the latter, that if he had got out at Shoe-lane too, he would have saved them the delay of another stoppage; whereupon the young men laugh again, and the old gentleman looks very solemn, and says nothing more till he gets to the Bank, when he trots off as fast as he can, leaving us to do the same, and to wish, as we walk away, that we could impart to others any portion of the amusement we have gained for ourselves.

CHAPTER XXII, Gin-Shops.

[212] It is a remarkable circumstance, that different trades appear to par-take of the disease to which elephants and dogs are especially liable, and to run stark, staring, raving mad, periodically. The great distinction between the animals and the trades, is, that the former run mad with a certain degree of propriety—they are very regular in their irregularities. We know the

period at which the emergency will arise, and provide against it accordingly. If an elephant run mad, we are all ready for him—kill or cure—pills or bullets, calomel in conserve of roses, or lead in a musket-barrel. If a dog happen to look unpleasantly warm in the summer months, and to trot about the shady side of the streets with a quarter of a yard of tongue hanging out of his mouth, a thick leather muzzle, which has been previously prepared in compliance with the thoughtful injunctions of the Legislature, is instantly clapped over his head, by way of making him cooler, and he either looks remarkably unhappy for the next six weeks, or becomes legally insane, and goes mad, as it were, by Act of Parliament. But these trades are as eccentric as comets; nay, worse, for no one can calculate on the recurrence of the strange appearances which betoken the disease. Moreover, the contagion is general, and the quickness with which it diffuses itself, almost incredible.

We will cite two or three cases in illustration of our [213] meaning. Six or eight years ago, the epidemic began to display itself among the linen-drapers and haberdashers. The primary symptoms were an inordinate love of plate-glass, and a passion for gas-lights and gilding. The disease gradually progressed, and at last attained a fearful height. Quiet, dusty old shops in different parts of town, were pulled down; spacious premises with stuccoed fronts and gold letters, were erected instead; floors were covered with Turkey carpets; roofs supported by massive pillars; doors knocked into windows; a dozen squares of glass into one; one shopman into a dozen; and there is no knowing what would have been done, if it had not been fortunately discovered, just in time, that the Commissioners of Bankruptcy were as competent to decide such cases as the Commissioners of Lunacy, and that a little confinement and gentle examination did wonders. The disease abated. It died away. A year or two of comparative tranquillity ensued. Suddenly it burst out again amongst the chemists; the symptoms were the same, with the addition of a strong desire to stick the royal arms over the shop-door, and a great rage for mahogany, varnish, and expensive floor-cloth. Then, the hosiers* were infected, and began to pull down their shop-fronts with frantic recklessness. The mania again died away, and the public began to congratulate themselves on its entire disappearance, when it burst forth with tenfold violence among the publicans, and keepers of "wine vaults." From that moment it has spread among them with unprecedented rapidity, exhibiting a concatenation of all the previous symptoms; onward it has rushed to every part of town, knocking down all the old public-houses, and depositing splendid mansions, stone balustrades, rosewood fittings, immense lamps, and illuminated clocks, at the corner of every street.

The extensive scale on which these places are established, and the ostentatious manner in which the business of even the smallest among them is divided into branches, is amusing. A handsome plate of ground glass in one door directs you [214] "To the Counting-house;" another to the "Bottle Department;" a third to the "Wholesale Department;" a fourth, to "The

* Merchants dealing in stockings, knitted underwear and other woolen goods.

Wine Promenade;" and so forth, until we are in daily expectation of meeting
with a "Brandy Bell," or a "Whiskey Entrance." Then, ingenuity is exhausted in devising attractive titles for the different descriptions of gin; and
the dram-drinking portion of the community as they gaze upon the gigantic
black and white announcements, which are only to be equalled in size by
the figures beneath them, are left in a state of pleasing hesitation between
"The Cream of the Valley," "The Out and Out," "The No Mistake," "The
Good for Mixing," "The real Knock-me-down," "The celebrated Butter
Gin," "The regular Flare-up," and a dozen other, equally inviting and wholesome *liqueurs*. Although places of this description are to be met with in
every second street, they are invariably numerous and splendid in precise
proportion to the dirt and poverty of the surrounding neighbourhood. The
gin-shops in and near Drury-lane, Holborn, St. Giles's, Covent-garden, and
Clare-market, are the handsomest in London. There is more of filth and
squalid misery near those great thoroughfares than in any part of this mighty
city.

We will endeavour to sketch the bar of a large gin-shop, and its ordinary
customers, for the edification of such of our readers as may not have had op-
portunities of observing such scenes; and on the chance of finding one well
suited to our purpose, we will make for Drury-lane, through the narrow
streets and dirty courts which divide it from Oxford-street, and that classical
spot adjoining the brewery at the bottom of Tottenham-court-road, best
known to the initiated as the "Rookery."

The filthy and miserable appearance of this part of London can hardly be
imagined by those (and there are many such) who have not witnessed it.
Wretched houses with broken windows patched with rags and paper: every
room let out to a different family, and in many instances to two or even three
[215]—fruit and "sweet-stuff" manufacturers in the cellars, barbers and red-
herring vendors in the front parlours, cobblers in the back; a bird-fancier in
the first floor, three families on the second, starvation in the attics, Irishmen
in the passage, a "musician" in the front kitchen, and a charwoman* and
five hungry children in the back one—filth everywhere—a gutter before the
houses and a drain behind—clothes drying and slops emptying, from the windows; girls of fourteen or fifteen, with matted hair, walking about barefoot,
and in white great-coats, almost their only covering; boys of all ages, in
coats of all sizes and no coats at all; men and women, in every variety of
scanty and dirty apparel, lounging, scolding, drinking, smoking, squabbling,
fighting, and swearing.

You turn the corner. What a change! All is light and brilliancy. The hum
of many voices issues from that splendid gin-shop which forms the commencement of the two streets opposite; and the gay building with the fan-
tastically ornamented parapet, the illuminated clock, the plate-glass windows
surrounded by stucco rosettes, and its profusion of gas-lights in richly-gilt
burners, is perfectly dazzling when contrasted with the darkness and dirt we

* A woman who does household work by the day.

have just left. The interior is even gayer than the exterior. A bar of French-polished mahogany, elegantly carved, extends the whole width of the place; and there are two side-aisles of great casks, painted green and gold, enclosed within a light brass rail, and bearing such inscriptions, as "Old Tom, 549;" "Young Tom, 360;" "Samson, 1421"—the figures agreeing, we presume, with "gallons," understood. Beyond the bar is a lofty and spacious saloon, full of the same enticing vessels, with a gallery running round it, equally well furnished. On the counter, in addition to the usual spirit apparatus, are two or three little baskets of cakes and biscuits, which are carefully secured at top with wicker-work, to prevent their contents being unlawfully abstracted. Behind it, are two showily-dressed damsels with large necklaces, dispensing the spirits and "compounds." They are assisted by the ostensible proprietor of [216] the concern, a stout, coarse fellow in a fur cap, put on very much on one side to give him a knowing air, and to display his sandy whiskers to the best advantage.

The two old washerwomen, who are seated on the little bench to the left of the bar, are rather overcome by the headdresses and haughty demeanour of the young ladies who officiate. They receive their half-quartern of gin and peppermint, with considerable deference, prefacing a request for "one of them soft biscuits," with a "Jist be good enough, ma'am." They are quite astonished at the impudent air of the young fellow in a brown coat and bright buttons, who, ushering in his two companions, and walking up to the bar in as careless a manner as if he had been used to green and gold ornaments all his life, winks at one of the young ladies with singular coolness, and calls for a "kervorten* and a three-out-glass," just as if the place were his own. "Gin for you, sir?" says the young lady when she has drawn it: carefully looking every way but the right one, to show that the wink had no effect upon her. "For me, Mary, my dear," replies the gentleman in brown. "My name an't Mary as it happens," says the young girl, rather relaxing as she delivers the change. "Well, if it an't, it ought to be," responds the irresistible one; "all the Marys as ever I see, was handsome gals." Here the young lady, not precisely remembering how blushes are managed in such cases, abruptly ends the flirtation by addressing the female in the faded feathers who has just entered, and who, after stating explicitly, to prevent any subsequent misunderstanding, that "this gentleman pays," calls for "a glass of port wine and a bit of sugar."

Those two old men who came in "just to have a drain," finished their third quartern a few seconds ago; they have made themselves crying drunk; and the fat comfortable-looking elderly women, who had "a glass of rum-shrub" † each, having chimed in with their complaints on the hardness of the times, one of the women has agreed to stand a glass round, jocularly observing that "grief never mended no broken [217] bones, and as good people's wery scarce, what I says is, make the most on 'em, and that's all about it!" a

* "Quartern" in a Cockney accent.
† Rum-shrub is a drink made of rum with sugar and orange or lemon juice.

sentiment which appears to afford unlimited satisfaction to those who have nothing to pay.

It is growing late, and the throng of men, women, and children, who have been constantly going in and out, dwindles down to two or three occasional stragglers—cold, wretched-looking creatures, in the last stage of emaciation and disease. The knot of Irish labourers at the lower end of the place, who have been alternately shaking hands with, and threatening the life of each other, for the last hour, become furious in their disputes, and finding it impossible to silence one man, who is particularly anxious to adjust the difference, they resort to the expedient of knocking him down and jumping on him afterwards. The man in the fur cap, and the potboy rush out; a scene of riot and confusion ensues; half the Irishmen get shut out, and the other half get shut in; the potboy is knocked among the tubs in no time; the landlord hits everybody, and everybody hits the landlord; the barmaids scream; the police come in; the rest is a confused mixture of arms, legs, staves, torn coats, shouting, and struggling. Some of the party are borne off to the station-house, and the remainder slink home to beat their wives for complaining, and kick the children for daring to be hungry.

We have sketched this subject very slightly, not only because our limits compel us to do so, but because, if it were pursued farther, it would be painful and repulsive. Well-disposed gentlemen, and charitable ladies, would alike turn with coldness and disgust from a description of the drunken besotted men, and wretched broken-down miserable women, who form no inconsiderable portion of the frequenters of these haunts; forgetting, in the pleasant consciousness of their own rectitude, the poverty of the one, and the temptation of the other. Gin-drinking is a great vice in England, but wretchedness and dirt are a greater; and until you improve [218] the homes of the poor, or persuade a half-famished wretch not to seek relief in the temporary oblivion of his own misery, with the pittance which, divided among his family, would furnish a morsel of bread for each, gin-shops will increase in number and splendour. If Temperance Societies would suggest an antidote against hunger, filth, and foul air, or could establish dispensaries for the gratuitous distribution of bottles of Lethe-water, gin-palaces would be numbered among the things that were.

Chapter XXIV, Criminal Courts.

[228] We shall never forget the mingled feelings of awe and respect with which we used to gaze on the exterior of Newgate in our schoolboy days. How dreadful its rough heavy walls, and low massive doors, appeared to us —the latter looking as if they were made for the express purpose of letting people in, and never letting them out again. Then the fetters over the debtors' door, which we used to think were a *bonâ fide* set of irons, just hung up

there, for convenience' sake, ready to be taken down at a moment's notice, and riveted on the limbs of some refractory felon! We were never tired of wondering how the hackney-coachmen on the opposite stand could cut jokes in the presence of such horrors, and drink pots of half-and-half so near the last drop.

Often have we strayed here, in sessions time, to catch a glimpse of the whipping-place, and that dark building on one side of the yard, in which is kept the gibbet with all its dreadful apparatus, and on the door of which we half expected to see a brass plate, with the inscription "Mr. Ketch;" * for we never imagined that the distinguished functionary could by possibility live anywhere else! The days of these childish dreams have passed away, and with them many other boyish ideas of a gayer nature. But we still retain so much of our original feeling, that to this hour we never pass the building without something like a shudder.

[229] What London pedestrian is there who has not, at some time or other, cast a hurried glance through the wicket at which prisoners are admitted into this gloomy mansion, and surveyed the few objects he could discern, with an indescribable feeling of curiosity? The thick door, plated with iron and mounted with spikes, just low enough to enable you to see, leaning over them, an ill-looking fellow, in a broad-brimmed hat, Belcher handkerchief †️ and top-boots: with a brown coat, something between a great-coat and a "sporting" jacket, on his back, and an immense key in his left hand. Perhaps you are lucky enough to pass, just as the gate is being opened; then, you see on the other side of the lodge, another gate, the image of its predecessor, and two or three more turnkeys, who look like multiplications of the first one, seated round a fire which just lights up the whitewashed apartment sufficiently to enable you to catch a hasty glimpse of these different objects. We have a great respect for Mrs. Fry, but she certainly ought to have written more romances than Mrs. Radcliffe.‡

We were walking leisurely down the Old Bailey,§ some time ago, when, as we passed this identical gate, it was opened by the officiating turnkey. We turned quickly round, as a matter of course, and saw two persons descending the steps. We could not help stopping and observing them.

They were an elderly woman, of decent appearance, though evidently poor, and a boy of about fourteen or fifteen. The woman was crying bitterly; she carried a small bundle in her hand, and the boy followed at a short distance behind her. Their little history was obvious. The boy was her son, to whose

---

* Jack Ketch, famous headsman of Charles II, who held his office from 1663 to 1686, was noted for his barbarity.

† A spotted or brightly-colored neckerchief.

‡ Elizabeth Fry (1780-1845) was a celebrated Quaker prison reformer who often visited such prisons as Newgate to preach to the inmates. Ann Radcliffe (1764-1823) was the leading writer of the type of horror tale called the Gothic novel.

§ The Central Criminal Court and the street outside it.

early comfort she had perhaps sacrificed her own—for whose sake she had
borne misery without repining, and poverty without a murmur—looking
steadily forward to the time, when he who had so long witnessed her struggles for himself, might be enabled to make some exertions for their joint
support. He had formed dissolute connexions; idleness had led to crime; and
he had been committed to take his trial [230] for some petty theft. He had
been long in prison, and, after receiving some trifling additional punishment,
had been ordered to be discharged that morning. It was his first offence, and
his poor old mother, still hoping to reclaim him, had been waiting at the
gate to implore him to return home.

We cannot forget the boy; he descended the steps with a dogged look,
shaking his head with an air of bravado and obstinate determination. They
walked a few paces, and paused. The woman put her hand upon his shoulder
in an agony of entreaty, and the boy sullenly raised his head as if in refusal.
It was a brilliant morning, and every object looked fresh and happy in the
broad, gay sunlight; he gazed round him for a few moments, bewildered with
the brightness of the scene, for it was long since he had beheld anything save
the gloomy walls of a prison. Perhaps the wretchedness of his mother made
some impression on the boy's heart; perhaps some undefined recollection of
the time when he was a happy child, and she his only friend, and best companion, crowded on him—he burst into tears; and covering his face with one
hand, and hurriedly placing the other in his mother's, walked away with her.

Curiosity has occasionally led us into both Courts at the Old Bailey. Nothing is so likely to strike the person who enters them for the first time, as the
calm indifference with which the proceedings are conducted; every trial seems
a mere matter of business. There is a great deal of form, but no compassion;
considerable interest, but no sympathy. Take the Old Court for example.
There sit the Judges, with whose great dignity everybody is acquainted, and
of whom therefore we need say no more. Then, there is the Lord Mayor in
the centre, looking as cool as a Lord Mayor *can* look, with an immense *bou-
quet* before him, and habited in all the splendour of his office. Then, there are
the Sheriffs, who are almost as dignified as the Lord Mayor himself; and the
Barristers, who are quite dignified enough in their own opinion; and the
spectators, who having paid for their [231] admission, look upon the whole
scene as if it were got up especially for their amusement. Look upon the
whole group in body of the Court—some wholly engrossed in the morning
papers, others carelessly conversing in low whispers, and others, again, quietly
dozing away an hour—and you can scarcely believe that the result of the
trial is a matter of life or death to one wretched being present. But turn
your eyes to the dock; watch the prisoner attentively for a few moments;
and the fact is before you, in all its painful reality. Mark how restlessly he
has been engaged for the last ten minutes, in forming all sorts of fantastic
figures with the herbs which are strewed upon the ledge before him; observe
the ashy paleness of his face when a particular witness appears, and how he

changes his position and wipes his clammy forehead, and feverish hands, when the case for the prosecution is closed, as if it were a relief to him to feel that the jury knew the worst.

The defence is concluded; the judge proceeds to sum up the evidence; and the prisoner watches the countenances of the jury, as a dying man, clinging to life to the very last, vainly looks in the face of his physician for a slight ray of hope. They turn round to consult; you can almost hear the man's heart beat, as he bites the stalk of rosemary, with a desperate effort to appear composed. They resume their places—a dead silence prevails as the foreman delivers in the verdict—"Guilty!" A shriek bursts from a female in the gallery; the prisoner casts one look at the quarter from whence the noise proceeded; and is immediately hurried from the dock by the gaoler. The clerk directs one of the officers of the Court to "take the woman out," and fresh business is proceeded with, as if nothing had occurred.

No imaginary contrast to a case like this, could be as complete as that which is constantly presented in the New Court, the gravity of which is frequently disturbed in no small degree, by the cunning and pertinacity of juvenile offenders. A boy of thirteen is tried, say for picking the [232] pocket of some subject of her Majesty, and the offence is about as clearly proved as an offence can be. He is called upon for his defence, and contents himself with a little declamation about the jurymen and his country—asserts that all the witnesses have committed perjury, and hints that the police force generally have entered into a conspiracy "again" him. However probable this statement may be, it fails to convince the Court, and some such scene as the following then takes place:

Court: Have you any witnesses to speak to your character, boy?

Boy: Yes, my Lord; fifteen gen'lm'n is a vaten outside, and vos a vaten all day yesterday, vich they told me the night afore my trial vos a comin' on.

Court: Inquire for these witnesses.

Here, a stout beadle* runs out, and vociferates for the witnesses at the very top of his voice; for you hear his cry grow fainter and fainter as he descends the steps into the court-yard below. After an absence of five minutes, he returns, very warm and hoarse, and informs the Court of what it knew perfectly well before—namely, that there are no such witnesses in attendance. Hereupon, the boy sets up a most awful howling; screws the lower part of the palms of his hands into the corners of his eyes; and endeavours to look the picture of injured innocence. The jury at once find him "guilty," and his endeavours to squeeze out a tear or two are redoubled. The governor of the gaol then states, in reply to an inquiry from the bench, that the prisoner has been under his care twice before. This the urchin resolutely denies in some such terms as—"S'elp me, gen'lm'n, I never vos in trouble afore—indeed, my Lord, I never vos. It's all a howen to my having a twin

* A minor official or attendant in courts, churches, guilds and universities who had the functions of keeping order and running errands.

brother, vich has wrongfully got into trouble, and vich is so exactly like me, that no vun ever knows the difference atween us."

This representation, like the defence, fails in producing the desired effect, and the boy is sentenced, perhaps, to seven [233] years' transportation. Finding it impossible to excite compassion, he gives vent to his feelings in an imprecation bearing reference to the eyes of "old big vig!" and as he declines to take the trouble of walking from the dock, is forthwith carried out, congratulating himself on having succeeded in giving everybody as much trouble as possible.

from

London

Charles Knight (ed.)

THE LARGE, six-volume *London* was one of the many publishing ventures of Charles Knight (1791-1873), who worked as an author, translator, editor and publisher. Knight usually aimed at a wide popular audience, producing inexpensive periodicals, encyclopedias, almanacs, and textbooks. Primarily a publisher, he was also a prolific writer and translator, specializing in journalism, economics, and history. After becoming associated with the Society for the Diffusion of Useful Knowledge in 1827, he served the cause of popular education by such publishing enterprises as the *Penny Magazine* (1832-35) and the *Penny Cyclopaedia* (1833-1844), a periodical called *Voice of the People* (1848), and the *Popular History of England* (1862). He had been interested in bibliographical matters since his youth, and between the years 1838 and 1841 published *The Pictorial Shakespeare*, an edition embodying his knowledge of textual problems. *London* was not one of Knight's inexpensive productions. A handsome set of books illustrated with many fine engravings, it was written by a number of collaborators under Knight's general editorship, and attempted to give the history of all the notable localities in London as well as a description of their contemporary appearance.

Six vols. London: Charles Knight and Co., 1843.

27

From VOLUME IV, CHAPTER XCV, "Public Refreshment" by G. Dodd.*

. . . [313] It is probable that itinerant piemen, such as Hogarth† gives to the life, have for centuries formed one class of London characters, and that various other eatables, and drinkables too, have been vended about in a similar manner, time out of mind; but by what steps the modern cook's-shop, or eating-house, has reached its present condition, it is not perhaps easy to say. There are, it appears, about two hundred places in London which can fittingly come under the denomination of eating-houses, occupying a place between the hotels on the one hand and the coffee-rooms on the other. At all of these places joints of meat are dressed every day, depending for variety on the extent of business done, but generally including boiled beef and roast beef, as well as the necessary appendages for the formation of a dinner. In some of these houses the quantity of meat dressed in a week is quite enormous; and it seems pretty evident that the greater the sale the better the quality of the articles sold—or perhaps we may take it in an inverse order, that the excellence of the provisions has led to the extent of the custom.

Some of these dining-rooms are the scenes of bustle during only a few hours of the day; while others, either from the extent of their trade, or the different classes of their visitors, present a never-ceasing picture of eating and drinking. Some, such as a celebrated house in Bishopsgate Street, are frequented almost entirely by commercial men and City clerks, who, during a few hours in the day, flock in by hundreds. Then again others, such as Williams's boiled-beef shop in the Old Bailey, and a few in the neighbourhood of Lincoln's Inn Fields, are frequented almost entirely by lawyers' clerks, witnesses, and others engaged in the law or criminal courts. In all such cases there is a "best" room for those whose purses are tolerably supplied; and a more humble room, generally nearer to the street, for such as can afford only a "sixpenny plate." Again, on going farther westward, we find, in the neighbourhood of Covent Garden and the Haymarket, dining-rooms in great plenty, the visitants at which are altogether of a different class. Here we may see actors, artists, paragraph-makers, and foreigners, most of whom seem in much less haste than the City diners. In this quarter of the town there are many French restaurateurs, whose rooms present the agreeable variety of ladies dining without any restraint from the observation of the male visitors.

It is observable that in some houses the waiter gives the diner a long detail

---

* George Dodd (1808-1881) was a free-lance writer who wrote on industry, manufacturing, and other informative subjects. He worked on a number of Knight's publications, and later wrote travel-guides, popular treatments of current events, and reference works.
† William Hogarth (1697-1764), the great eighteenth-century artist, was famous for his scenes of London life.

of the good things which are "just ready," while in others there is a printed
bill-of-fare placed before him. The latter is certainly the most systematic
method; for, by the time the nimble waiter has got through his speech, we
almost forget the first items to which he directed attention. In the "bill of
fare" all the dishes customarily prepared at the house are printed in certain
groups, and the prices are *written* opposite those which are to be had hot on
any particular day, so that a customer can at once see what provisions are
ready, and how much he shall have to pay for them. In the opposite case,
where the visitor knows nothing of the matter but what the waiter tells him,
the routine of proceedings may be thus sketched:—The guest, perhaps a man
of business who has but little time to spare for his dinner, enters the room,
takes the first seat he can find (the one nearest the fire in cold weather),
takes off his hat, and asks for the 'Times' or the [314] 'Chronicle.' While he
is glancing his eye rapidly over the daily news, the active, tidy waiter, with
a clean napkin on his left arm, comes to his side, and pours into his ear, in a
rapid but monotonous tone, some such narrative as the following:—"Roast
beef, boiled beef, roast haunch of mutton, boiled pork, roast veal and ham,
salmon and shrimp-sauce, pigeon-pie, rump-steak pudding." The visitor is
perhaps deep in the perusal of 'Spanish Scrip' or 'Colombian Bonds,' or
some other newspaper intelligence, and the waiter is obliged to repeat his
catalogue; but, generally speaking, the order is quickly given, and quickly
attended to. A plate of roast beef, which may be taken as a standard of comparison, is charged for at these places at prices varying from 4*d.* to 10*d.*,
generally from 6*d.* to 8*d.*; and other articles are in a corresponding ratio.
When the meat and vegetables have disappeared, the nimble waiter is at your
elbow, to ask whether pastry or cheese is wanted; and when the visitor is
about to depart, the waiter adds up, with characteristic rapidity, the various
items constituting the bill. "Meat 8*d.*, potatoes 1*d.*, bread 1*d.*, cheese 1*d.*,"
&c., are soon summed up; the money is paid, and the diner departs.

   At the alamode-beef* houses the routine is still more rapid. Here a visitor
takes his seat, and the waiter places before him a knife, a fork, and a spoon;
and gives him the choice among sundry lumps of bread kept in an open
basket. Meanwhile the visitor asks for a "sixpenny plate;" and it may happen
that two other customers ask at the same time, the one for a sixpenny and
the other for a fourpenny plate. Out goes the waiter, calling, in a quick
tone, for "two sixes and a four;" a brevity which is perfectly well understood
by those who are to lade out the soup from the cauldron wherein it is prepared. Presently he returns with a pile of pewter plates, containing the "two
sixes and a four," and places them before the diners. There is a house near
the theatres where this scene of operation continues almost uninterruptedly
from twelve o'clock at noon till an hour or two after the theatres are over in
the evening; some taking soup as a luncheon, some as an early dinner, some
as a late dinner, some as a substitute for tea, and the remainder as a supper.

   There is a lower class of soup-houses, where persons to whom sixpence is

* Beef stew.

even too much for a dinner may obtain wherewithal to dine. Whoever has had
to walk through Broad Street, St. Giles's, or down the northern side of
Holborn Hill, may have seen shops, in the windows of which a goodly array
of blue and white basins is displayed, and from which emanate abundant
clouds of odour-giving steam. Around the windows, too, a crowd of hungry
mortals assemble on a cold day, and partake (in imagination) of the enticing
things within. A poor fellow, all in tatters, with a countenance which speaks
strongly of privation, gazes eagerly through the window at what is going on
within, and thinks how rich a man must be who can afford to pay twopence
or threepence for "a basin of prime soup, potatoes, and a slice of bread;"—
for it is at some such charge as this that the viands are sold. As for the quality of the soup, we should, perhaps, only be just in supposing that it is good
enough for the price. One thing is certain, that the quantity sold every day
at these houses is extremely large.

The "chop-houses" in the City form a class by themselves. They are
neither eating-houses nor taverns, nor do they belong to classes hereafter to
be noticed. The solid food here to be procured is chiefly in the form of a
steak or a chop, with [315] such small appendages as are necessary to form
a meal. There is no hot joint from which a guest may have a "sixpenny" or
a "ninepenny" plate; nor are there the various dishes which fill up the bill-of-
fare at a dining-room. Every guest knows perfectly well what he can procure
there. If a chop or a steak will suffice, he can obtain it; if not, he goes to
some house where greater variety is provided. With his chop he can have
such liquor as his taste may prefer. There are some of these houses which
have been attended by one generation after another of guests, comprising
merchants, bankers, and commercial men of every grade. The portrait of the
founder, or a favourite waiter, may perhaps be seen over the fireplace in the
best room; and the well-rubbed tables, chairs, and benches tell of industry
oft repeated. Sometimes the older houses exhibit a waiter who has gone
through his daily routine for half a century. There is a dingy house in a
court in Fleet Street where the chops and steaks are unrivalled. Who that
has tasted there that impossible thing of private cookery—a *hot* mutton chop,
a second brought when the first is despatched—has not pleasant recollections
of the never-ending call to the cook of "Two muttons to follow"?

At most of the respectable eating and chop houses it is a pretty general
custom to give a penny or twopence to the waiter when the "reckoning" is
paid. This is a bad system. It would be much better to pay an extra penny
for the price of the dinner, and let the waiter be paid by the master; instead
of, as is at present the case, the waiter giving the master a *douceur* for
permission to hold the situation. But whether such a change would change
the characteristics of a waiter, we cannot say; certain it is that a London
waiter is quite a character. Here is Mr. Leigh Hunt's picture of one:—"He
has no feeling of noise, but as the sound of dining, or of silence, but as a thing
before dinner. Even a loaf with him is hardly a loaf; it is so many 'breads.'
His longest speech is the making out of a bill *vivâ voce*—'Two beefs—one

potatoes—three ales—two wines—six and twopence,'—which he does with an indifferent celerity amusing to new comers who have been relishing their fare, and not considering it as a mere set of items."

Many houses have what is termed in France a *table-d'hôte,* or in England an *ordinary;* that is, a dinner ready for all comers at a fixed hour in the day, and at a fixed charge. The host determines on the choice of good things to constitute the bill of fare; and the diner partakes of such as may best accord with his palate. Some of these places are attended day after day by nearly the same persons, while others see a constant succession of new faces. There is one such house near or in Billingsgate, celebrated for the excellence of the *fish,* which forms a component part of the cheer; and which is, on this account, much frequented by the connoisseurs in fish. Nay, we have heard that so far does the demand for table-room exceed the supply, that the "knowing ones" have their seat at the table half an hour before the prescribed dinner-time, as the only way to be prepared for the fish by the time the fish is prepared for them. A public-house (really one) in a street near Covent Garden has an ordinary of three courses, which the lovers of economical good eating, who cannot dine without fish and pastry, delight to haunt. But there are few of these. The *ordinaries* of the days of Elizabeth have left few successors.

Besides the dining-rooms and chop-houses, properly so called, there are many places where a man can get a dinner by a sort of indirect arrangement. Not to [316] mention oyster-rooms, which are frequented rather for suppers than dinners, or pastry-cooks' shops, which are rather for lady-like delicacies than for stout hearty food which will enable a man to buffet through the world, or Garraway's, and one or two similar houses, where a sandwich and a glass of wine or ale may be rapidly swallowed, there are public-houses where a *gridiron* is kept always at hand for cooking a steak or a chop belonging to a customer. If we draw a circle of a few hundred yards radius round the Royal Exchange, we shall find more than one place of which the following is a sketch. A butcher's shop within a door or two of a public-house supplies a purchaser with a steak or a chop at a reasonable price. He carries it into the public-house (or tavern, if the name be preferred) and places it in the hands of a waiter or servant, who speedily dresses it on an enormous gridiron, the bars of which are so constructed as to save a great portion of the fat from the meat. For this service the small sum of *one penny* only is charged, in addition to an equally moderate charge for bread, potatoes, and whatever drink may be called for.

Some of these houses are celebrated for the "fine old cheese," or the "baked potatoes," or the "mutton pies," which they provide for their customers; each place having a reputation for some one or other welcome dish. In humble neighbourhoods, again, all such dainties as "sheeps' trotters," "sheeps' heads," "pigs' faces," "faggots," &c. are to be had hot at certain hours of the day;* but these are not supplied by the owners of public-houses; they are procured

* "Trotters" are sheep's feet; "faggots" were an economical dish made of chopped pork-liver rolled into a ball.

at shops adjacent, and very often demolished in the tap-rooms of the public-houses. . . .

Volume V, Chapter CIX, "Covent Garden" by J. Saunders* and J. C. Platt.

. . . [140] The market-days at Covent Garden are Tuesday, Thursday, and Saturday, the last being by far the most important. There is no particular hour for commencing business, but it varies at different seasons, and by daybreak there are always a few retail dealers present. Waggons and carts have been arriving for some time before, and porters are busied in transferring their contents to the different stations of the salesmen while the dawn is yet grey. The houses of refreshment around the market are open at half-past one in summer; and little tables are set out against the pillars of the piazzas by the venders of tea and coffee. Here the porters and carters can obtain refreshment without needing to resort to exciting liquors; and few greater benefits have been conferred on the laborious classes whose occupation is in the public markets than that of substituting tea and coffee for ardent spirits. There is some separation of the [141] different classes of articles, and potatoes and coarser produce are assigned a distinct quarter. Vegetables and fruit are tolerably well separated, and flowers and plants are found together. The west side of the square is covered with potted flowers and plants in bloom, and a gay, beautiful, and fragrant display they make. The supply of "cut" flowers for bouquets, or, to use the old-fashioned word, nose-gays, is very large, including "walls," daffodils, roses, pinks, carnations, &c., according to the season. The carts and waggons with vegetables are drawn up close together on three sides of the market. A waggon-load of fine fresh cabbages, of clean-washed turnips, carrots, or cauliflowers, or an area of twenty square yards covered with the latter beautiful vegetable, or either of the others piled in neat stacks, is a pleasing sight. Here are onions from the Bedfordshire sands or Deptford, cabbages from Battersea, asparagus from Mortlake and Deptford, celery from Chelsea, peas from Charlton, these spots being each famous for the production of these particular articles, though the supply may be larger from other places. By and by the greengrocers come jogging in; and the five spacious streets leading to the market in time become crowded with a double row of their vehicles. The costermongers and venders of water-cresses, and itinerant dealers who have taken up the trade as a temporary resource, arrive with their donkey-carts, trucks, or baskets. The Irish basket-women, who ply as porteresses, and will carry your purchase to

* John Saunders (1810-1895) was an editor, playwright, journalist and novelist who worked for Knight as a young man. Later he founded his own periodical, edited a magazine and wrote a large number of plays and novels, many of them about working-class life.

any part of the town, jabber in Erse,* and a subdued clamouring sound tells you that the business of the day has really begun. As fast as the retail dealer makes his bargains a porter carries the articles to his market-cart, pushing through the crowd with the load on his head as well as he can. The baskets of "spring onions" † and young radishes are thronged by the itinerant dealers trying to drive hard bargains. It is interesting to watch for a short time the business of the flower-market. [142] This is the Londoners' flower-garden, and is resorted to in the early summer morning by many a lover of flowers compelled by his occupation to live in the densely-crowded parts of London, and who steals a few moments from the busy day to gratify one of the purest tastes. This out-of-door floral exhibition has undergone an extraordinary improvement within the last few years, and it is really an attractive show. It keeps alive a taste which in many instances would otherwise languish; and it is not a little "refreshing" to see the humble mechanic making a purchase of a root of "hen and chicken daisies," a "black" wall-flower, or a primrose, to ornament the window of his workshop. Some who love flowers better than they understand how to treat them, while making their purchase, gather instructions for keeping them fresh and healthy. The "pot" plants are bought in ones and twos by private persons; but the itinerant dealer fills his basket or donkey-cart, and will be met with in his perambulations during the day in most parts of London in spring and summer. The most common plants are pelagorniums [sic], fuchsias, verbenas, heliotropes, amaranthus, cockscombs, calceolarias, roses, myrtles, and other greenhouse plants. The cut flowers are purchased for the decoration of public rooms, and by persons who love the exquisite beauty of flowers, and by itinerant dealers, chiefly females, who make them up into small bouquets and vend them in the streets. The smart clerk purchases them for a posy, and to stick a fine pelagornium in the button hole is not a practice to be despised, albeit a glass phial filled with water on a corner of his desk would perhaps be as good a destination. The sweet-briar which the flower-girl offers for sale in the crowded street gives out a fragrance which is most delicious, as its odours are momentarily inhaled by the hasty passenger proceeding to scenes so different from those which it recalls. The costermongers, who may be seen in all the great wholesale markets of London, Smithfield excepted, unless they may go there to speculate in horse-flesh for the boiler, or to buy a donkey, are a very singular race, and in their sharp commercial habits come nearer to the Jews than any other class. From their appearance any one would infer that their purchases would be confined to a few bunches of water-cresses, but they often buy considerable quantities of the best description of articles; and though, still judging from appearances, it would seem to display a very reckless degree of confidence in each other, they not unfrequently club their money and buy up an advantageous lot on favourable terms, though it is not easy to perceive by what

* The Irish variant of Gaelic.
† Leeks.

arrangement they can divide the bargain amongst each other without serious disputes. The narrow and dirty streets which they inhabit may often be seen gay with a rich display of potted flowers and plants which they are about to carry through the town for sale; and at other times an unwonted aspect of purity is given to the vicinity by a profuse supply of the finest cauliflowers. The costermongers may be divided into several ranks, the lowest being scarcely worthy of the name, as he only purchases in small quantities which he can carry off in his basket. A considerable degree above him is he who carries his commodities from street to street on a truck with a capacious board on the top, shelved at the edges; but it must be stated that the truck is only a hired one, either for the day or the [143] week; the costermonger who owns a donkey, and a rough cart which seems to have been rudely made by his own hands, is indeed worthy of his name and character, and he may save money if he is not too fond of low sports; but a prince among the tribe is he who has not only cash for any chance speculation which may turn up, but possesses accumulated capital in the shape of trucks which he lets out at a fixed rent to his less fortunate or less steady brethren. One man of this class, who lives near the 'Elephant and Castle,' has forty of these trucks. They cost from 2*l.* to 2*l.* 10*s.* when new: he is not so extravagant as to buy them fresh from the maker, but picks them up when misfortune obliges one of the fraternity to descend to a humbler rank in the profession. The charge for letting them out is 4*d.* a-day, or 2*s.* a-week, but without the board at the top 3*d.* and 1*s.* 6*d.*; and in winter the price for each sort is only 1*s.* 6*d.* Sometimes one of these wealthy truck-men will buy up on very advantageous terms large quantities of such articles as are in season, and he can sell again to the drawers of his trucks cheaper than they can buy in small quantities in the market. He knows better than to employ the buyers as his servants, but is content with a small profit and no risk, and as he gets so handsome an income from his trucks he ought to be content. A boy of the lowest class commencing his career in Covent Garden Market, if he be prudent, sharp, and intelligent, and is fortunately exempt from the vices of his companions, has a better and surer prospect of making a fortune, if he pursues a right course, than most of the youths of the middle class. . . .

From VOLUME V, CHAPTER CXXI,
"Prisons and Penitentiaries" by J. C. Platt.

[321] About 36,000 criminals and other persons (exclusive of debtors) pass through the Metropolitan gaols, houses of correction, bridewells, and penitentiaries, every year. In the year 1839 the number of persons taken into custody by the metropolitan police was equal to the whole population of some of our largest towns, being 65,965. The disproportion of the sexes was not greater than in the colony of New South Wales, there being 22,467 females and 43,498 males. The numbers taken up for drunkenness were 13,952

males and 7317 females, or nearly one-third of the whole number: the amount taken from drunken persons and restored to them when sober was 9430*l*., in 1837. The number of disorderly characters apprehended in 1839, was 4957 males and 3217 females; together 8174 persons; besides 3154 disorderly prostitutes, 4436 for common assaults, and 1448 for assaults on the police; and of vagrants the number was 3780. There were 6764 common larceny cases; and 3196 persons were apprehended as 'suspicious characters.' In the class of cases already enumerated are included 52,221 persons. Altogether, of the 65,965 persons taken into custody there were 33,882 at once discharged by the magistrates; 28,488 were summarily convicted or held to bail, and 3595 were committed for trial, of whom 2813 were convicted. Larcenies in a dwelling-house were most numerous in Whitechapel in 1837, and in St. George's in the Borough, in 1836. Larcenies from the person were most common in Covent Garden in the one year and in Shadwell in the other. Highway robberies, burglaries, house and shop-breaking occurred [322] most frequently in the suburbs—as in Whitechapel, Southwark, Lambeth, Mile End, and Poplar; but the number of this class of offences, in the whole of the metropolitan district in 1839, was under 200. The parish of St. James's furnished, in 1837, the largest proportionate number of cases for the police under the head of drunkenness, disorderly prostitutes, and vagrancy. Clerkenwell was distinguished for the largest number of cases of horse-stealing, assaults with attempt to rescue, and wilful damage. Common assaults were most frequent in Covent Garden in 1837, and in St. George's in the East in 1836; coining and uttering counterfeit coin in Clerkenwell and Covent Garden; embezzlement in Whitechapel and Clerkenwell; and pawning illegally in Mile End and Lambeth. Murder was most prevalent in Clerkenwell and Whitechapel; manslaughter in Islington and Clerkenwell; and arson in Marylebone and Westminster. One thing is at least clear, that Clerkenwell holds a bad pre-eminence for the number and nature of the offences committed within its limits; but district returns must be continued for a series of years before the character of any particular division of the metropolis can be fully brought out. Comparing Middlesex (including London) with England and Wales, we find that in assaults the county is very much above the average, a result which probably arises in a great degree from the presence of a numerous and efficient police force, which, by affording the means of immediate arrest in cases of this nature, augments the number of cases brought before the magistrates; and the same cause will account for the smaller proportion of murders, as interference frequently takes place before quarrels proceed to a fatal termination. The assaults on peace-officers are also few in number, from its being well known that the aid of additional policemen can be easily obtained. The valuable property in shops and warehouses is usually so well protected in London, both by the presence of a police force and internally by bolts and bars, that the average of burglaries is also fewer than in the country; and the same may be said of housebreaking, which crime, as already stated, chiefly occurs in the suburbs. Robbery, with violence, is also below the average; but in malicious offences against property, the disproportion in Middlesex is very striking, which is to be accounted for by the difficulty of finding means to gratify private vengeance in this way, while, in the country, stackburning, and killing and maiming cattle are crimes of easy commission. But in crimes which call for dexterity and intelligence the preponderance in Middlesex is very great, as in the case of larceny from the person (pocket-picking) and forgery. Lastly, the disproportion of female criminals in the metropolis is very considerable. In 1842, out of 5569 female offenders, 989 were committed in Middlesex, or between one-fifth and one-sixth, instead of about one-ninth. In the Metropolitan police district the amount of loss by 11,589 robberies in 1838 was 28,619*l*., and the number for which a police force could fairly be responsible was 2919, involving a loss of 10,914*l*., including 446 cases of robbery by "means unknown." At the commencement of the present century Mr. Colquhoun, himself a police magistrate, estimated the amount of depredations on property committed in the metropolis and its vicinity at 2,000,000*l*.! Is it to be supposed that, with the present most efficient police force of about 3500 persons, less than 2 per cent. of the felonies should now become known? It is quite clear, indeed, that Mr. Colquhoun's statement was either very far wide of the mark, or that a most enormous saving had been effected by an improved system of police.

[323] Still there is no manner of doubt, that, from the number of persons living habitually by depredations on property, the amount of loss must be very great. The Constabulary Commissioners, who had access to the best sources of information, made a return of the number of depredators and offenders against the law, or who had been subjected to the law, or brought within the cognizance of the police in the metropolitan police district, and the following was the result of their investigation. They divided the whole number into three classes:—1. Persons who have no visible means of subsistence, and who are believed to live by violation of the law, as by habitual depredation, by fraud, by prostitution, &c. 2. Persons following some ostensible and legal occupation, but who are known to have committed an offence, and are believed to augment their gains by habitual or occasional violation of the law. 3. Persons not known to have committed any offences, but known as associates of the above classes, and otherwise deemed to be suspicious characters. The following is the return:

Character and Description of Offenders	1st Class	2nd Class	3rd Class
Burglars	77	22	8
Housebreakers	59	17	34
Highway robbers	19	8	11
Pickpockets	544	75	154
Common thieves	1667	1338	652
Forgers	—	3	—
Obtainers of goods by false pretences	33	108	—
Persons committing frauds of any other description	23	118	41
Receivers of stolen goods	51	158	134
Horse-stealers	7	4	—

Character and Description of Offenders	1st Class	2nd Class	3rd Class
Cattle-stealers	—	—	—
Dog-stealers	45	48	48
Coiners	25	1	2
Utterers of base coin	202	54	61
Habitual disturbers of the public peace	723	1866	179
Vagrants	1089	186	20
Begging-letter writers	12	17	21
Bearers of begging-letters	22	40	24
Prostitutes, well-dressed, living in brothels	813	62	20
Prostitutes, well-dressed, walking the streets	1460	79	73
Prostitutes, low, infesting low neighbourhoods	3533	147	184
Classes not before enumerated	40	2	438
Total	10444	4353	2104

This return, tested as it was by the average length of career of offenders passing through the prisons of the metropolis, is no doubt as near the truth as possible. Besides this return, the Constabulary Commissioners also obtained another, giving the number of houses open for the accommodation of delinquency and vice in the same district; and this return we subjoin:

Houses for the reception of stolen goods	227
Ditto suppressed since the establishment of the police	131
Houses for the resort of thieves	276
Ditto suppressed since the establishment of the police	159
Average number of thieves daily resorting to each	17
Number of brothels where prostitutes are kept	933
Average number of prostitutes kept in each	4
Number of houses of ill-fame where prostitutes resort	848
Number of houses where prostitutes lodge	1554
Number of gambling-houses	32
Average number of persons resorting to each daily	20
Mendicants' lodging-houses	221
Average daily number of lodgers at each house	11

. . . [328] Notwithstanding that gradually a number of improvements have taken place in the discipline and administration of Newgate, it is still defective, and radically so, for the present building does not admit of the application of a proper system of discipline. In 1836 the Inspectors of Prisons justly found fault with the evils of gaol-contamination which prevail within its walls. The prisoners were enabled to amuse themselves with gambling, card-playing and draughts. They could obtain, by stealth it is true, the luxury of tobacco and a newspaper. Sometimes they could get drunk. Instruments to facilitate prison-breaking were found in the prison. Combs and towels were not provided, and the supply of soap was insufficient. In 1838 the Inspectors reported, that "this great metropolitan prison, while it continues in its present state, is a fruitful source of demoralization." In their last Report (the Seventh), dated 5th April, 1843, the Inspectors say:—"It has been our painful duty again and again to point attention to the serious evils resulting from gaol association and consequent necessary contamination in this prison. The importance of this prison in this point of view is very great. As the great metropolitan prison for the untried, it is here that those most skilled in crime of every form, those whom the temptations, the excesses, and the experience of this great city have led through a course of crime to the highest skill in the arts of depredation and to the lowest degradation of infamy, meet together with those who are new to such courses, and who are only too ready to learn how they may pursue the career they have just entered upon, with most security from detection and punishment, and with greater success and indulgence. The numbers committed, nearly 4000 per annum, which have rapidly increased, and are still increasing, render this a subject of still greater moment. Of this number about one-fifth are acquitted; many of these return to their associates with increased knowledge and skill in crime; with lost characters; with more hardened dispositions from their association here with others worse than themselves; and with their sense of shame and self-respect sadly diminished, if not utterly destroyed, by exposure to others, and by increased gaol acquaintances. Many others are sentenced to short terms of imprisonment, and in like manner soon get back again to their former courses and companions; and each of these becomes a source of greater mischief to the public, and of danger and seduction to the unwary and inexperienced. We most seriously protest against Newgate as a great school of crime. Associated together in large numbers and in utter idleness, frequently moved from ward to ward, and thereby their prison acquaintance much enlarged, we affirm that the prisoners must quit this prison worse than they enter it. It is said that prisoners are here but for a short time, and therefore that much mischief cannot be done. Many of them are here for three weeks and more, and are locked up together in numbers from three to twenty, for twenty out of twenty-four hours, without the restraining presence even of an officer, without occupation or resource, without instruction, except that afforded by the daily chapel service, and by the short visits which a chaplain can pay from ward to ward in so large a prison, and by the books which are [329] placed in the wards. At the end of three weeks what remains to be learnt that any inmate of a ward can teach? what narrative of guilty or sensual adventure remains untold? what anticipation of future success and indulgence that has not been dwelt upon? Some few have courage to fly from such mischievous companionship, and ask, after a few hours' experience of the wards of Newgate, to be placed in the separate cells; but it is not to be expected that many will voluntarily fly from company which distracts thought, to seclusion and their own unhappy reflections. The arrangements however for these few are such as to deter them from availing themselves of them. The solitary cells are the old condemned cells of Newgate, which are now used as refractory cells for those who offend against the discipline of the prison, or for those charged with unnatural offences, or with the most brutal crimes; and if a young man, who has never before been in prison—who wishes to retain the little good that remains to him—and who is disgusted with the characters he has met in the prison, and the language and conversation he has been obliged to hear, requests to be put apart, he is removed to one of these cells. They are cold, ill ventilated, dark, small, and even without a seat to sit upon. At our last inspection we found two young men of comparatively respectable appearance, who, disgusted with the bad conversation, the oaths, and the indecent language which they said they had heard in the wards, requested to be alone; and who preferred solitude in these wretched cells to such companionship. One had been a month in separate confinement under the most unfavourable circumstances possible; and yet did not regret the choice he had made."

From VOLUME V, CHAPTER CXXV,
"London Shops and Bazaars" by G. Dodd.

. . . [389] In the first place, then—and pity 't is that the first place should be so occupied—we have the public-houses, taverns, and gin-palaces. Those shops have been among the first to introduce a decorative style of shop-architecture; and, what seems to many persons most strange, the poorer the neighborhood, the more splendid do these places become. There are about four thousand regularly-licensed public-houses in London, besides a large number of drinking-houses of various kinds which cannot come under this designation. The change between past and present times is more marked in respect to public-houses than to almost any other kind of retail shop in London. All the descriptions which writers have given of the older houses of this character bear a strong family likeness, as do the pictures which Hogarth and others have left. The tavern-keeper was a jolly, portly man, with a red face, knee-breeches (into the pockets of which his hands were often thrust), and buckled shoes. His shop or "bar" was small but well filled, exhibiting punch-bowls on a shelf, a little gilt Bacchus sitting across a barrel, a bunch of grapes of impossible dimensions, and a sign-board creaking on its hinges outside. But now how great is the change! We are first dazzled with the splendid gas-lamps ranged on the outside of the house, and shedding a ray of surpassing brilliancy (there was a public-house, three or four years ago, whose exterior exhibited a lamp ten feet high, containing seventy jets of gas!). When we come nearer we see that the interior is fully as brilliant as the exterior: elegantly-formed branches of pipes descend from the ceiling, or ascend from the counter, and yield a vast number of gas-flames. The bar-furniture, such as counters, [390] beer-machines, spirit-machines, are all of the finest workmanship and highest polish; while behind the counter, instead of the jolly Boniface of old, we see smartly-dressed females, dispensing the pennyworths or small quantities of liquor. It may be that a man or a boy draws the malt-liquor; but the chances are ten to one that one of the other sex—though strange it may seem—is serving those small portions of the burning liquid which so often bring ruin as their attendants. There is one feature in a modern public-house for which our times need not be envied: in front of the counter are the ragged, the depraved, the impoverished, spending perhaps their last penny for gin, and cursing and quarrelling under the influence of the inebriation which it brings. It is, however, only fair to bear in mind that this is not a feature of all these houses: some derive the chief part of their business from serving families with beer, and such are, though much less splendid, much better ordered, than the real "gin-palaces." To arrive at something like a general rule, we may say that those public-houses which are situated in or near the lowest dens of poverty, such as Seven Dials, White-chapel, and some spots on the south of the river, have been becoming more and more splendid every year; while those situated near the squares and private streets have a decent air of respectability about them, as far removed from the desolating splendour of the former, as from the hearty jollity of the olden taverns.

[391] The Bakers' and the Chemists' shops are among those which have adopted the luxury of plate-glass windows and bright gas-lamps. Twenty years ago most of the bakers' shops had small flat windows, and were very modestly lighted in the evening by a lamp or two: the baker, with his woollen cap on his head, stood behind the counter rasping his loaves and rolls; while his wife, a plain, decent body, served the "quarterns" and "half-quarterns." But now the window displays its large squares of plate-glass, its brightly-blazing gas-jets, and its long array of neat trays filled with biscuits, whose shape would defy Euclid. The Chemists, or, as they ought more properly to be called, the Druggists, have made a notable advance in shop-architecture and arrangements. Most London walkers will remember the time when the large red, and green, and yellow bottles, shedding a ghastly light on the passer-by, were the chief indications of the presence of a Druggist's shop; but now the plate-glass window exhibits a most profuse array of knick-knacks, not only such as pertain to "doctors' stuff," but lozenges, perfumery, soda-water powders, &c.; while the well-dressed shopmen or "assistants" within—one of the most lowly-paid class of respectable persons in London—ply their avocation of semi-chemists and semi-shopmen.

The Butchers' shops are pretty nearly what butchers' shops have always been: they have undergone but little change. They are still open shops, with their stout counters, provided with bins underneath for containing salt-meat, their huge chopping-blocks, their rows of hooks whereon to hang the meat, their rough floors covered with saw-dust, and their window-board next the street. A sash-window to a butcher's shop would be quite a solecism; but still there are at the west-end of the town symptoms of smartness and cleanli-ness to which the east makes no pretensions. The Grocers' shops—not the Greengrocers, for they remain open-fronted shops, as they were in former days, and in many cases exhibit the same heap of coals in one corner, to be sold in pecks or pen'orths—have advanced in the march of improvement. The grocer is no longer content to place a solitary box of raisins, a chest which may or may not contain tea, and a few other articles, in his window. He has his extensive prairie of moist sugar, crossed with rivulets of pre-

served lemon-peel; his samples of tea are contained in elegant little polished
vases, guarded by mandarins in splendid attire; his coffee is exhibited in various states and qualities; he has a highly polished steam-engine in his window,
to imply that he sells so much coffee that he must have steam power to grind
it; his loaves of white sugar are broken in half, to show that they are not
"dummies," and that they have the right crystalline grain; and he does not
fail to inform you that he has taken advantage of the recent intelligence from
China to make extensive ready-money purchases, by which he can sell tea
lower than his neighbours. His shop is redolent of plate-glass and gas-lights,
and is altogether an attractive affair. There are, however, a few old establishments in this line whose celebrity renders these showy displays unnecessary;
and there are also two or three new ones which command a large business by
advertising rather than by shop-window display.

The shops devoted to the sale of wearing apparel are, however, the most
remarkable in London. The principle of competition has been driven further
in the drapery business than in most others, and hence the linen-drapers'
shops exhibit the effects which this competition produces more strikingly perhaps than most others. The rise of the cotton manufacture in England has
had much to [392] do with this matter; for when woollen fabrics were the
staple of English dress, the comparative costliness prevented any very eager
competition, and the fabrics themselves were not of so showy a character.
It is true the mercer had attractive silken goods to display in his window; but
the immense consumption of cotton in female dress has been the chief moving power towards the production of the present remarkable display in the
drapers' shops. The mills, the labour, the capital employed in this manufacture have led to so large a production that the manufacturer is anxious to
"do business" in any quarter, and this anxiety leads to a constant increase
in the number of retail shops.

To whatever part of London we direct our steps, we shall find that the
Drapers' shops—including in this term those which sell cotton, linen, silk,
and worsted goods—are among the handsomest. We may commence a tour
from the East, and we shall find it everywhere pretty nearly alike; that is, in
the busy streets, for in the by-streets the shops of this kind, what few there
are, are of a much humbler description. In Whitechapel and other wide
thoroughfares at the east end, the goods exposed in these windows are generally rather of a humble and cheap kind; but the windows are nevertheless
glazed with plate-glass, and lighted with a profusion of gas-jets, such as only
the gin-palaces can equal. On approaching Aldgate we find, among many
shops of this character, one for the sale of garments for the male sex; and a
most extraordinary shop it is, for it may be said to reach from the ground to
the roof, every story being fronted with plate-glass, and filled with goods.
From Aldgate to St. Paul's, whether we go by way of Fenchurch Street and
Lombard Street, or Leadenhall Street and Cornhill, the shops of this character
are not particularly observable; but when we arrive at St. Paul's Churchyard
we come to a very world of show. Here we find a shop whose front presents

an uninterrupted mass of glass from the ceiling to the ground; no horizontal
sash bars being seen, and the vertical ones made of brass. Here, too, we see
on a winter's evening a mode of lighting recently introduced, by which the
products of combustion are given off in the street, instead of being left to soil
the goods in the window: the lamps are fixed outside the shop, with a reflector
so placed as to throw down a strong light upon the commodities in the
window. . . .

[394] Nor is the method of conducting business at these shops less remarkable than their appearance. Everything is on the "high-pressure" system of
competition; and many of the most notable changes in shop arrangements
have originated there. At one time well-shaped gilt letters written on the
facia* over the window sufficed; but they have been nearly superseded by
letters carved in wood and then gilt, or by letters cast in porcelain or glass,
and decorated or partly gilt. Then, as well-shaped letters may be feared to
attract no notice, others have been invented which shall seduce by their odd-
ness. Some are very thick and short; some thin and lofty; some have thick
strokes where there ought to be thin, and *vice versá;* some are represented
perspectively, as if standing one behind another like a file of soldiers; some
follow each other vertically up the front of the house; and in one instance
that we have seen, the letters are placed upside down. If, instead of looking
at the inscription over the window, we read those in the window, we are led
almost to believe that man was made to fatten on the misfortunes of his
fellow-man:—"dreadful conflagration," "awful inundation," "manufacturing
distress," "ruinous sacrifice," "bankruptcy"—are the written horrors which
stare the reader in the face, and which are intended to make them believe that
those misfortunes happening to other men have been the means of enabling
the shopkeeper to sell countless thousands of bales of goods at —— per yard
—of course, 50 per cent. under what the raw materials cost. One would think
that the joke had become a stale one, that it had been worn to death by such
constant usage; but there still seem to be persons willing to be deceived.
There are also numberless little catchwords to attract the notice of the
passerby: such as "Look here!"—"Stop!"—"Tariff!"—"Income-tax!"—
"Given away!"—"Sale closes to-day!" &c.: anything, in short, which may
make the rapid walker stay his, or her, pace. The price of a commodity, too,
may be so ticketed as to deceive a reader: thus, two guineas, by a dexterous
smallness in the £, may look remarkably like twenty-two shillings. It is only
fair to admit, however, that so far as the linen-drapery business is concerned,
the higher class of shops do not push this system to so great an extent as those
of humble rank. Still the practice is so far general as to constitute a marked
feature in retail trade, and to furnish a fair source of reflection on the commercial causes which have led to so keen a spirit of competition. . . .

* The plate or tablet on the front of the shop.

from

London Labour and the London Poor: *A Cyclopedia of the Condition and Earnings of Those That* Will Work, *Those That* Cannot Work, *and Those That* Will Not Work.

Henry Mayhew

HENRY MAYHEW was a journalist and comic dramatist born in 1812 who turned to journalism after running away to sea as a boy and later serving as a clerk in his father's law office. Between 1831 and 1841 he started or helped to start a number of popular periodicals, including the famous comic weekly, *Punch. London Labour and the London Poor* was originally written, in collaboration with John Binny and others, as a series of articles for the *Morning Chronicle,* the same newspaper for which Dickens had worked, and which had published some of the *Sketches by Boz* about fifteen years earlier. Mayhew's reports describe the London of the late forties; part of his work was published in two volumes in 1851, but the rest of it was delayed by legal difficulties.

Mayhew is the originator of an important school of reporting which took as its mission the task of calling the attention of the general public to the plight of the poor. He was a natural sociologist who did his work without ever hearing of the science of sociology, a forerunner of such investigators as Beatrice Webb and Charles Booth. Mayhew's work contains valuable facts and statistics that could be gathered

43

only by interviewing hundreds of people and by making elaborate investigations. But it has more than utilitarian value; its immediacy and wealth of detail capture the imagination and set the scene vividly before the reader. Perhaps the most valuable aspect of his work is its demonstration that the intolerable conditions of slum life could be reported in an objective, matter-of-fact manner, without horror or indignation. Mayhew is sympathetic and humane without being maudlin. He enters into the situations of thieves and prostitutes without abandoning ordinary moral standards, but also without a trace of condemnation or condescension.

Four vols. London: Griffin, Bohn, and Company, 1861.

From VOLUME I, The Homes of the Costermongers.

[47] The homes of the costermongers in these places, may be divided into three classes; firstly, those who, by having a regular trade or by prudent economy, are enabled to live in comparative ease and plenty; secondly, those who, from having a large family or by imprudent expenditure, are, as it were, struggling with the world, and thirdly, those who for want of stock-money, or ill success in trade are nearly destitute.

The first home I visited was that of an old woman, who with the assistance of her son and girls, contrived to live in a most praiseworthy and comfortable manner. She and all her family were teetotallers, and may be taken as a fair type of the thriving costermonger.

As I ascended a dark flight of stairs, a savory smell of stew grew stronger at each step I mounted. The woman lived in a large airy room on the first floor ("the drawing-room" as she told me laughing at her own joke), well lighted by a clean window, and I found her laying out the savory smelling dinner looking most temptingly clean. The floor was as white as if it had been newly planed, the coke fire was bright and warm, making the lid of the tin saucepan on it rattle up and down as the steam rushed out. The wall over the fire-place was patched up to the ceiling with little square pictures of saints, and on the mantel-piece, between a row of bright tumblers and wine glasses filled with odds and ends, stood glazed crockeryware images of Prince Albert and M. Jullien.* Against the walls, which were papered with "hangings" of four different patterns and colours, were hung several warm shawls, and in the band-box, which stood on the stained chest of drawers, you could tell that the Sunday bonnet was stowed safely away from the dust. A turn-up bed-

* Albert, the husband of Queen Victoria, held the title of Prince Consort. Louis Antoine Julien (or Jullien) was a popular conductor of opera and concert music.

stead thrown back, and covered with a many-coloured patch-work quilt, stood opposite to a long dresser with its mugs and cups dangling from the hooks, and the clean blue plates and dishes ranged in order at the back. There were a few bushel baskets piled up in one corner, "but the apples smelt so," she said, "they left them in a stable at night."

By the fire sat the woman's daughter, a pretty meek-faced gray-eyed girl of sixteen, who "was home nursing" for a cold. "Steve" (her boy) I was informed, was out working. With his help, the woman assured me, she could live very comfortably—"God be praised" and when he got the barrow he was promised, she gave me to understand, that their riches were to increase past reckoning. Her girl too was to be off at work as soon as sprats came in. "Its on Lord Mayor's-day they comes in," said a neighbour who had rushed up to see the strange gentleman, "they says he has 'em on his table, but I never seed 'em. They never gives us the pieces, no not even the heads," and every one laughed to their utmost. The good old dame was in high spirits, her dark eyes sparkling as she spoke about her "Steve." The daughter in a little time lost her bashfulness, and informed me "that one of the Polish refugees was a-courting Mrs. M——, who had given him a pair of black eyes."

On taking my leave I was told by the mother that their silver gilt Dutch clock—with its glass face and blackleaded weights—"was the best one in London, and might be relied on with the greatest safety."

As a specimen of the dwellings of the struggling costers, the following may be cited:

The man, a tall, thick-built, almost good-looking fellow, with a large fur cap on his head, lived with his family in a front kitchen, and as there were, with his mother-in-law, five persons, and only one bed, I was somewhat puzzled to know where they could *all* sleep. The barrow standing on the railings over the window, half shut out the light, and when any one passed there was a momentary shadow thrown over the room, and a loud rattling of the [48] iron gratings above that completely prevented all conversation. When I entered, the mother-in-law* was reading aloud one of the threepenny papers to her son, who lulled on the bed, that with its curtains nearly filled the room. There was the usual attempt to make the fireside comfortable. The stone sides had been well whitened, and the mantel-piece decorated with its small tin trays, tumblers, and a piece of looking-glass. A cat with a kitten were seated on the hearth-rug in front. "They keeps the varmint away," said the woman, stroking the "puss," "and gives a look of home." By the drawers were piled up four bushel baskets, and in a dark corner near the bed stood a tall measure full of apples that scented the room. Over the head, on a string that stretched from wall to wall, dangled a couple of newly-washed shirts, and by the window were two stone barrels, for lemonade, when the coster visited the fairs and races.

Whilst we were talking, the man's little girl came home. For a poor man's child she was dressed to perfection; her pinafore was clean, her face shone

* Stepmother.

with soap, and her tidy cotton print gown had clearly been newly put on that morning. She brought news that "Janey" was coming home from auntey's, and instantly a pink cotton dress was placed by the mother-in-law before the fire to air. (It appeared that Janey was out at service, and came home once a week to see her parents and take back a clean frock.) Although these people were living, so to speak, in a cellar, still every endeavour had been made to give the home a look of comfort. The window, with its paper-patched panes, had a clean calico blind. The side-table was dressed up with yellow jugs and cups and saucers, and the band-boxes had been stowed away on the flat top of the bedstead. All the chairs, which were old fashioned mahogany ones, had sound backs and bottoms.

Of the third class, or the very poor, I chose the following "type" out of the many others that presented themselves. The family here lived in a small slant-ing-roofed house, partly stripped of its tiles. More than one half of the small leaden squares of the first-floor window were covered with brown paper, puffing out and crackling in the wind, while through the greater part of the others were thrust out ball-shaped bundles of rags, to keep out the breeze. The panes that did remain were of all shapes and sizes, and at a distance had the appearance of yellow glass, they were so stained with dirt. I opened a door with a number chalked on it, and groped my way up a broken tottering stair-case.

It took me some time after I had entered the apartment before I could get accustomed to the smoke, that came pouring into the room from the chimney. The place was filled with it, curling in the light, and making every thing so indistinct that I could with difficulty see the white mugs ranged in the corner-cupboard, not three yards from me. When the wind was in the north, or when it rained, it was always that way, I was told, "but otherwise," said an old dame about sixty, with long grisly hair spreading over her black shawl, "it is pretty good for that."

On a mattrass, on the floor, lay a pale-faced girl—"eighteen years old last twelfth-cake day" *—her drawn-up form showing in the patch-work counter-pane that covered her. She had just been confined, and the child had died! A little straw, stuffed into an old tick, was all she had to lie upon, and even that had been given up to her by the mother until she was well enough to work again. To shield her from the light of the window, a cloak had been fastened up slantingly across the panes; and on a string that ran along the wall was tied, amongst the bonnets, a clean nightcap—"against the doctor came," as the mother, curtsying, informed me. By the side of the bed, almost hidden in the dark shade, was a pile of sieve baskets, crowned by the flat shallow† that the mother "worked" with.

The room was about nine feet square, and furnished a home for three women. The ceiling slanted like that of a garret, and was the colour of old leather, excepting a few rough white patches, where the tenants had rudely

* January 6th, the twelfth day after Christmas, celebrated as the feast of the Epiphany.
† A basket or tray used by costermongers.

mended it. The white light was easily seen through the laths, and in one corner a large patch of the paper looped down from the wall. One night the family had been startled from their sleep by a large mass of mortar—just where the roof bulged in—falling into the room. "We never want rain water," the woman told me, "for we can catch plenty just over the chimney-place."

They had made a carpet out of three or four old mats. They were "obligated to it, for fear of dropping anything through the boards into the donkey stables in the parlour underneath. But we only pay ninepence a week rent," said the old woman, "and mustn't grumble."

The only ornament in the place was on the mantel-piece—an old earthenware sugar-basin, well silvered over, that had been given by the eldest girl when she died, as a remembrance to her mother. Two cracked tea-cups, on their inverted saucers, stood on each side, and dressed up the fire-side into something like tidiness. The chair I sat on was by far the best out of the three in the room, and that had no back, and only half its quantity of straw.

The parish, the old woman told me, allowed her 1s. a week and two loaves. But the doctor ordered her girl to take sago and milk, and she was many a time sorely puzzled to get it. The neighbours helped her a good deal, and often sent her part of their unsold greens;—even if it was only the outer leaves of the cabbages, she was thankful for them. Her other girl—a big-boned wench, with a red shawl crossed over her bosom, and her black hair parted on one side—did all she could, and so they lived on. "As long as they kept out of the 'big house' (the workhouse) she would not complain."

I never yet beheld so much destitution borne with so much content. Verily the acted philosophy of the poor is a thing to make those who write and preach about it hide their heads.

From Volume II, Boy Crossing-Sweepers and Tumblers.

[494] A remarkably intelligent lad, who, on being spoken to, at once consented to give all the information in his power, told me the following story of his life.

It will be seen from this boy's account, and the one or two following, that a kind of partnership exists among some of these young sweepers. They have associated themselves together, appropriated several crossings to their use, and appointed a captain over them. They have their forms of trial, and "jury-house" for the settlement of disputes; laws have been framed, which govern their commercial proceedings, and a kind of language adopted by the society for its better protection from its arch-enemy, the policeman.

I found the lad who first gave me an insight into the proceedings of the associated crossing-sweepers crouched on the stone steps of a door in Adelaide-street, Strand; and when I spoke to him he was preparing to settle down in a corner and go to sleep—his legs and body being curled round almost as closely as those of a cat on a hearth.

The moment he heard my voice he was upon his feet, asking me to "give a halfpenny to poor little Jack."

He was a good-looking lad, with a pair of large mild eyes, which he took good care to turn up with an expression of supplication as he moaned for his halfpenny.

A cap, or more properly a stuff bag, covered a crop of hair which had matted itself into the form of so many paint-brushes, while his face, from its roundness of feature and the complexion of dirt, had an almost Indian look about it; the colour of his hands, too, was such that you could imagine he had been shelling walnuts.

He ran before me, treading cautiously with his naked feet, until I reached a convenient spot to take down his statement, which was as follows:—

[495] brother, my uncle, did all his. He used to go up to High Park, and then go round by the Hospital, and then turn up a yard, where all the men are who play for money [Tattersall's]; and there he'd lose his money, or sometimes win,—but that wasn't often. I remember he used to come home tipsy, and say he'd lost on this or that horse, naming wot one he'd laid on; and then mother would coax him to bed, and afterwards sit down and begin to cry.

"I was not with father when he died (but I was when he was dying), for I was sent up along with eldest sister to London with a letter to uncle, who was head servant at a doctor's. In this letter, mother asked uncle to pay back some money wot he owed, and wot father let him, and she asked him if he'd like to come down and see father before he died. I recollect I went back again to mother by the Orwell steamer. I was well dressed then, and had good clothes on, and I was given to the care of the captain—Mr. King his name was. But when I got back to Ipswich, father was dead.

"Mother took on dreadful; she was ill for three months afterwards, confined to her bed. She hardly eat anything: only beaf-tea—I think they call it— and eggs. All the while she kept on crying.

"Mother kept a servant; yes, sir, we always had a servant, as long as I can recollect; and she and the woman as was there—Anna they called her, an old lady—used to take care of me and sister. Sister was fourteen years old (she's married to a young man now, and they've gone to America; she went from a place in the East India Docks, and I saw her off). I used, when I was with mother, to go to school in the morning, and go at nine and come home at twelve to dinner, then go again at two and leave off at half-past four,— that is, if I behaved myself and did all my lessons right; for if I did not I was kept back till I *did* them so. Mother used to pay one shilling a-week, and extra for the copy-books and things. I can read and write—oh, yes, I mean read and write well—read anything, even old English; and I write pretty fair, —though I don't get much reading now, unless it's a penny paper—I've got one in my pocket now—it's the *London Journal*—there's a tale in it now about two brothers, and one of them steals the child away and puts another in his place, and then he gets found out, and all that, and he's just been falling off a bridge now.

"After mother got better, she sold all the furniture and goods and came up to London;—poor mother! She let a man of the name of Hayes have the greater part, and he left Ipswich soon after, and never gave mother the money. We came up to London, and mother took two rooms in Westminster, and I and sister lived along with her. She used to make hair-nets, and sister helped her, and used to take 'em to the hair-dressers to sell. She made these nets for two or three years, though she was suffering with a bad breast;—she died of that—poor thing!—for she had what doctors calls cancer—perhaps you've heard of 'em, sir,—and they had to cut all round here (making motions with his hands from the shoulder to the bosom). Sister saw it, though I didn't.

"Ah! she was a very good, kind mother, and very fond of both of us; though father wasn't, for he'd always have a noise with mother when he come home, only he was seldom with us when he was making his goods.

"After mother died, sister still kept on making nets, and I lived with her for some time, until she told me she couldn't afford to keep me no longer, though she seemed to have a pretty good lot to do; but she would never let me go with her to the shops, though I could crochet, which she'd learned me, and used to run and get her all her silks and things what she wanted. But she was keeping company with a young man, and one day they went out, and came back and said they'd been and got married. It was him as got rid of me.

"He was kind to me for the first two or three months, while he was keeping her company; but before he was married he got a little cross, and after he was married he begun to get more cross, and used to send me to play in the streets, and tell me not to come home again till night. One day he hit me, and I said I wouldn't be hit about by him, and then at tea that night sister gave me three shillings, and told me I must go and get my own living. So I bought a box and brushes (they cost me just the money) and went cleaning boots, and I done pretty well with them, till my box was stole from me by a boy where I was lodging. He's in prison now—got six calendar for picking pockets.

"Sister kept all my clothes. When I asked her for 'em, she said they was disposed of along with all mother's goods; but she gave me some shirts and stockings, and such-alike, and I had very good clothes, only they was all worn out. I saw sister after I left her, many times. I asked her many times to take me back, but she used to say, 'It was not her likes, but her husband's, or she'd have had me back;' and I think it was true, for until he came she was a kind-hearted girl; but he said he'd enough to do to look after his own living; he was a fancy-baker by trade.

"I was fifteen the 24th of last May, sir, and I've been sweeping crossings now near upon two years. There's a party of six of us, and we have the crossings from St. Martin's Church as far as Pall Mall. I always go along with them as lodges in the same place as I do. In the daytime, if it's dry, we do anythink what we can—open cabs, or anythink; but if it's wet, we separate, and I and another gets a crossing—those who gets on it first, keeps it,—and we stand on each side and take our chance.

[496] "We do it in this way:—if I was to see two gentlemen coming, I should cry out, 'Two toffs!' and then they are mine; and whether they give me anythink or not they are mine, and my mate is bound not to follow them; for if he did he would get a hiding from the whole lot of us. If we both cry out together, then we share. If it's a lady and gentleman, then we cries, 'A toff and a doll!' Sometimes we are caught out in this way. Perhaps it is a lady and gentleman and a child; and if I was to see them, and only say, 'A toff and a doll,' and leave out the child, then my mate can add the child; and as he is right and I wrong, then it's his party.

"If there's a policeman close at hand we mustn't ask for money; but we are always on the look-out for the policemen, and if we see one, then we calls out 'Phillup!' for that's our signal. One of the policemen at St. Martin's Church—Bandy, we calls him—knows what Phillup means, for he's up to us; so we had to change the word. (At the request of the young crossing-sweeper the present signal is omitted.)

"Yesterday on the crossing I got threepence halfpenny, but when it's dry like to-day I do nothink, for I haven't got a penny yet. We never carries no pockets, for if the policemen find us we generally pass the money to our mates, for if money's found on us we have fourteen days in prison.

"If I was to reckon all the year round, that is, one day with another, I think we make four-pence every day, and if we were to stick to it we should make more, for on a very muddy day we do better. One day, the best I ever had, from nine o'clock in the morning till seven o'clock at night, I made seven shillings and sixpence, and got not one bit of silver money among it. Every shilling I got I went and left at a shop near where my crossing is, for fear I might get into any harm. The shop's kept by a women we deals with for what we wants—tea and butter, or sugar, or brooms—anythink we wants. Saturday night week I made two-and-sixpence; that's what I took altogether up to six o'clock.

"When we see the rain we say together, 'Oh! there's a jolly good rain! we'll have a good day to-morrow.' If a shower comes on, and we are at our room, which we general are about three o'clock, to get somethink to eat—besides, we general go there to see how much each other's taken in the day—why, out we run with our brooms.

"We're always sure to make money if there's mud—that's to say, if we look for our money, and ask; of course, if we stand still we don't. Now, there's Lord Fitzhardinge, he's a good gentleman, what lives in Spring-gardens, in a large house. He's got a lot of servants and carriages. Every time he crosses the Charing-cross crossing he always gives the girl half a sovereign." (This statement was taken in June 1856.) "He doesn't cross often, because, hang it, he's got such a lot of carriages, but when he's on foot he always does. If they asks him he doesn't give nothink, but if they touches their caps he does. The housekeeper at his house is very kind to us. We run errands for her, and when she wants any of her own letters taken to the post then she calls, and if we are on the crossing we takes them for her. She's a very nice lady, and gives us broken victuals. I've got a share in that crossing,—there are three of us, and when he gives the half sovereign he always gives it to the girl, and those that are in it shares it. She would do us out of it if she could, but we all takes good care of that, for we are all cheats.

"At night-time we tumbles—that is, if the policemen ain't nigh. We goes general to Waterloo-place when the Opera's on. We sends on one of us ahead, as a looker-out, to look for the policeman, and then we follows. It's no good tumbling to gentlemen *going* to the Opera; it's when they're coming back they gives us money. When they've got a young lady on their arm they laugh at us tumbling; some will give us a penny, others threepence, sometimes a sixpence or a shilling, and sometimes a halfpenny. We either do the cat'un-wheel, or else we keep before the gentleman and lady, turning head-over-heels, putting our broom on the ground and then turning over it.

"I work a good deal fetching cabs after the Opera is over; we general open the doors of those what draw up at the side of the pavement for people to get into as have walked a little down the Haymarket looking for a cab. We gets a month in prison if we touch the others by the columns. I once had half a sovereign give me by a gentleman; it was raining awful, and I run all about for a cab, and at last I got one. The gentleman knew it was half a sovereign, because he said—'Here, my little man, here's half a sovereign for your trouble.' He had three ladies with him, beautiful ones, with nothink on their heads, and only capes on their bare shoulders; and he had white kids on, and his regular Opera togs, too. I liked him very much, and as he was going to give me somethink the ladies says—'Oh, give him somethink extra!' It was pouring with rain, and they couldn't get a cab; they were all engaged, but I jumped on the box of one as was driving along the line. Last Saturday Opera night I made fifteen pence by the gentlemen coming from the Opera.

[497] "We always meet at St. Martin's steps—the 'jury house,' we calls 'em—at three o'clock in the morning, that's always our hour. We reckons up what we've taken, but we don't divide. Sometimes, if we owe anythink where we lodge, the women of the house will be waiting on the steps for us: then, if we've got it, we pay them; if we haven't, why it can't be helped, and it goes on. We gets into debt, because sometimes the women where we live gets lushy; then we don't give them anythink, because they'd forget it, so we spends it ourselves. We can't lodge at what's called model lodging-houses, as our hours don't suit them folks. We pays threepence a-night for lodging. Food, if we get plenty of money, we buys for ourselves. We buys a pound of bread, that's two-pence farthing—best seconds, and a farthing's worth of dripping—that's enough for a pound of bread—and we gets a ha'porth of tea and a ha'porth of sugar; or if we're hard up, we gets only a penn'orth of bread. We make our own tea at home; they lends us a kittle, tea-pot, and cups and saucers, and all that.

"Once or twice a-week we gets meat. We all club together, and go into

Newgate Market and gets some pieces cheap, and biles them at home. We tosses up who shall have the biggest bit, and we divide the broth, a cupful in each basin, until it's lasted out. If any of us has been unlucky, we each gives the unlucky one one or two halfpence. Some of us is obliged at times to sleep out all night; and sometimes, if any of us gets nothink, then the others gives him a penny or two, and *he* does the same for us when *we* are out of luck.

"Besides, there's our clothes: I'm paying for a pair of boots now. I paid a shilling off Saturday night.

"When we gets home at half-past three in the morning, whoever cries out 'first wash' has it. First of all we washes our feet, and we all uses the same water. Then we washes our faces and hands, and necks, and whoever fetches the fresh water up has first wash; and if the second don't like to go and get fresh, why he uses the dirty. Whenever we come in the landlady makes us wash our feet. Very often the stones cuts our feet and makes them bleed; then we bind a bit of rag round them. We like to put on boots and shoes in the daytime, but at night-time we can't, because it stops the tumbling.

"On the Sunday we all have a clean shirt put on before we go out, and then we go and tumble after the omnibuses. Sometimes we do very well on a fine Sunday, when there's plenty of people out on the roofs of the busses. We never do anythink on a wet dry day, but only when it's been raining and then dried up. I have run after a Cremorne bus, when they've thrown us money, as far as from Charing-cross right up to Piccadilly, but if they don't throw us nothink we don't run very far. I should think we gets at that work, taking one Sunday with another, eightpence all the year round.

"When there's snow on the ground we puts our money together, and goes and buys an old shovel, and then, about seven o'clock in the morning, we goes to the shops and asks them if we shall scrape the snow away. We general gets twopence every house, but some gives sixpence, for it's very hard to clean the snow away, particular when it's been on the ground some time. It's awful cold, and gives us chilblains on our feet; but we don't mind it when we're working, for we soon gets hot then.

"Before winter comes, we general save up our money and buys a pair of shoes. Sometimes we makes a very big snowball and rolls it up to the hotels, and then the gentlemen laughs and throws us money; or else we pelt each other with snowballs, and then they scrambles money between us. We always go to Morley's Hotel, at Charing-cross. The police in winter times is kinder to us than in summer, and they only laughs at us;—p'rhaps it is because there is not so many of us about then,—only them as is obligated to find a living for themselves; for many of the boys has fathers and mothers as sends them out in summer, but keeps them at home in winter when it's piercing cold.

"I have been to the station-house, because the police always takes us up if we are out at night; but we're only locked up till morning,—that is, if we behaves ourselves when we're taken before the gentleman. Mr. Hall, at Bow-street, only says, 'Poor boy, let him go.' But it's only when we've done noth-ink but stop out that he says that. He's a kind old gentleman; but mind, it's only when you have been before him two or three times he says so, because if it's a many times, he'll send you for fourteen days.

From VOLUME IV, Pickpockets and Shoplifters.

. . . [304] We say there are a few exceptions to the general rule, that the most of our habitual thieves have sprung from the loins of felon parents. We blush to say that some have joined the ranks of our London thieves, and are living callous in open crime, who were trained in the homes of honest and industrious parents, and were surrounded in early life with all those influences which are fitted to elevate and improve the mind. But here our space forbids us to enlarge.

The chief sources whence our pickpockets spring are from the low lodging-houses—from those dwellings in low neighbourhoods, where their parents are thieves, and where improvident and drunken people neglect their children, such as Whitechapel, Shoreditch, Spitalfields, New Cut, Lambeth, the Borough, Clerkenwell, Drury Lane, and other localities. Many of them are the children of Irish parents, costermongers, bricklayers' labourers, and others. They often begin to steal at six or seven years of age, sometimes as early as five years, and commit petty sneaking thefts, as well as pick handkerchiefs from gentlemen's pockets. Many of these ragged urchins are taught to steal by their companions, others are taught by trainers of thieves, young men and women, and some middle-aged convicted thieves. They are learned to be expert in this way. A coat is suspended on the wall with a bell attached to it, and the boy attempts to take the handkerchief from the pocket without the bell ringing. Until he is able to do this with proficiency he is not considered well trained. Another way in which they are trained is this: The trainer—if a man—walks up and down the room with a handkerchief in the tail of his coat, and the ragged boys amuse themselves abstracting it until they learn to do it in an adroit manner. We could point our finger to three of these execrable wretches, who are well known to train schools of juvenile thieves—one of them, a young man at Whitechapel; another, a young woman at Clerkenwell; and a third, a middle-aged man residing about Lambeth Walk. These base wretches buy the stolen handkerchiefs from the boys at a paltry sum. We have also heard of some being taught to pick pockets by means of an effigy; but this is not so well authenticated.

Great numbers of these ragged pickpockets may be seen loitering about our principal streets, ready to steal from a stall or shop-door when they find an opportunity. During the day they generally pick pockets two or three in a little band, but at dusk a single one can sometimes do it with success. They not only steal handkerchiefs of various kinds, but also pocketbooks from the tails of gentlemen's coats. We may see them occasionally engaged at this work on Blackfriars Bridge and London Bridge, also along Bishopsgate, Shoreditch,

Whitechapel, Drury Lane, and similar localities. They may be seen at any hour of the day, but chiefly from 10 to 2 o'clock. They are generally actively on the look-out on Saturday evening in the shopping streets where the labouring people get their provisions in for the Sunday. At this early stage the boys occasionally pick pockets, and go about cadging and sneaking (begging and committing petty felonies).

The next stage commences—we shall say—about fourteen years of age, when the stripling lays aside his rags, and dresses in a more decent way, though rather shabby. Perhaps in a dark or gray frock-coat, dark or dirty tweed trousers, and a cap with peak, and shoes. At this time many of them go to low neighbourhods, or to those quieter localities where the labouring people reside, and pick the pockets of the wives and daughters of this class of persons; others steal from gentlemen passing along thoroughfares, while a few adroit lads are employed by men to steal from ladies' pockets in the fashionable streets of the metropolis.

These young thieves seldom commit their depredations in the localities where they are known, but prowl in different parts of the metropolis. They are of a wandering character, changing from one district to another, and living in different lodging-houses—often leaving their parent's houses as early as ten years of age. Sometimes they are driven by drunken loafing parents to steal, though in most cases they leave their comfortable homes and live in lodging-houses.

When they have booty, they generally bring it to some person to dispose of, as suspicion would be aroused if they went to sell or pawn it themselves. In some cases they give it to the trainer of thieves, or they take it to some low receiving house, where wretches encourage them in stealing; sometimes to low coffee-houses, low hairdressers or tailors, who act as middlemen to dispose of the property, generally giving them but a small part of the value.

In the event of their rambling to a distant part of London, they sometimes arrange [305] to get one of their number to convey the stolen goods to these parties. At other times they dispose of them to low wretches connected with the lodging-houses, or other persons in disreputable neighbourhoods.

At this time many of them cohabit with girls in low lodging-houses; many of whom are older than themselves, and generally of the felon class.

These lads frequently steal at the "tail" of gentlemen's coats, and learn the other modes of picking pockets.

Stealing the handkerchief from the "tail" of a gentleman's coat in the street is generally effected in this way. Three or four usually go together. They see an old gentleman passing by. One remains behind, while the other two follow up close beside him, but a little behind. The one walking by himself behind is the looker out to see if there are any police or detectives near, or if any one passing by or hovering around is taking notice of them. One of the two walking close by the gentleman adroitly picks his pocket, and coils the handkerchief up in his hand so as not to be seen, while the other brings his body close to him, so as not to let his arm be seen by any passer by.

If the party feel him taking the handkerchief from his pocket, the thief passes it quickly to his companion, who runs off with it. The looker-out walks quietly on as if nothing had occurred, or sometimes walks up to the gentleman and asks him what is the matter, or pretends to tell him in what direction the thief has run, pointing him to a very different direction from the one he has taken.

They not only abstract handkerchiefs but also pocketbooks from the tail of gentlemen's coats, or any other article they can lay their fingers on.

This is the common way in which the coat-pocket is picked when the person is proceeding along the street. Sometimes it happens that one thief will work by himself, but this is very seldom. In the case of a person standing, the coat-tail pocket is picked much in the same manner.

These boys in most cases confine themselves to stealing from the coat-pocket on the streets, but in the event of a crowd on any occasion, they are so bold as to steal watches from the vest-pocket. This is done in a different style, and generally in the company of two or three in this manner: One of them folds his arms across his breast in such a way that his right hand is covered with his left arm. This enables him to use his hand in an unobserved way, so that he is thereby able to abstract the watch from the vest-pocket of the gentleman standing by his side.

A police-officer informed us, that when at Cremorne about a fortnight ago, a large concourse of people was assembled to see the female acrobat, termed the "Female Blondin," cross the Thames on a rope suspended over the river, he observed two young men of about twenty-four years of age, and about the middle height, respectably dressed, whom he suspected to be pickpockets. They went up to a smart gentlemanly man standing at the riverside looking eagerly at the Female Blondin, then walking the rope over the middle of the river. As his attention was thus absorbed, the detective saw these two men go up to him. One of them placed himself close on the right hand side of him, and putting his right arm under his left, thus covered his right hand, and took the watch gently from the pocket of the gentleman's vest. The thief made two attempts to break the ring attached to the watch, termed the "bowl" or swivel, with his finger and thumb.

After two ineffective endeavours he bent it completely round, and yet it would not break. He then left the watch hanging down in front of the vest, the gentleman meanwhile being unaware of the attempted felony. The detective officer took both the thieves into custody. They were brought before the Westminster police-court and sentenced each to three months' imprisonment for an attempt to steal from the person.

The same officer informed us that about a month or six weeks ago, in the same place, on a similar occasion, he observed three persons, a man, a boy, and a woman, whom he suspected to be picking pockets. The man was about twenty-eight years of age, rather under the middle size. The woman hovered by his side. She was very good-looking, about twenty-four years of age, dressed in a green coloured gown, Paisley shawl, and straw bonnet trimmed with red velvet and red flowers. The man was dressed in a black frock-coat, brown trousers, and black hat. The boy, who happened to be his brother, was about fourteen years old, dressed in a brown shooting-coat, corduroy trousers, and black cap with peak. The boy had an engaging countenance, with sharp features and smart manner. The officer observed the man touch the boy on the shoulder and point him towards an old lady. The boy placed himself on her right side, and the man and woman kept behind. The former put his left hand into the pocket of the lady's gown and drew nothing from it, then left her and went [306] about two yards farther; there he placed himself by other two ladies, tried both their pockets and left them again. He followed another lady and succeeded in picking her pocket of a small sum of money and a handkerchief. The officer took them all to the police station with the assistance of another detective officer, when they were committed for trial at Clerkenwell sessions. The man was sentenced to ten years' penal servitude, the boy to two months' hard labour, and three months in a reformatory, and the woman was sentenced to two years' imprisonment, with hard labour, in the House of Correction at Westminster.

It appeared, in the course of evidence at the trial, that this man had previously been four years in penal servitude, and since his return had decoyed his little brother from a situation he held, for the purpose of training him to pick pockets, having induced him to rob his employer before leaving service.

The *scarf pin* is generally taken from the breast in this way. The thief generally has a handkerchief in his hand, pretending to wipe his nose, as he walks along the street. He then places his right hand across the breast of the person he intends to rob, bringing his left hand stealthily under his arm. This conceals his movements from the eyes of the person. With the latter hand he snatches out the pin from the scarf. It is sometimes done with the right hand, at other times with the left, according to the position of the person, and is generally done in the company of one or more. The person robbed is rarely aware of the theft. Should he be aware, or should any one passing by have observed the movement, the pin got from the scarf is suddenly passed into the hands of the other parties, when all of them suddenly make off in different directions soon to meet again in some neighbouring locality.

At other times the thief drives the person with a push, in the street, bringing his hands to his breast as if he had stumbled against him, at the same time adroitly laying hold of the pin. This is done in such a way that the person is seldom aware of the robbery until he afterwards finds out the loss of the article.

The *trousers pocket* is seldom picked on the public street, as this is an operation of considerable difficulty and danger. It is not easy to sip [sic] the hand into the trousers pocket without being felt by the person attempted to be robbed. This is generally done in crowds where people are squeezed together, when they contrive to do it in this way: They cut up the trousers with a knife or other sharp instrument, lay open the pocket, and adroitly rifle the money from it; or they insert the fingers or hand into it in a push, often without being observed, while the person's attention is distracted, possibly by some of the accomplices or stalls. They often occasion a disturbance in crowds, and create a quarrel with people near them, or have sham fights with each other, or set violently on the person they intend to rob. Many rough expedients are occasionally had recourse to, to effect this object.

Sometimes the pocket is picked in a crowd by means of laying hold of the party by the middle as if they had jostled against him, or by pressing on his back from behind, while the fingers or hand are inserted into the pocket of his trousers to snatch any valuables, money or otherwise, contained therein.

This mode of stealing is sometimes done by one person, at other times by the aid of accomplices. It is most commonly done in the manner now described.

By dint of long experience and natural skill, some attain great perfection in this difficult job, and accomplish their object in the most clever and effective manner. They are so nimble and accomplished that they will accost a gentleman in the street, and while speaking to him, and looking him in the face, will quietly insert their hand into his vest pocket and steal his watch.

In a crowd, the pin is sometimes stolen with dexterity by a person from behind inserting his hand over the shoulder. Sometimes the watch is stolen by a sudden snatch at the guard, when the thief runs off with his booty. This is not so often done in the thoroughfares, as it is attended with great danger of arrest. It is oftener done in quiet by-streets, or by-places, where there are many adjacent courts and alleys intersecting each other, through which the thief has an opportunity of escaping.

These are the various modes by which gentlemen's pockets are generally picked. . . .

from

Household Words

Household Words was a family magazine founded by Dickens in 1850. As a way of capitalizing upon his fame, he had the words, "Conducted by Charles Dickens" printed at the top of every page. *Household Words* was intended for a broad and unimaginative public more interested in factual and amusing information than in fiction or ideas. It carried some stories, a little poetry, and a serialization of Dickens' *Child's History of England*, but most of its space was devoted to articles about contemporary life and customs. Dickens wrote regularly for *Household Words* (though his contributions, like all the others, were unsigned), and the magazine is an accurate reflection of his interests, but all of the articles reprinted here were written by other contributors.

VOLUME I, NUMBER 1, Saturday, March 30th, 1850, "The Amusements of the People."

. . . [13] There is a range of imagination in most of us, which no amount of steam-engines will satisfy; and which The-great-exhibition-of-the-works-of-industry-of-all-nations, itself, will probably leave unappeased. The lower we go, the more natural it is that the best-relished provision for this should be found in dramatic entertainments; as at once the most obvious, the least troublesome, and the most real, of all escapes out of the literal world. Joe Whelks, of the New Cut, Lambeth, is not much of a reader, has no great store of books, no very commodious room to read in, no very decided inclination to read, and no power at all of presenting vividly before his mind's eye what he reads about. But, put Joe in the gallery of the Victoria Theatre; show him doors and windows in the scene that will open and shut, and that people can get in and out of; tell him a story with these aids, and by the help of live men and women dressed up, confiding to him their innermost secrets, in voices audible half a mile off; and Joe will unravel a story through all its entanglements, and sit there as long after midnight as you have anything left to show him. Accordingly, the Theatres to which Mr. Whelks resorts, are always full; and whatever changes of fashion the drama knows elsewhere, it is always fashionable in the New Cut. . . .

A few weeks ago, we went to one of Mr. Whelks's favourite Theatres, to see an attractive Melo-Drama called MAY MORNING, OR THE MYSTERY OF 1715, AND THE MURDER! We had an idea that the former of these titles might refer to the month in which either the Mystery or the Murder happened, but we found it to be the name of the heroine, the pride of Keswick Vale; who was 'called May Morning' (after a common custom among the English Peasantry) 'from her bright eyes and merry laugh.' Of this young lady, it may be observed, in passing, that she subsequently sustained every possible calamity of human existence, in a white muslin gown with blue tucks; and that she did every conceivable and inconceivable thing with a pistol, that [14] could anyhow be effected by that description of fire-arms.

The Theatre was extremely full. The prices of admission were, to the boxes, a shilling; to the pit, sixpence; to the gallery, threepence. The gallery was of enormous dimensions (among the company, in the front row, we observed Mr. Whelks); and overflowing with occupants. It required no close observation of the attentive faces, rising one above another, to the very door in the roof, and squeezed and jammed in, regardless of all discomforts, even there, to impress a stranger with a sense of its being highly desirable to lose no possible chance of effecting any mental improvement in that great audience.

The company in the pit were not very clean or sweet-savoured, but there were some good-humoured young mechanics* among them, with their wives. These were generally accompanied by 'the baby,' insomuch that the pit was a perfect nursery. No effect made on the stage was so curious, as the looking down on the quiet faces of these babies fast asleep, after looking up at the staring sea of heads in the gallery. There were a good many cold fried soles in the pit, besides; and a variety of flat stone bottles, of all portable sizes.

The audience in the boxes was of much the same character (babies and fish excepted) as the audience in the pit. A private in the Foot Guards sat in the next box; and a personage who wore pins on his coat instead of buttons, and was in such a damp habit of living as to be quite mouldy, was our nearest neighbour. In several parts of the house we noticed some young pickpockets of our acquaintance; but as they were evidently there as private individuals, and not in their public capacity, we were little disturbed by their presence. For we consider the hours of idleness passed by this class of society

* Manual laborers.

as so much gain to society at large; and we do not join in a whimsical sort of lamentation that is generally made over them, when they are found to be unoccupied.

As we made these observations the curtain rose, and we were presently in possession of the following particulars.

Sir George Elmore, a melancholy Baronet with every appearance of being in that advanced stage of indigestion in which Mr. Morrison's patients usually are, when they happen to hear, through Mr. Moat, of the surprising effects of his Vegetable Pills,* was found to be living in a very large castle, in the society of one round table, two chairs, and Captain George Elmore, 'his supposed son, the Child of Mystery, and the Man of Crime.' The Captain, in addition to an undutiful habit of bullying his father on all occasions, was a prey to many vices: foremost among which may be mentioned his desertion of his wife, 'Estella de Neva, a Spanish lady,' and his determination unlawfully to possess himself of May Morning; M. M. being then on the eve of marriage to Will Stanmore, a cheerful sailor, with very loose legs.

The strongest evidence, at first, of the Captain's being the Child of Mystery and the Man of Crime was deducible from his boots, which, being very high and wide, and apparently made of sticking-plaister,† justified the worst theatrical suspicions of his disadvantage. And indeed he presently turned out as ill as could be desired: getting into May Morning's Cottage by the window after dark; refusing to 'unhand' May Morning when required to do so by that lady; waking May Morning's only surviving parent, a blind old gentleman with a black ribbon over his eyes, whom we shall call Mr. Stars, as his name was stated in the bill thus * * * * * * ; and showing himself desperately bent on carrying off May Morning by force of arms. Even this was not the worst of the Captain; for, being foiled in his diabolical purpose—temporarily by means of knives and pistols, providentially caught up and directed at him by May Morning, and finally, for the time being, by the advent of Will Stanmore—he caused one Slink, his adherent, to denounce Will Stanmore as a rebel, and got that cheerful mariner carried off, and shut up in prison. At about the same period of the Captain's career, there suddenly appeared in his father's castle, a dark complexioned lady of the name of Manuella, 'a Zingara Woman from the Pyrenean mountains; the wild wanderer of the heath, and the pronouncer of the prophecy,' who threw the melancholy baronet, his supposed father, into the greatest confusion by asking him what he had upon his conscience, and by pronouncing mysterious rhymes concerning the Child of Mystery and the Man of Crime, to a low trembling of fiddles. Matters were in this state when the Theatre resounded with applause, and Mr. Whelks fell into a fit of unbounded enthusiasm, consequent on the entrance of 'Michael the Mendicant.'

At first we referred something of the cordiality with which Michael the Mendicant was greeted, to the fact of his being 'made up' with an excessively

---

* James Morrison's Vegetable Universal Medicine was a celebrated nostrum of the time.
† The Victorian equivalent of adhesive tape.

dirty face, which might create a bond of union between himself and a large majority of the audience. But it soon came out that Michael the Mendicant had been hired in old time by Sir George Elmore, to murder his (Sir George Elmore's) elder brother—which he had done; notwithstanding which little affair of honour, Michael was in reality a very good fellow; quite a tender-hearted man; who, on hearing of the Captain's determination to settle Will Stanmore, cried out, 'What! more bel-ood!' and fell flat—overpowered by his nice sense of humanity. In like manner, in describing that small error of judgment into which he had allowed himself to be tempted by money, this gentleman exclaimed, 'I ster-ruck him down, and fel-ed in er-error!' and further he remarked, with honest pride, 'I have liveder as a beggar—a road-ersider vaigerant, but no ker-rime since then has stained these hands!' All these sentiments of the worthy man were hailed with showers of [15] applause; and when, in the excitement of his feelings on one occasion, after a soliloquy, he 'went off' *on his back,* kicking and shuffling along the ground, after the manner of bold spirits in trouble, who object to be taken to the station-house, the cheering was tremendous.

And to see how little harm he had done, after all! Sir George Elmore's elder brother was NOT dead. Not he! He recovered, after this sensitive creature had 'fel-ed in er-error,' and, putting a black ribbon over his eyes to disguise himself, went and lived in a modest retirement with his only child. In short, Mr. Stars was the identical individual! When Will Stanmore turned out to be the wrongful Sir George Elmore's son, instead of the Child of Mystery and Man of Crime, who turned out to be Michael's son, (a change having been effected, in revenge, by the lady from the Pyrenean Mountains, who became the Wild Wanderer of the Heath, in consequence of the wrongful Sir George Elmore's perfidy to her and desertion of her), Mr. Stars went up to the Castle, and mentioned to his murdering brother how it was. Mr. Stars said it was all right; he bore no malice; he had kept out of the way, in order that his murdering brother (to whose numerous virtues he was no stranger) might enjoy the property; and now he would propose that they should make it up and dine together. The murdering brother immediately consented, embraced the Wild Wanderer, and it is supposed sent instructions to Doctors' Commons for a license to marry her. After which, they were all very comfortable indeed. For it is not much to try to murder your brother for the sake of his property, if you only suborn such a delicate assassin as Michael the Mendicant!

All this did not tend to the satisfaction of the Child of Mystery and Man of Crime, who was so little pleased by the general happiness, that he shot Will Stanmore, now joyfully out of prison and going to be married directly to May Morning, and carried off the body, and May Morning to boot, to a lone hut. Here, Will Stanmore, laid out for dead at fifteen minutes past twelve, P.M., arose at seventeen minutes past, infinitely fresher than most daisies, and fought two strong men single-handed. However, the Wild Wanderer, arriving with a party of male wild wanderers, who were always at her disposal—and the murdering brother arriving arm-in-arm with Mr. Stars—stopped the combat, confounded the Child of Mystery and Man of Crime, and blessed the lovers.

The adventures of 'RED RIVEN THE BANDIT' concluded the moral lesson of the evening. But, feeling by this time a little fatigued, and believing that we already discerned in the countenance of Mr. Whelks a sufficient confusion between right and wrong to last him for one night, we retired: the rather as we intended to meet him, shortly, at another place of dramatic entertainment for the people.

VOLUME I, NUMBER 3, Saturday, April 13th, 1850, "The Amusements of the People."

[57] Mr. Whelks being much in the habit of recreating himself at a class of theatres called 'Saloons,' we repaired to one of these, not long ago, on a Monday evening; Monday being a great holiday-night with Mr. Whelks and his friends.

The Saloon in question is the largest in London (that which is known as The Eagle, in the City Road, should be excepted from the generic term, as not presenting by any means the same class of entertainment), and is situate not far from Shoreditch Church. It announces 'The People's Theatre,' as its second name. The prices of admission are, to the boxes, a shilling; to the pit, sixpence; to the lower gallery, fourpence; to the upper gallery and back seats, threepence. There is no half-price. The opening piece on this occasion was described in the bills as 'the greatest hit of the season, the grand new legendary and traditionary drama, combining supernatural agencies with historical facts, and identifying extraordinary superhuman causes with material, terrific, and powerful effects.' All the queen's horses and all the queen's men could not have drawn Mr. Whelks into the place like this description. Strengthened by lithographic representations of the principal superhuman causes, combined with the most popular of the material, terrific, and powerful effects, it became irresistible. Consequently, we had already failed, once, in finding six square inches of room within the walls, to stand upon; and when we now paid our money for a little stage box, like a dry shower-bath, we did so in the midst of a stream of people who persisted in paying their's for other parts of the house in despite of the representations of the Money-taker that it was 'very full, everywhere.'

The outer avenues and passages of the People's Theatre bore abundant testimony to the fact of its being frequented by very dirty people. Within, the atmosphere was far from odoriferous. The place was crammed to excess, in all parts. Among the audience were a large number of boys and youths, and a great many very young girls grown into bold women before they had well ceased to be children. These last were the worst features of the whole crowd, and were more prominent there than in any other sort of public assembly that we know of, except at a public execution. There was no drink supplied, beyond the contents of the porter-can (magnified in its dimensions, perhaps), which may be usually seen traversing the galleries of the largest Theatres as well as the least, and which was here seen everywhere. Huge ham-sandwiches, piled on trays like deals in a timber-yard, were handed about for sale to the hungry; and there was no stint of oranges, cakes, brandy-balls, or other similar refreshments. The Theatre was capacious, with a very large capable stage, well lighted, well [58] appointed, and managed in a business-like, orderly manner in all respects; the performances had begun so early as a quarter past six, and had been then in progress for three-quarters of an hour.

It was apparent here, as in the theatre we had previously visited, that one of the reasons of its great attraction was its being directly addressed to the common people, in the provision made for their seeing and hearing. Instead of being put away in a dark gap in the roof of an immense building, as in our once National Theatres, they were here in possession of eligible points of view, and thoroughly able to take in the whole performance. Instead of being at a great disadvantage in comparison with the mass of the audience, they were here *the* audience, for whose accommodation the place was made. We believe this to be one great cause of the success of these speculations. In whatever way the common people are addressed, whether in churches, chapels, schools, lecture-rooms, or theatres, to be successfully addressed they must be directly appealed to. No matter how good the feast, they will not come to it on mere sufferance. If, on looking round us, we find that the only things plainly and personally addressed to them, from quack medicines upwards, be bad or very defective things,—so much the worse for them and for all of us, and so much the more unjust and absurd the system which has haughtily abandoned a strong ground to such occupation.

We will add that we believe these people have a right to be amused. A great deal that we consider to be unreasonable, is written and talked about not licensing these places of entertainment. We have already intimated that we believe a love of dramatic representations to be an inherent principle in human nature. In most conditions of human life of which we have any knowledge, from the Greeks to the Bosjesmen, some form of dramatic representation has always obtained.* We have a vast respect for county magistrates, and for the lord chamberlain; but we render greater deference to such extensive and immutable experience, and think it will outlive the whole existing court and commission. We would assuredly not bear harder on the four-

* In the remote interior of Africa, and among the North American Indians, this truth is exemplified in an equally striking manner. Who that saw the four grim, stunted, abject Bush-people at the Egyptian Hall—with two natural actors among them out of that number, one a male and the other a female—can forget how something human and imaginative gradually broke out in the little ugly man, when he was roused from crouching over the charcoal fire, into giving a dramatic representation of the tracking of a beast, the shooting of it with poisoned arrows, and the creature's death? [Original footnote.]

penny theatre, than on the four shilling theatre, or the four guinea theatre; but we would decidedly interpose to turn to some wholesome account the means of instruction which it has at command, and we would make that office of Dramatic Licenser, which, like many other offices, has become a mere piece of Court favour and dandy conventionality, a real, responsible, educational trust. We would have it exercise a sound supervision over the lower drama, instead of stopping the career of a real work of art, as it did in the case of Mr. Chorley's play at the Surrey Theatre, but a few weeks since, for a sickly point of form.

To return to Mr. Whelks. The audience, being able to see and hear, were very attentive. They were so closely packed, that they took a little time in settling down after any pause; but otherwise the general disposition was to lose nothing, and to check (in no choice language) any disturber of the business of the scene.

On our arrival, MR. WHELKS had already followed Lady Hatton the Heroine (whom we faintly recognised as a mutilated theme of the late Thomas Ingoldsby) to the 'Gloomy Dell and Suicide's Tree,' where Lady H. had encountered the 'apparition of the dark man of doom,' and heard the 'fearful story of the Suicide.' She had also 'signed the compact in her own Blood;' beheld 'the Tombs rent asunder;' seen 'skeletons start from their graves, and gibber Mine, mine, for ever!' and undergone all these little experiences, (each set forth in a separate line in the bill) in the compass of one act. It was not yet over, indeed, for we found a remote king of England of the name of 'Enerry,' refreshing himself with the spectacle of a dance in a Garden, which was interrupted by the 'thrilling appearance of the Demon.' This 'superhuman cause' (with black eyebrows slanting up into his temples, and red-foil cheekbones,) brought the Drop-Curtain down as we took possession of our Shower-Bath.

It seemed, on the curtain's going up again, that Lady Hatton had sold herself to the Powers of Darkness, on very high terms, and was now overtaken by remorse, and by jealousy too; the latter passion being excited by the beautiful Lady Rodolpha, ward to the king. It was to urge Lady Hatton on to the murder of this young female (as well as we could make out, but both we and MR. WHELKS found the incidents complicated) that the Demon appeared 'once again in all his terrors.' Lady Hatton had been leading a life of piety, but the Demon was not to have his bargain declared off, in right of any such artifices, and now offered a dagger for the destruction of Rodolpha. Lady Hatton hesitating to accept this trifle from Tartarus, the Demon, for certain subtle reasons of his own, proceeded to entertain her with a view of the 'gloomy court-yard of a convent,' and the apparitions of the 'Skeleton Monk,' and the 'King of Terrors.' Against these superhuman causes, another superhuman cause, to wit, the ghost of Lady H.'s mother came into play, and greatly confounded the Powers of Darkness, by waving the 'sacred emblem' over the head of the else devoted Rodolpha, and causing her to sink into the earth. Upon this [59] the Demon, losing his temper, fiercely invited

Lady Hatton to 'Be-old the tortures of the damned!' and straightway conveyed her to a 'grand and awful view of Pandemonium, and Lake of Transparent Rolling Fire,' whereof, and also of 'Prometheus chained, and the Vulture gnawing at his liver,' MR. WHELKS was exceedingly derisive.

The Demon still failing, even there, and still finding the ghost of the old lady greatly in his way, exclaimed that these vexations had such a remarkable effect upon his spirit as to 'sear his eyeballs,' and that he must go 'deeper down,' which he accordingly did. Hereupon it appeared that it was all a dream on Lady Hatton's part, and that she was newly married and uncommonly happy. This put an end to the incongruous heap of nonsense, and set MR. WHELKS applauding mightily; for, except with the lake of transparent rolling fire (which was not half infernal enough for him), MR. WHELKS was infinitely contented with the whole of the proceedings.

Ten thousand people, every week, all the year round, are estimated to attend this place of amusement. If it were closed to-morrow—if there were fifty such, and they were all closed to-morrow—the only result would be to cause that to be privately and evasively done, which is now publicly done; to render the harm of it much greater, and to exhibit the suppressive power of the law in an oppressive and partial light. The people who now resort here, *will be* amused somewhere. It is of no use to blink that fact, or to make pretences to the contrary. We had far better apply ourselves to improving the character of their amusement. It would not be exacting much, or exacting anything very difficult, to require that the pieces represented in these Theatres should have, at least, a good, plain, healthy purpose in them. . . .

VOLUME I, NUMBER 16, Saturday, July 13th, 1850, "The Modern Science of Thief-Taking."

[368] If thieving be an Art (and who denies that its more subtle and delicate branches deserve to be ranked as one of the Fine Arts?), thief-taking is a Science. All the thief's ingenuity; all his knowledge of human nature; all his courage; all his coolness; all his imperturbable powers of face; all his nice discrimination in reading the countenances of other people; all his manual and digital dexterity; all his fertility in expedients, and promptitude in acting upon them; all his Protean cleverness of disguise and capability of counterfeiting every sort and condition of distress; together with a great deal more patience, and the additional qualification, integrity, are demanded for the higher branches of thief-taking.

If an urchin picks your pocket, or a bungling "artist" steals your watch so that you find it out in an instant, it is easy enough for any private in any of the seventeen divisions of London Police to obey your panting demand to "Stop thief!" But the tricks and contrivances of those who wheedle money out of your pocket rather than steal it; who cheat you with your eyes open; who clear every vestige of plate out of your pantry while your servant is on the stairs; who set up imposing warehouses, and ease respectable firms of large parcels of goods; who steal the acceptances of needy or dissipated young men;—for the detection and punishment of such impostors a superior order of police is requisite.

To each division of the Force is attached two officers, who are denominated "detectives." The staff, or head-quarters, consists of six sergeants and two inspectors. Thus the Detective Police, of which we hear so much, consists of only forty-two individuals, whose duty it is to wear no uniform, and to perform the most difficult operations of their craft. They have not only to counteract the machinations of every sort of rascal whose only means of existence is avowed rascality, but to clear up family mysteries, the investigation of which demands the utmost delicacy and tact.

One instance will show the difference between a regular and a detective policeman. Your wife discovers on retiring for the night, that her toilette has been plundered; her drawers are void; except the ornaments she now wears, her beauty is as unadorned as that of a quakeress: not a thing is left; all the fond tokens you gave her when her prenuptial lover, are gone; your own miniature, with its setting of gold and brilliants; her late mother's diamonds; the bracelets "dear papa" presented on her last birth-day; the top of every bottle in the dressing-case brought from Paris by Uncle John, at the risk of his life, in February 1848, are off—but the glasses remain. Every valuable is swept away with the most discriminating villainy; for no other thing in the chamber has been touched; not a chair has been moved; the costly pendule on the chimney-piece still ticks; the entire apartment is as neat and trim as when it had received the last finishing sweep of the housemaid's duster. The entire establishment runs frantically up stairs and down stairs; and finally congregates in my Lady's Chamber. Nobody knows anything whatever about it; yet everybody offers a suggestion, although they have not an idea "who ever did it." The housemaid bursts into tears; the cook declares she thinks she is going into hysterics; and at last you suggest sending for the Police; which is taken as a suspicion of, and insult on the whole assembled household, and they descend into the lower regions of the house in the sulks.

X 49 arrives. His face betrays sheepishness, combined with mystery. He turns his bull's-eye into every corner, and upon every countenance (including that of the cat), on the premises. He examines all the locks, bolts, and bars, bestowing extra diligence on those which enclosed the stolen treasures. These he declares have been "Wiolated;" by which he means that there has been more than one "Rape of the Lock." He then mentions about the non-disturbance of other valuables; takes you solemnly aside, darkens his lantern, and asks if you suspect any of your servants, in a mysterious whisper, which implies that *he* does. He then examines the upper bedrooms, and in that of the female servants he discovers the least valuable of the rings, and a cast-off silver tooth-pick between the mattresses. You have every confidence in your maids; but what *can* you think? You suggest their safe custody; but your wife intercedes, and the policeman would prefer speaking to his inspector before he locks anybody up.

Had the whole matter remained in the hands of X 49, it is possible that your troubles would have lasted you till now. A train of legal proceedings— actions for defamation of character and suits for damages—would have followed, which would have cost more than [369] the value of the jewels, and the entire execration of all your neighbours and every private friend of your domestics. But, happily, the Inspector promptly sends a plain, earnest-looking man, who announces himself as one of the two Detectives of the X division. He settles the whole matter in ten minutes. His examination is ended in five. As a connoisseur can determine the painter of a picture at the first glance, or a wine-taster the precise vintage of a sherry by the merest sip; so the Detective at once pounces upon the authors of the work of art under consideration, by the style of performance; if not upon the precise executant, upon the "school" to which he belongs. Having finished the toilette branch of the inquiry, he takes a short view of the parapet of your house, and makes an equally cursory investigation of the attic window fastenings. His mind is made up, and most likely he will address you in these words:—

"All right, Sir. This is done by one of 'The Dancing School!' "

"Good Heavens!" exclaims your plundered partner. "Impossible, why *our* children go to Monsieur Pettitoes, of No. 81, and I assure you he is a highly respectable professor. As to his pupils, I—"

The Detective smiles and interrupts. "Dancers," he tells her, "is a name given to the sort of burglar by whom she had been robbed; and every branch of the thieving profession is divided into gangs, which are termed 'Schools.' " From No. 82 to the end of the street the houses are unfinished. The thief made his way to the top of one of these, and crawled to your garret—"

"But we are forty houses distant, and why did he not favour one of my neighbours with his visit?" you ask.

"Either their uppermost stories are not so practicable, or the ladies have not such valuable jewels."

"But how do they know that?"

"By watching and inquiry. This affair may have been in action for more than a month. Your house has been watched; your habits ascertained; they have found out when you dine—how long you remain in the dining-room. A day is selected; while you are busy dining, and your servants busy waiting on you, the thing is done. Previously, many journeys have been made over the roofs, to find out the best means of entering your house. The attic is chosen; the robber gets in, and creeps noiselessly, or 'dances' into the place to be robbed."

"Is there *any* chance of recovering our property?" you ask anxiously, seeing the whole matter at a glance.

"I hope so. I have sent some brother officers to watch the Fences' houses."
"Fences?"

"Fences," explains the Detective, in reply to your innocent wife's inquiry, "are purchasers of stolen goods. Your jewels will be forced out of their settings, and the gold melted."

The lady tries, ineffectually, to suppress a slight scream.

"We shall see, if, at this unusual hour of the night, there is any bustle in or near any of these places; if any smoke is coming out of any one of their furnaces, where the melting takes place. *I* shall go and seek out the precise 'garretter'—that's another name these plunderers give themselves—whom I suspect. By his trying to 'sell' your domestics by placing the ring and toothpick in their bed, I think I know the man. It is just in his style."

The next morning, you find all these suppositions verified. The Detective calls, and obliges you at breakfast—after a sleepless night—with a complete list of the stolen articles, and produces some of them for identification. In three months, your wife gets nearly every article back; her damsels' innocence is fully established; and the thief is taken from his "school" to spend a long holiday in a penal colony.

This is a mere common-place transaction, compared with the achievements of the staff of the little army of Detective policemen at head-quarters. Sometimes they are called upon to investigate robberies; so executed, that no human ingenuity appears to ordinary observers capable of finding the thief. He leaves not a trail or a trace. Every clue seems cut off; but the experience of a Detective guides him into tracks quite invisible to other eyes. Not long since, a trunk was rifled at a fashionable hotel. The theft was so managed, that no suspicion could rest on any one. The Detective sergeant who had been sent for, fairly owned, after making a minute examination of the case, that he could afford no hope of elucidating the mystery. As he was leaving the bed-room, however, in which the plundered portmanteau stood, he picked up an ordinary shirt-button from the carpet. He silently compared it with those on the shirts in the trunk. It did not match them. He said nothing, but hung about the hotel for the rest of the day. Had he been narrowly watched, he would have been set down for an eccentric critic of linen. He was looking out for a shirt-front or wristband without a button. His search was long and patient; but at length it was rewarded. One of the inmates of the house showed a deficiency in his dress, which no one but a Detective would have noticed. He looked as narrowly as he dared at the pattern of the remaining fasteners. It corresponded with that of the little tell-tale he had picked up. He went deeper into the subject, got a trace of some of the stolen property, ascertained a connexion between it and the suspected person, confronted him with the owner of the trunk, and finally succeeded in convicting him of the theft.—At another hotel-robbery, the blade of a knife, broken in the lock of a [370] portmanteau, formed the clue. The Detective employed in that case was for some time indefatigable in seeking out knives with broken blades. At length he found one belonging to an under-waiter, who proved to have been the thief.

The swell-mob*—the London branch of which is said to consist of from

* A gang of thieves who dressed fashionably in order to escape detection.

one hundred and fifty to two hundred members—demand the greatest amount of vigilance to detect. They hold the first place in the "profession."

Their cleverness consists in evading the law; the most expert are seldom taken. One "swell," named Mo. Clark, had an iniquitous career of a quarter of a century, and never was captured during that time. He died a "prosperous gentleman" at Boulogne, whither he had retired to live on his "savings," which he had invested in house property. An old hand named White lived unharmed to the age of eighty; but he had not been prudent, and existed on the contributions of the "mob," till his old acquaintances were taken away, either by transportation or death, and the new race did not recognise his claims to their bounty. Hence he died in a workhouse. The average run of liberty which one of this class counts upon is four years.

The gains of some of the swell mob are great. They can always command capital to execute any especial scheme. Their travelling expenses are large; for their harvests are great public occasions, whether in town or country. As an example of their profits, the exploits of four of them at the Liverpool Cattle Show some seven years ago, may be mentioned. The London Detective Police did not attend, but one of them waylaid the rogues at the Euston Station. After an attendance of four days, the gentlemen he was looking for appeared, handsomely attired, the occupants of first-class carriages. The Detective, in the quietest manner possible, stopped their luggage; they entreated him to treat them like "gentlemen." He did so, and took them into a private room, where they were so good as to offer him fifty pounds to let them go. He declined, and over-hauled their booty; it consisted of several gold pins, watches, (some of great value,) chains and rings, silver snuff-boxes, and bank-notes of the value of one hundred pounds! Eventually, however, as owners could not be found for some of the property, and some others would not prosecute, they escaped with a light punishment.

In order to counteract the plans of the swell mob, two of the sergeants of the Detective Police make it their business to know every one of them personally. The consequence is, that the appearance of either of these officers upon any scene of operations is a bar to anything or anybody being "done." This is an excellent characteristic of the Detectives, for they thus become as well a Preventive Police. We will give an illustration:—

You are at the Oxford commemoration.† As you descend the broad stairs of the Roebuck to dine, you overtake on the landing a gentleman of foreign aspect and elegant attire. The variegated pattern of his vest, the jetty gloss of his boots, and the exceeding whiteness of his gloves—one of which he crushes in his somewhat delicate hand—convince you that he is going to the grand ball, to be given that evening at Merton. The glance he gives you while passing, is sharp, but comprehensive; and if his eye does rest upon any one part of your person and its accessories more than another, it is upon the gold watch which you have just taken out to see if dinner be "due." As you step aside to make room for him, he acknowledges the courtesy with "Par-r-r-

† A ceremony honoring the founders of the university.

don," in the richest Parisian *gros parle,* and a smile so full of intelligence and courtesy, that you hope he speaks English, for you set him down as an agreeable fellow, and mentally determine that if he dines in the Coffee-room, you will make his acquaintance.

On the mat at the stair-foot there stands a man. A plain, honest-looking fellow, with nothing formidable in his appearance, or dreadful in his countenance; but the effect his apparition takes on your friend in perspective, is remarkable. The poor little fellow raises himself on his toes, as if he had been suddenly overbalanced by a bullet; his cheek pales, and his lip quivers, as he endeavours ineffectually to suppress the word *"coquin!"* He knows it is too late to turn back (he evidently would, if he could), for the man's eye is upon him. There is no help for it, and he speaks first; but in a whisper. He takes the new comer aside, and all you can overhear is spoken by the latter, who says he insists on Monsieur withdrawing his "School" by the seven o'clock train.

You imagine him to be some poor wretch of a schoolmaster in difficulties; captured, alas, by a bailiff. They leave the inn together, perhaps for a sponging house. So acute is your pity, that you think of rushing after them, and offering bail. You are, however, very hungry, and, at this moment, the waiter announces that dinner is on table.

In the opposite box there are covers for four, but only three convives. They seem quiet men—not gentlemen, decidedly, but well enough behaved.

"What has become of Monsieur?" asks one. None of them can divine.

"Shall we wait any longer for him?"

"Oh, no—Waiter—Dinner!"

By their manner, you imagine that the style of the Roebuck is a "cut above them." They have not been much used to plate. The silver forks are so curiously heavy, that one of the guests, in a dallying sort of way, balances a prong across his fingers, while the chasing of the castors engages the attention of a second. This is all done while they talk. When the fish is brought, the third casts a careless glance or two at the dish cover, and when the waiter has gone for the sauce, he taps it with his nails, and says [371] enquiringly to his friend across the table, "Silver?"

The other shakes his head, and intimates a hint that it is *only* plated. The waiter brings the cold punch, and the party begin to enjoy themselves. They do not drink much, but they mix their drinks rather injudiciously. They take sherry upon cold punch, and champagne upon that, dashing in a little port and bottled stout between. They are getting merry, not to say jolly, but not at all inebriated. The amateur of silver dish-covers has told a capital story, and his friends are revelling in the heartiest of laughs, when an apparition appears at the end of the table. You never saw such a change as his presence causes, when he places his knuckles on the edge of the table and looks at the diners *seriatim;* the courtiers of the sleeping beauty suddenly struck somniferous were nothing to this change. As if by magic, the loud laugh is turned to silent consternation. You now, most impressively, understand the meaning of the term "dumbfoundered." The mysterious stranger makes some enquiry about "any cash?"

The answer is "Plenty."

"All square with the landlord, then?" asks the same inflexible voice as—to my astonishment—that which put the Frenchman to the torture.

"To a penny," the reply.

"*Quite* square?" continues the querist, taking with his busy eye a rapid inventory of the plate.

"S'help me——"

"Hush!" interrupts the dinner spoiler, holding up his hand in a cautionary manner. "Have you done anything to-day?"

"Not a thing."

Then there is some more in a low tone; but you again distinguish the word "school," and "seven o'clock train." They are too old to be the Frenchman's pupils; perhaps they are his assistants. Surely they are not all the victims of the same *capias*** and the same officer!

By this time the landlord, looking very nervous, arrives with his bill: then comes the head waiter, who clears the table; carefully counting the forks. The reckoning is paid, and the trio steal out of the room with the man of mystery behind them,—like sheep driven to the shambles.

You follow to the Railway station, and there you see the Frenchman, who complains bitterly of being "sold for noting" by his enemy. The other three utter a confirmative groan. In spite of the evident omnipotence of their persevering follower, your curiosity impels you to address him. You take a turn on the platform together, and he explains the whole mystery. "The fact is," he begins, "I am Sergeant Witchem, of the Detective police."

"And your four victims are?"—

"Members of a crack school of swell-mobsmen."

"What do you mean by 'school?'"

"Gang. There is a variety of gangs—that is to say, of men who 'work' together, who play into one another's hands. These gentlemen hold the first rank, both for skill and enterprise, and had they been allowed to remain would have brought back a considerable booty. Their chief is the Frenchman."

"Why do they obey your orders so passively?"

"Because they are sure that if I were to take them into custody, which I could do, knowing what they are, and present them before a magistrate, they would all be committed to prison for a month, as rogues and vagabonds."

"They prefer then to have lost no inconsiderable capital in dress and dinner, to being laid up in jail."

"Exactly so."

The bell rings, and all five go off into the same carriage to London.

This is a circumstance that actually occurred; and a similar one happened when the Queen went to Dublin. The mere appearance of one of the Detec-

* Latin; a legal document directing that an arrest be made.

tive officers before a "school" which had transported itself in the Royal train, spoilt their speculation; for they all found it more advantageous to return to England in the same steamer with the officer, than to remain with the certainty of being put in prison for fourteen or twenty-eight days as rogues and vagabonds.

So thoroughly well acquainted with these men are the Detective officers we speak of, that they frequently tell what they have been about by the expression of their eyes and their general manner. This process is aptly termed "reckoning them up." Some days ago, two skilful officers, whose personal acquaintance with the swell mob is complete, were walking along the Strand on other business, when they saw two of the best dressed and best mannered of the gang enter a jeweller's shop. They waited till they came out, and, on scrutinising them, were convinced, by a certain conscious look which they betrayed, that they had stolen something. They followed them, and in a few minutes something was passed from one to the other. The officers were convinced, challenged them with the theft, and succeeded in eventually convicting them of stealing two gold eye-glasses, and several jewelled rings. "The eye," said our informant, "is the great detector. We can tell in a crowd what a swell-mobsman is about by the expression of his eye."

It is supposed that the number of persons who make a trade of thieving in London is not more than six thousand; of these, nearly two hundred are first-class thieves or swell mobsmen; six hundred "macemen," and trade swindlers, bill-swindlers, dog-stealers, &c.; About forty burglars, "dancers," "garretteers," and other adepts with the skeleton-keys. The rest are pickpockets, "gonophs—" † mostly young thieves who sneak into areas, and rob tills—and other pilferers.

VOLUME III, NUMBER 55, Saturday, April 12th, 1851, "Common-Sense on Wheels."

[61] A London cab-stand is one of our great national, real original ill-regulated public inconveniences. As an existing buttress of our liberties, it is to be presumed that it is inseparably connected with the glory of the country, and that the country would receive a fatal shock if it were in anywise improved; but I diffidently incline to the opinion, nevertheless, that it is capable of some small changes for the better.

It has never been clearly made out—except by prescription and precedent —why it is indispensable that a London cab should be dirty; why the palsied window-sashes must be artfully made not to fit the window; why one door must never open, and the other never shut; why there must be, at least, one broken window, replaced (in the genteeler sort of cab) with a wooden shutter; why the check-line must be broken or gone, and the bands for pulling up the glasses cropped short off; why the nose-bags of the horses must be

† Slang for "thieves"; it is derived ultimately from Hebrew.

under the seat; why there must be a view of the pavement through the chinks in the bottom; why the fare must sit in a foot-bath of foul straw; why the cab must be damp; why the driver must be dirty; why the rate of fares and distances must be nominal; why everything connected with the crazy, ricketty, jolting, ramshackle, ugly, unsavoury, cheating, dear Institution must be exactly the reverse of what it ought to be.

Suppose the cab were clean and comfortable. Suppose the driver were civil and sober. Suppose eightpence were understood to mean not more than a shilling, and three-quarters of a mile not more than a mile. Suppose the complicated back-fare question were set at rest by the abolition of back fares. Suppose we had Inspectors of public vehicles, and that neither Lords nor younger sons were eligible for those offices. Suppose, in the event of my being overturned, abused, or overcharged, I had some easy means of redress, which did not involve my dancing attendance at a villanous police-office, among the scum of the land;—I am afraid the Constitution would go by the board directly?

Otherwise, I really think we might do something to reform it altogether. The Railway Companies have tried, but they have not a great deal in their power without the aid of the Government. Consider the materials with which they have to deal. Look at an ordinary cab-stand. Here is one, under my window!

Fifteen cabs on the rank, and three piratical cabs hovering about the street, on kidnapping expeditions. One of the fifteen is a Hansom—clean and well-built, but with a perilous driver up behind—a reckless man at street-corners—not at all accustomed to the care of children—a neck or nothing sort of fellow, and much more neck than nothing. Of the other fourteen drivers, eight don't know how to drive, and six don't care. Some are on their boxes, some at their horses' heads, some "chaffing" a common acquaintance outside the tap-room window of the Red Lion, where there are three shallow tubs, a little pump, and that wonderful character the waterman, in a suit of door-mat. What is the fiction concerning this mysterious waterman? Is he supposed to be the father of the stand? Has he any place of residence besides the stand? Has he any relations or friends? Had he any youth? Was he ever anything but a waterman? Was his father a waterman? Was his mother the bride of a waterman? Will his son (if he have one) be a waterman? Was he always red in the face, and full of gin and beer? What does he do here? What does he mean? Is he what Mr. Carlyle calls a self-constituted Impostor, or did anybody ever constitute him what he is? And if so, why so, and what is he?

He can't be on the stand to inspect the cabs. Look at the cabs, in every degree of ramshacklement, and each cab puts its veto on the supposition! He can't be on the stand to inspect the horses. Look at the horses! He can't be on the stand to inspect the drivers. Look at the drivers! He can't be here to preserve order; for, see, when the elderly gentleman with the brown umbrella calls a cab; seven cabs draw off the rank, block up the street, dash into

one another, and imperil the elderly gentleman's life. Then why is this strange
being perpetually stumping, day and night, about the stand, in his suit of
door-mat, with shoes four inches high in the sole, soliciting "a copper" of all
engagers of cabs? What a wonderful people we are in some of our institutions,
and how constantly we jog on, never so much as guessing at the riddles of
our Deputy Chaff-Waxes and our watermen, and many other such puzzling
matters.

A sensible Belgravian has put forth his might in the "Times" newspaper,
towards effecting Jehuicular* reform. He states very truly, that cab-stands
are, in the abstract and to their immediate neighbours, simply nuisances. He
proposes to convert them into urban ornaments. He would have them properly
paved and drained. He would promote the waterman to the dignity of an
important public officer; making him a member of the police force, to be
paid out of the police-rates, instead of the drivers' pockets. He is not to
[62] be a lord or a younger son, but a genuine functionary, bred to his work,
and not born to it. A handsome sentry-box to be his official residence. "In
front should be a paved space, where the stand post should be erected and
the pails placed. On the top of the box should be a lamp, glazed with coloured glass, so that any stranger might at night see from a distance where he
might find a cab rank. It should be the duty of the waterman, at least three
times a day, to sweep the stand and turn on the water to wash it down.
Inside the waterman's box should be hung up most extensive tables of cab-
fares from that particular stand to all parts of London, and in every direction; also rules for the good order of the cab-rank, and tables of fines for
disobedience." The waterman should be provided with writing materials, and
a book, in which he might register all complaints, and take the number of
the cabman, for insolence, overcharge, and other indiscretions. The waterman
would also act as arbiter in case of disputes, as fireman in case of fire, as
policeman in case of robbery, as gaoler until a perambulating colleague cus-
todier should come by; as a general patron, supervisor, umpire of the cabman
on his stand—commander, in short, of the vehicular ranks. The army is not
a small one. In London alone eight thousand men earn their bread by the flick
of the whip. One ray of common-sense in reference to them shines from the
prospectus of a "Provident and Benevolent Institution for the Hackney-
Coach Trade," which now lies on our table.

All this is very much needed. In all small things our nation are bad sys-
tematisers; abroad, they beat us hollow in sumptuary and municipal regulations and little public facilities and conveniences. In France, for instance,
public conveyances are infinitely better managed. The tariff for hackney
conveyances in Paris is very simple: there can be no dispute. You pay a fixed
price per journey (*par course*). Provided you do not go beyond the barriers
of the city, and do not stop on the road, one franc and a quarter is the
charge for an ordinary cab, holding two persons besides the driver, be the

* A jocular coining based on the name of Jehu, a chariot-driver mentioned in 2 Kings
IX. 20.

ride ever so long. If you make a call, that is two courses, and you are charged accordingly. If you want two horses and a better sort of vehicle, you may pay as much as two francs and a half for your course. Or you can, if you choose, hire by time. The price of the course is painted on the lamps of the carriage, and generally inside too. In justice to the British Cab it must be owned that the pace of the Parisian vehicle is much slower; because the horses are much less powerful, or rather much more helpless. . . .

Volume III, Number 56, Saturday, April 19th, 1851, "London Sparrows."

[85] A nice light dinner at my club, to-day—no politics after it—too wise for that—bad for digestion at my age. I will go home at once. As the evening is fine, I will take Cockspur Street in my way, in order to have a look at the window of Squires' (late Colnaghi and Puckle's) print-shop. How it shines with rich effects of light and shade!

Now, let me see. What is that? My spectacles. So, I thought it was his. Carlo Dolce's "Madonna colle Stelle." How beautiful! how more than beautiful! A divine light, like an inward tear, gleams in the eye, as though the soul were melting with grief, too sacred to be allowed to gush forth upon the cheek, far less to fall upon the earth. Moreover, the deep sorrow is tempered with a resigned and loving sweetness—a looking upward to One whose presence to her inspired vision, or rapt and devout imagination, gives balm and consolation to her mute heart's anguish. A window full of prints like this, and those of Paul and Dominic Colnaghi, and one or two others——

But what is this fidgetting behind me—this twitching at my coat-skirts? I turn round. Nobody is behind me. There is nobody close to me. Some people passing by—but not near. I must have fancied it.

Anything new in the window, since I last came by. Yes—"Les Saintes Femmes vont au tombeau du Christ." The painter, judging by those two heads, for I don't recollect the design—must be Raphael. Let me see—my spectacles again. "Charles Landell, *pinxit!*" Astonishing audacity! The deliberate imitation in style and character of two of the heads, and the direct robbery of the third! This latter one is Raphael's "St. Anne." Why, I know it as well as I know my own face, and better. It is in Raphael's "Holy Family" entitled "La Perle," and was, some years ago, in possession of the King of Spain. The cool and barefaced way in which artists continually purloin——

There, again!—certainly something pushed along close behind me; yet there's no crowd, nor any one at my side. To be sure, at the other end of the window-front there is a little urchin looking in at a print. It could not have been he. How earnestly he gazes at Raphael's "Madonna, with the infant Christ!" But now I look again at him, what a face he has! what bad features and expression. How can he feel any sympathy with what he gazes upon. It must be mere curiosity. Yet how intent he seems. He is very diminutive, and cannot be above eight or nine years of age; yet he has the face of a bad man of fifty. He has a sallow complexion, a retreating forehead, with dirty light hair, very coarse and short. No cap; so that I see the shape of his head, which is very small, and compressed in front and at the sides, and rises behind very high, and expands. His nose is mean and pinched, with a sharp ridge, his eyes very small, his cheek-bones and the lower jaw, very large for such a child; his mouth also is large, and projects, and his chin juts out sharply—the little Tartar. But what is this on the other side of me, and close under my elbow? Another poor little imp of about ten years of age. How extremely plain—not to say ugly—street-children often are! Their hard life and the characters of their parents, causes it. This child, who is now staring in at the window upon a print of Sir Robert Peel, and flattening his nose against the glass, has a forehead "villanous low," with dark eyes, and short dark hair, and his diminutive face, both in features and expression, is uncommonly like one end of a cocoa-nut.

What a sad lot for these children to be left thus,—perhaps even turned adrift by their parents, to wander about the streets, and pick up, here and there, a precarious crumb! And now, as I turn round, I see three others, apparently in the same wretched outcast condition—two boys and a girl. The elder boy seems not to care much about it; he has, no doubt, become more accustomed to his lot. He is between twelve and thirteen. His voice [86] is hoarse, cracked, and discordant; perhaps by some street-cry. He has a large projecting nose, red pulpy lips, a long chin, and a long throat, uncovered. No collar—indeed, now I look again, no shirt; and he wears a greasy jacket and trowsers, both much too small for him; so that his large red hands and wrists, swollen with chilblains, hang listlessly far below the end of his sleeves; and his long, thin ankles, and large unshapely feet are so far below the end of his trowsers as to give the appearance of the legs and feet of a bird. He is whistling a sort of jig tune, and beating time with one of his heels. Poor boy!—I dare say he would be very glad to work if he had an opportunity. A girl, of about twelve, stands on one side of him. She is so scantily clad as to be scarcely decent. Her shoulder-blades stick up, she is so meagre, and she shivers with the cold. But I do not like the expression of her face; for, though I pity her eager, hungry look, and evidently bad state of health, I cannot help seeing that she has very much the look of a sickly rat. On the other side of the elder boy, stands a younger one—of some ten years of age. He is very pale, and has fair hair, a rueful mouth, rather dropping at the corners, large sad eyes, with very long lashes, and an expression at once timid, yet indifferent—innocent, and guilty. Guilty!—of what can such a child be guilty? They slowly walk away, all three—perhaps in consequence of my observing them so attentively. They quicken their pace as they turn the corner. Why was I so tardy to relieve them? It would have become me, as a Christian, to have thought of relieving their necessities, even for the night, far better than to have speculated upon their physiognomies as a philosopher. But it is time for me to return home. Sad addition to my experience. My wife waiting tea for——bless my so——where?—it can't be?—yes, it can—my watch is gone! Slipt down through my pocket—no doubt—there's a hole in it—no—or it fell out while I was stooping to fasten my gaiter-button, in Pall Mall. Most vexatious. A family watch! Gold chain, and seals, too! Well—it can't be helped. In these cases a pinch of snuff often—often—pshaw!—often relieves—relieves one—hillo!—have I been relieved of that, also! Perhaps it's in my side pocket, with my purse—purse! why, my purse is gone! I really begin to think I must have been robbed!

It was but too true. I had been robbed. Nor have I recounted the extent; for, on arriving at home, I found that I had also lost a white cambric handkerchief, and a silk snuff handkerchief; and my wife, making a further examination, discovered that I had lost my gold spectacles and case, a diamond shirt-pin, a box of Tolu lozenges, which I had purchased in the morning, and a handsomely bound edition of Izaak Walton's delightful "Treatise on Angling." But where, and when, I could have lost all these things—by what means, and by whom I could have been robbed—I was utterly at a loss to conjecture.

I remained in this condition of perfect innocence and bewilderment as to the nimble fingers that had picked my pockets, till this morning, when, casually looking over a newspaper, of a week or two back, I alighted upon the following Police Report:—

PRECOCIOUS CRIME AND IMPUDENCE.—At the Mansion House, three boys, the eldest only eleven, and the two others *under nine* years of age, were charged with picking pockets. A lad had, to his suprise, seen one of them slide a small stick into the pocket of a gentleman, and open it for inspection; and he had seen the process repeated on several succeeding customers, but, as it chanced, without disclosing any prospect of spoil. The two companions kept close, covering their leader's operations, and ready to receive his booty and make off.

"On this statement being made, the smallest of the boys exclaimed, 'Don't you believe a word he says, my Lord; it's all nothing but out-and-out lies.'

"Lord Mayor. 'What did you carry that stick for?'

"Boy. 'What for? why, to keep away any boys that might want to whack me, to be sure.'

"The other urchin, looking the Lord Mayor full in the face, assured him that their accuser was a regular liar, and he would nap it some day for what he said against innocent people. The eldest of the boys said he had neither father nor mother; that he lived with a woman in Mint Street, to whom he paid a penny a-night for his bed; and that he grubbed about for his victuals in the day.

"Lord Mayor. 'I shall cause inquiries to be made about you, and send you to the House of Occupation.'

"Boy. 'Don't do that. If you let me go, you shan't have me any more, I'll promise you.'

"Lord Mayor. 'No; you shall have some protection. As for the other two, they shall be whipped in the presence of their parents, who are here, and discharged.'

A light—a lurid beam, but still a light—broke upon me, as I laid down the paper, and snatched off my spectacles. The children!—the little objects looking in at the print-shop in Cockspur Street—looking in at Sir Robert Peel —and the Madonna—and lurking round about, behind me!—those were the poor innocents who had so adroitly dipped into my pockets, and relieved me of the contents. Those were the London Sparrows, who "grubbed about" the streets for their victuals in the day, and picked up whatever they could find by night! To think of a gentleman at my time of life, being robbed by infants of eight or nine years of age!—and to think of a wise and paternal government being able to devise no better remedy for so shocking an employment for infants, than that of giving them a whipping!

Discoursing on these matters last night at my club, there happened to be present a gentleman (Mr. Joseph Tweezer), a member of the Statistical Society, who had paid much [87] attention to the subject of infant thieves, and he informed me, that the fact, of which I made so much, though it might be much to me on account of the loss, was a common occurrence.

"Yes, Sir," said I, "but, if I seem to make much of it, you must also add my first shock at such very early depravity—a depravity that makes but one step between the cradle and the gallows! Surely, Mr. Tweezer, you do not call *that* a common occurrence?"

Mr. Tweezer assured me that it was. He told me he had often attended at the Police Courts, and had been an eye and ear-witness to scenes quite equal to the one I mentioned having recently read in a newspaper police report. Only two days ago he was present when a little boy of nine years of age was brought up for examination. It was proved that he had robbed a till in a shop in broad day, and while the shopman was there. He had watched the man till he moved away from behind the counter, and then dropping on all-fours, the diminutive thief crawled along the floor on his hands and knees, got underneath the counter, and raising one hand, softly drew out the till-drawer, and took three shillings and sixpence. He would have got safe off, but for a customer entering the door just as he was creeping out.

"Dreadful precocity!" said I. "My oil and Italian merchant* told me that a short time ago three little boys came to his shop door, and begged in the most eloquent terms, for a half-penny, 'to buy a bit of bread.' He did not give them the half-penny, but he gave each of them a piece of bread. They had been gone about five minutes, when he discovered they had stolen a bottle of olives to eat with it. He consoled himself, however, with the reflection that the boys, no doubt, took the olives for preserved gooseberries, or nice plums; so that whether they ate them direct out of the bottle, or had a pud-

* A merchant dealing in olive oil, groceries, fruit, etc.

ding made of them, the expression of face with which he knew they would look at each other on the first mouthful, would well repay him for the loss. But as to the impudence of infant thieves, even in the presence of the magistrate, of which you tell me, surely this is not a common occurrence?"

"It continually happens," replied Mr. Tweezer: "I once saw a little imp, of not more than ten years of age—and very small even for that age—brought before the magistrate for attempting to steal a bundle of dried sprats from a fishmonger's, simply watching a moment when nobody was in the shop. He was caught by a policeman happening to pass the door just as he darted out with his prize. But the sprats were not found upon him. He had contrived to get rid of them, the instant he found himself seized. When the magistrate asked him what he had to say for himself, he replied, 'Ax fifty-two' (the number of the policeman) 'what *he* has to say, your worship, for taking hold on a hinnocent boy in that way, all for nothink?' The magistrate was amazed. 'For nothing! you little rascal,' said he, 'why, did you not steal a bundle of dried sprats?' 'No, your worship, not a bit on it—on my hoath, if I did.' The magistrate fixed his eye upon the little imp. 'Then what did you do in the shop?' said he, 'why did you go in there when nobody else was in sight?' Without an instant's hesitation, the imp aforesaid replied, 'A boy flung my cap into the shop for a lark—and I went arter it—that's all, your worship!'"

"But this," said I, "did not get him off?"

"Of course not," replied Mr. Tweezer; "his defence was received with a burst of laughter, and he was ordered two days' imprisonment, and to be whipped."

"Some private room, then, is attached to the magistrate's office for this summary process of whipping;" said I, "and the boy is afterwards taken to a place of confinement near at hand, I suppose?"

"Oh, by no means," exclaimed Mr. Tweezer; "don't imagine that matters are conducted in any such simple, convenient, and inexpensive form as that. Something elaborate, costly, and quite unnecessary, is the rule on these occasions. There is no private room attached to any magistrates' office for the summary castigation of infant criminals; neither are they confined in any House of Correction near at hand, for the four-and-twenty, or eight-and-forty, hours' imprisonment, which they are sometimes ordered. No, no; a far more imposing paraphernalia is considered requisite. The little urchin—and, of course, it often occurs that there is only one—is duly conducted to the huge, black, close-covered police-van, with its pair of fine horses, coachman, police-guard outside behind, and, perhaps, a second policeman seated inside with 'the prisoner.' Away they drive, in dark solemnity, through the streets, 'the observed of all observers,' and take their way to Westminster, and then through a variety of squalid streets and ways, till they arrive at the great Tothill Fields Bridewell.* The massive gates are unlocked—inward rolls the sombre van—more gates are unlocked—the prisoners are ordered to alight—

* A London correctional institution; hence, any jail or prison.

and, behold! out gets a little, dirty, ragged, trembling, half-fledged London
Sparrow, and is deposited on the broad gravel-walk leading up to the Governor's house! He is then left standing, with scared looks, staring round at the
great stony solitude of dead walls and blind buildings, and walls with black
*chevaux-de-frize** of iron along the top of them, till relieved by the arrival of
an officer, who 'conducts him to his apartment,' where, in presence of 'his
medical attendant,' he is duly introduced by the proper officer to 'his birch-
rod,' and is then placed in solitary confinement during the remaining four-
and-twenty hours of the term of his sentence!"

"And you have seen all this, sir?" said I.

"No," replied Mr. Tweezer, "not with my own eyes. I have never been
to Bridewell; [88] but I was told it all—in fact, the whole scene was described to me, and many such, by one of the policemen who attended the
van, and was, no doubt, indignant at so much trouble, expense, and for-
mality for so insignificant a result. He was a very large-made, powerful man
—has since left 'the force,' and gone as porter on the Great Western Railway."

"But, good heavens, Mr. Tweezer!" exclaimed I, "can a wise and paternal
government devise no better machinery than all this for the prevention of
juvenile and infant crime? Prevention do I say?—why there's no attempt at
prevention in this. It is simply a costly arrangement for inflicting small
punishments, the effect of which may not, perhaps, be of much longer dura-
tion than the period of confinement—unless, indeed, it tends to harden and
exasperate, and render the culprits more cunning for the future."

"You are quite right," replied my friend Tweezer, "as to the view you take
of these trivial and numerous punishments of the infant thieves; but you
are not doing justice to the arrangements of the Tothill Fields Bridewell, if
you suppose they do no more than this. In this prison are hundreds of
women of all ages, as well as hundreds of boys of all ages, from six to fifteen;
many of these are ordered imprisonment for periods of two or three years;
and when this is the case, they are each taught to read and write, and are
instructed in some trade, according to the aptitude they evince. In many
instances—for picking pockets, you know, my dear sir, requires an expert
hand, especially when they contrive to take everything a gentleman has about
him—in many instances, therefore, the prisoners became skilful workmen,
so that on leaving the prison, they are able to earn an honest living. And
this. at least fifty per cent. of them are found to do."

"But, my dear sir," said I; "excellent and comforting as all this is, which
you tell me, it really seems like beginning at the wrong end. First, the paternal government allows its children to become thieves without a single
effort at prevention; and then, when prevention is a work of very great difficulty, and requires a great expenditure of money and time, to produce a
doubtful result—or only fifty per cent. of ultimate good—then, only, the idea

* An obstacle, originally used in warfare, consisting of a heavy wooden beam with spikes.

of education, instruction, and training in moral and personal habits, seems to occur to the sagacious brains of our legislators. Look at the scurvy sum granted for what they dared to call 'National Education!'—and look at the taxes I pay for all sorts of other things! Protection, forsooth! and taxes for the 'Public Service!' why are my contributions to the public service of so little good to me, in respect of the safety of my personal property, that I must needs pay, in addition, the sum total of a gold watch—a silver snuff-box—two handkerchiefs—a diamond shirt-pin—a pair of gold spectacles—a box of Tolu lozenges, and a handsomely bound copy of Izaac Walton's 'Complete Angler,' [sic]—in order to be protected, in certain statistical ratios and degrees, from a similar occurrence in future, which may, nevertheless, happen to-morrow!"

VOLUME IV, NUMBER 84, Saturday, November 1st, 1851, "Down Whitechapel Way."

[126] . . . Those who care to know a little about what their neighbours in the far East are doing this Saturday night, are very welcome to accompany me in the little excursion I am about to make. A thick pair of boots, and perhaps a mackintosh, or some light covering of that sort, would not be out of place; for it is as rainy, slushy, and muddy a Saturday night as you would desire to have (or not to have) in the month of October. Stay, here is a friend with us who has known Whitechapel and its purlieus any time this five-and-twenty years, on all sorts of days and nights. Here is another who is an enthusiast in the noble art of self-defence, and who insists on forming one of our party, on the principle that a night excursion to Whitechapel must necessarily involve a "scrimmage," and an opportunity to develop the celebrated tactics of the prize-ring on a grand scale. Those who patronise the deleterious weed may light cigars; and so onward towards Whitechapel!

On, through Fleet Street—passing St. Dunstan's as eight strikes; noting the newspaper offices blazing with gas from basement to garret; jostled occasionally by the well-looking (though ruined) agricultural gentlemen, with massy watch-chains (and bankrupt purses) who have been discussing port and Protection after an ample dinner at Peele's or Anderton's. On, and up Ludgate the lofty, watching the red and blue lights of the doctors' shops as they are mirrored in the wet pavement; and thinking, perhaps, that, after all, there may be some good in that early-closing movement which has fastened the portals of all those magnificent palaces of linen-drapery, and sent those shoals of spruce clerks and assistants forth for health and recreation—many, it is to be hoped, to the Literary and Scientific Institute, the class-room, and the singing lesson, and not *all* (as some kind souls would insinuate) to the taproom or the cigar shop. On, round the solemn dome of St. Paul's, and by that remarkable thoroughfare on the left-hand side, where, to my mind, the odours of a pastrycook's shop, of a tallow-manufactory, of the Chapter Coffee House, and all the newly-bound books in Paternoster Row are irrevocably combined and blended. On, by Cheapside, the magnificent, where rows of dazzling gas-reflectors illumine shop-fronts, teeming with yet more dazzling stores of watches, rich jewellery, and bales of silver spoons and forks. There are desolate ragged wretches staring wistfully at the glittering heaps of baubles, just as they would at the pennyworth of pudding in the window of a cook's shop. Are they speculating on the possibility of a gold watch filling a hungry belly? or are they, haply, contemplating one bold dash through the frail sheet of glass—one hasty snatch at the watches, and rings, and bracelets —one desperate [127] throw for luxury and riot at the best, or at the worst for the comfortable gaol, the warm convict's dress, and the snug cell with its hot-water pipes? . . . A hundred yards to the left, and here we are, not absolutely in Whitechapel itself, but at the entrance of that peculiar and characteristic district, which I take to be bounded by Mile-end gate on the east, and by the establishment of Messrs. Aaron and Son on the west.

First, Aaron. Gas, splendour, wealth, boundless and immeasurable, at a glance. Countless stories of gorgeous show-rooms, laden to repletion with rich garments. Gas everywhere. Seven hundred burners, they whisper to me. The tailoring department; the haberdashery department; the hat, boots, shawl, outfitting, cutlery department. Hundreds of departments. Legions of "our young men" in irreproachable coats, and neckcloths void of reproach. Corinthian columns, enriched cornices, sculptured panels, arabesque ceilings, massive chandeliers, soft carpets of choice patterns, luxury, elegance, the riches of a world, the merchandise of two, everything that anybody ever could want, from a tin shaving-pot to a cashmere shawl. Astonishing cheapness—wonderful celerity—enchanting civility! Great is Aaron of the Minories! Of the Minories? of everywhere. He pervades Aldgate; he looms on Whitechapel; an aërial suspension bridge seems to connect his Minorial palace with his West End Branch. Aaron is everywhere. When I came from Weedon the other day, his retainers pelted me with his pamphlets as I quitted the railway station. Aaron has wrenched the lyre and the bays from our laureate's hands; he and his son are the monarchs of Parnassus. His circulars are thrown from balloons and fired out of cannon. I believe they must grow in market gardens somewhere out of town—they are so numerous. Of course, Aaron is a great public benefactor.

Crossing the Minories, and keeping on the right-hand side of the road, we are in the very thick of "Butcher Row" at once. A city of meat! The gas, no longer gleaming through ground-glass globes, or aided by polished reflectors, but flaring from primitive tubes, lights up a long vista of beef, mutton, and veal. Legs, shoulders, loins, ribs, hearts, livers, kidneys, gleam in all the gaudy panoply of scarlet and white on every side. "Buy, buy, buy!" resounds shrilly through the greasy, tobacco-laden, gas-rarefied air. There are eloquent butchers, who rival Orator Henley in their encomiums on the legs and briskets they expose; insinuating butchers, who wheedle the softer sex into purchasing, with sly jokes and well-turned compliments; dignified butchers (mostly plethoric, double-chinned men, in top-boots, and doubtless wealthy), who seem to think that the mere appearance of their meat, and of themselves, is sufficient to ensure custom, and seldom condescend to mutter more than an occasional "Buy!" Then, there are bold butchers—vehement rogues, in stained frocks—who utter frantic shouts of "Buy, buy, buy!" ever and anon making a ferocious sally into the street, and seizing some unlucky wight, who buys a leg of mutton or a bullock's heart, *nolens, volens!*

Bless the women! how they love marketing! Here they are by scores. Pretty faces, ugly faces, young and old, chaffering, simpering, and scolding vehemently. Now, it is the portly matron—housekeeper, may be, to some wealthy, retired old bachelor; she awes the boldest butcher, and makes even the dignified one incline in his top-boots. And here is the newly-married artisan's wife—a fresh, rosy-cheeked girl, delightfully ignorant of housekeeping, though delighted with its responsibilities—charmingly diffident as to what she shall buy, and placing implicit, and, it is to be hoped, not misplaced, confidence in the insinuating butcher, who could, I verily believe, persuade her that a pig's fry is a [128] saddle of mutton. Poor thing! she is anxious to be at home and get Tom's supper ready for him; and as for Tom, the sooner he gets away from the public-house, where his wages are paid him every Saturday night, the better it will be for his wife and for him, too, I opine. There are but few male purchasers of butcher's meat. Stay, here is one—a little, rosy man, in deep black, and with a very big basket, and holding by the hand a little rosy girl, in black as deep. He is a widower, I dare say, and the little girl his daughter. How will it be, I wonder, with that couple, a dozen years hence? Will the little girl grow big enough to go to market by herself, while father smokes his pipe at home? or, will father marry again, and a shrewish stepmother ill-treat the girl, till she runs away and——Well, well! we have other matters beside Butcher Row to attend to. We can but spare a glance at that gaunt old man, with the bristly beard and the red eyelids, who is nervously fingering, while he endeavours to beat down the price of those sorry scraps of meat yonder. His history is plain enough to read, and is printed in three letters on his face. G.I.N.

On the pavement of this Butcher Row, we have another market, and a grand one too. Not confined, however, to the sale of any one particular article, but diversified in an eminent degree. Half-way over the curbstone and the gutter, is an apparently interminable line of "standings" and "pitches," consisting of trucks, barrows, baskets, and boards on tressels, laden with almost every imaginable kind of small merchandise. Oysters, vegetables, fruit, combs, prints in inverted unbrellas, ballads, cakes, sweet stuff, fried fish, artificial flowers,(!) chairs, brushes and brooms, soap, candles, crockery?ware, ironmongery, cheese, walking-sticks, looking-glasses, frying-pans, bibles, waste-paper, toys, nuts, and firewood. These form but a tithe of the contents of this Whitechapel Bezesteen.* Each stall is illuminated, and each in its own peculiar manner. Some of the vendors are careless, and their lamps are but primitive, consisting of a rushlight stuck in a lump of clay, or a turnip cut in half. But there is a degree of luxury in not a few; "Holliday's lamps," green paper shades, "fishtail" burners,† and, occasionally, camphine lamps, being freely exhibited. I don't think you could collect together, in any given place in Europe, a much queerer assortment than the sellers of the articles exposed, were it not the buyers thereof. Here are brawny costermongers by dozens, in the orthodox corduroys, fur caps, and "king's man" handkerchiefs.‡ Lungs of leather have they, marvellous eloquence, also, in praising carrots, turnips, and red herrings. Here, too, are street mechanics, manufacturers of the articles they sell, and striving with might and main to sell them: and you will find very few, or rather, *no* Irish among this class. I see women among the street sellers, as I move along—some, poor widow souls—some, who have grown old in street trading—some, little puny tottering things, sobbing and shivering as they sell. The buyers are of all descriptions, from the middle to the very lowest class, inclusive. Ruddy mechanics, with their wives on their arms, and some sallow and shabby, reeling to and from the gin-shops. Decent married women, and comely servant girls, with latch-keys and market-baskets. Beggars, by dozens. Slatternly, frowsy, drabs of women, wrangling with wrinkled crones, and bating down the price of a bunch of carrots fiercely. Blackguard boys, with painted faces, tumbling head over heels in the mud. Bulky costers, whose day's work is over, or who do not care to work at all. Grimy dustmen, newly emancipated from the laystall. The bare-headed, or battered-bonneted members of the class called (and truly) unfortunate, haunt the other side of the road. There is too much light and noise here for them.

But the noise! the yelling, screeching, howling, swearing, laughing, fighting saturnalia; the combination of commerce, fun, frolic, cheating, almsgiving, thieving, and devilry; the Geneva-laden§ tobacco-charged atmosphere! The thieves, now pursuing their vocation, by boldly snatching joints of meat from the hooks, or articles from the stalls; now, peacefully, basket in hand, making their Saturday night's marketing (for even thieves must eat). The short pipes, the thick sticks, the mildewed umbrellas, the dirty faces, the ragged coats! Let us turn into the gin-shop here, for a moment.

It is a remarkably lofty, though not very spacious, edifice—the area, both before and behind the bar, being somewhat narrow. There are enormous tubs of gin, marked with an almost fabulous number of gallons each; and there are composite columns, and mirrors, and handsome clocks, and ormolu

* A Bezesteen is an Oriental bazaar or market-place.
† Gas burners with spreading flames.
‡ Handkerchiefs having a yellow pattern on a green background; they were favored as neckwear by costermongers.
§ "Geneva" is a synonym for "gin;" it has no connection with the Swiss city.

candelabra, in the approved Seven Dials style. But the company are different. They have not the steady, methodical, dram-drinking system of the Seven Dials, Drury Lane, and Holborn gin-shop *habitués;* the tremulous deposition of the required three-halfpence; the slow, measured, draining of the glass; the smack of the lips, and quick passing of the hand over the mouth, followed by the speedy exit of the regular dram-drinker, who takes his "drain" and is off, even if he is in again in a short time. These Whitechapel gin-drinkers brawl and screech horribly. Blows are freely exchanged, and sometimes pewter measures fly through the air like Shrapnel shells. The stuff itself, which in the western gin-shops goes generally by the name of "blue ruin" or "short," is here called, indifferently, "tape," "max," "duke," "gatter," and "jacky." Two more peculiarities I observe also. One is, that there are no spruce barmaids, or smiling landladies—stalwart men in white aprons supply their place. The second is, that there are a multiplicity of doors, many more than [129] would at first seem necessary, and for ever on the swing; but the utility of which is speedily demonstrated to me by the simultaneous ejection of three "obstropelous" Irish labourers, by three of the stalwart barmen.

The trucks and barrows, the fried fish and artificial flowers, are not quite so abundant when we have passed a thoroughfare called Somerset Street. They get even more scarce when we see, on the other side of the road, two stone posts, or obelisks on a small scale, marking at once the boundaries of the City, and the commencement of that renowned thoroughfare, politely called Middlesex Street, but known to Europe in general, and the nobility and gentry connected with the trade in old clothes in particular, as Petticoat Lane. It is no use going down there this Saturday, for the Hebrew community, who form its chief delight and ornament, are all enjoying their "shobbhouse," * and we shall meet with them elsewhere. We will, if you please, cross over, leaving the curbstone market (which only exists on one side), and, allured by the notes of an execrably played fiddle, enter one of those dazzling halls of delight, called a "penny gaff."

The "gaff" throws out no plausible puffs, no mendacious placards, respecting the entertainment to be found therein. The public take the genuineness of the "gaff" for granted, and enter by dozens. The "gaff" has been a shop— a simple shop—with a back parlour to it, and has been converted into a hall of delight, by the very simple process of knocking out the shop front, and knocking down the partition between the shop and parlour. The gas-fittings yet remain, and even the original counters, which are converted into "reserved seats," on which, for the outlay of twopence, as many costers, thieves, Jew-boys, and young ladies, as can fight for a place, are sitting, standing, or lounging. For the common herd—the οἱ πολλοί—the *conditio vivendi*† is simply the payment of one penny, for which they get standing rooms in what

* The Jewish sabbath.
† The Greek *hoi polloi* means the common people. The Latin *conditio vivendi* means, very loosely, the right to remain.

are somewhat vaguely termed the "stalls,"—plainly speaking, the body of the shop. The proscenium is marked by two gas "battens" or pipes, perforated with holes for burners, traversing the room horizontally, above and below. There are some monstrous engravings, in vile frames, suspended from the walls, some vilely coloured plaster casts, and a stuffed monstrosity or two in glass cases. The place is abominably dirty, and the odour of the company generally, and of the shag tobacco they are smoking, is powerful.

A capital house though, to-night: a bumper, indeed. Such a bumper, in fact, that they have been obliged to place benches on the stage (two planks on tressels), on which some of the candidates for the reserved seats are accommodated. As I enter, a gentleman in a fustian suit deliberately walks across the stage and lights his pipe at the footlights; while a neighbour of mine, of the Jewish persuasion, who smells fearfully of fried fish, dexterously throws a cotton handkerchief, containing some savoury condiment from the stalls to the reserved seats, where it is caught by a lady whom he addresses by the title of "Bermondsey Bet." Bet is, perhaps, a stranger in these parts, and my Hebrew friend wishes to show her that Whitechapel can assert its character for hospitality.

Silence for the manager, if you please!—who comes forward with an elaborate bow, and a white hat in his hand, to address the audience. A slight disturbance has occurred, it appears, in the course of the evening; the Impresario complains bitterly of the "mackinnations" of certain parties "next door," who seek to injure him by creating an uproar, after he has gone to the expense of engaging "four good actors" for the express amusement of the British public. The "next door" parties are, it would seem, the proprietors of an adjacent public-house, who have sought to seduce away the supporters of the "gaff," by vaunting the superior qualities of their cream gin, a cuckoo clock, and the "largest cheroots in the world for a penny."

Order is restored, and the performances commence. "Mr. and Mrs. Stitcher," a buffo duet of exquisite comicality, is announced. Mr. Stitcher is a tailor, attired in the recognised costume of a tailor *on* the stage, though, I must confess, I never saw it *off*. He has nankeen pantaloons, a red nightcap— a redder nose, and a cravat with enormous bows. Mrs. Stitcher is "made up" to represent a slatternly shrew, and she looks it all over. They sing a verse apiece; they sing a verse together; they quarrel, fight, and make it up again. The audience are delighted. Mr. S. reproaches Mrs. S. with the possession of a private gin-bottle; Mrs. S. inveighs against the hideous turpitude of Mr. S. for pawning three pillow-cases to purchase beer. The audience are in ecstacies. A sturdy coalheaver in the "stalls" slaps his thigh with delight. It is *so* real. Ugh! terribly real; let us come away, even though murmurs run through the stalls that "The Baker's Shop" is to be sung. I see, as we edge away to the door, a young lady in a cotton velvet spencer, bare arms, and a short white calico skirt, advance to the footlights. I suppose she is the Fornarina, who is to enchant the dilettanti with the flowery song in question.

We are still in Whitechapel High Street; but in a wider part. The curb-stone market has ceased; and the head quarters of commerce are in the shops. Wonderful shops, these! Grocers, who dazzle their customers with marvellous Chinese paintings, and surmount the elaborate vessels (Properties for a Pantomime) containing their teas and sugars with startling acrostics—pungent conundrums. Is it in imagination only, or in reality, that I see, perched above these groceries, an imp—a fantastic imp, whose head-dress is shaped like a retort, who has [130] a lancet in his girdle, and on whose brow is written *"Analysis?"*—that, when I read the placards relative to "Fine young Hyson," "Well-flavoured Pekoe," "Strong family Souchong," "Imperial Gunpowder," this imp, putting his thumb to his nose, and spreading his fingers out demoniacally, whispers, "Sloe-leaves, China-clay, Prussian blue, yellow ochre, gum, tragacanth, garbage, poison?"—that, pointing to Muscovado, and "Fine West India," and "superfine lump," he mutters "Sand, chalk, poison?" —that when I talk of cocoa, he screams, "Venetian Red, and desiccated manure?"—that, when I allude to coffee, mocking gibes of burnt beans, chicory, poison?—* that he dances from the grocer's to the baker's, next door, and executes maniacal gambadoes on the quartern loaves and French rolls, uttering yells about chalk, alum, and dead men's bones?—that he draws chalk and horses' brains from the dairyman's milk; and horse-flesh, and worse offal still, from sausages?—that he shows me everywhere fraud, adulteration and poison! Avaunt, imp! I begin to think that there is nothing real in the eating and drinking line—that nothing is but what is not—that all beer is *cocculus Indicus*†—all gin, turpentine, in this delusive Whitechapel. And not in Whitechapel alone. Art thou immaculate, Shoreditch? Art thou blameless, Borough? Canst thou place thy hand on thy waistcoat, Oxford Street, the aristocratic, and say thy tea knows no "facing or glazing," thy sugar no potato starch, thy beer no doctoring?

But one of my friends is clamorous for beer; and, to avoid adulteration, we eschew the delusive main thoroughfare for a moment, and strike into a maze of little, unsavoury backstreets, between Whitechapel Church and Goodman's Fields. Here is a beer-shop—a little, blinking, wall-eyed edifice, with red curtains in the window, and a bar squeezed up in one corner, as though it were ashamed of itself. From the door of the tap-room which we open, comes forth a thick, compact body of smoke. There are, perhaps, twenty people in the room, and they are all smoking like limekilns. From a kiln at the upper extremity, comes forth the well-remembered notes of the old *trink-lied*, "Am Rhein, am Rhein." We are in Vaterland at once. All these are Teutons—German sugar-bakers. There are hundreds more of their countrymen in the nar-

---

* The imp is suggesting that adulterants have been added to sound products. "Pekoe," "Souchong" and "Gunpowder" are varieties of tea. "China-clay" or kaolin is a fine white potter's clay. "Muscovado" is raw, unrefined sugar. "Fine West India" is probably also a variety of sugar.
† The poisonous berry of a plant found in Malabar and Ceylon.

row streets about here, and dozens of low lodging-houses, where the German emigrants are crimped and boarded and robbed. Here, also, live the German buy-a-broom girls. There are little German public-houses, and German bakers, and little shops, where you can get sauerkraut and potato-salad, just as though you were in Frankfort or Mayence. Dear old Vaterland! pleasant country of four meals a-day, and featherbed counterpanes—agreeable land, where you can drink wine in the morning, and where everybody takes off his hat to everybody else! Though thy cookery is execrable, and thy innkeepers are robbers, I love thee, Germany, still!

My experienced friend, when we have refreshed ourselves at this hostelry, brings us by a short cut, into Union Street, and so into the broad White-chapel-road. Here the curbstone market I have alluded to, crosses the road itself, and stretches, in a straggling, limping sort of way, up to Whitechapel Workhouse. We come here upon another phase of Saturday-night Whitechapel life. The children of Jewry begin to encompass us, not so much in the way of business; for though their Sabbath is over, and work is legal—though Aaron, at the other extremity, is in full swing of money-making activity, yet the majority of the Israelites prefer amusing themselves on a Saturday night. They are peculiar in their amusements, as in everything else. The public-house—the mere bar, at least, has no charms for them; but almost all the low coffee-shops you pass are crowded with young Jews, playing dominoes and draughts; while in the publics, where taprooms are attached, their elders disport themselves with cards, bagatelle, and the excitement of a sing-song meeting. Smoking is universal. Cigars the rule—pipes the exception. Hounds-ditch, the Minories, Leman Street, Duke's Place, St. Mary Axe, Bevis Marks, and Whitechapel itself, have all contributed their quota to fill these places of amusement; and here and there you will see some venerable Israelite, with long beard and strange foreign garb, probably from Tangier or Constanti-nople, on a visit to his brethren in England. There are legends, too, of obscure places in this vicinity, where what the French call *"gros jeu,"* or high play, is carried on. In Butcher Row, likewise, are Jew butchers, where you may see little leaden seals, inscribed with Hebrew characters, appended to the meat, denoting that the animal has been slaughtered according to the directions of the Synagogue. In the daytime you may see long bearded rabbins examining the meat, and testing the knives on their nails.

What have we here? "The grand Panorama of Australia, a series of moving pictures." Admission, one penny. Just a-going to begin. Some individuals, dressed as Ethiopian serenaders, hang about the door; and one with the largest shirt-collar I have ever seen, takes my penny, and admits me, with some score or two more, where, though it *is* just a-going to begin, I and my friends wait a good quarter of an hour. There are two policemen off duty beside me, who are indulging in the *dolce far niente,** and cracking nuts.

* An Italian phrase meaning "pleasant idleness."

There is a decent, civil-spoken silk-weaver from Spitalfields, too, whose ancestors, he tells me, came over to England at the time of the revocation of the Edict of Nantes, and who has a romantically French name. He has the old Lyons indentures of his ancestors at home, he says.

We give up the panorama in despair; and, [131] for aught we know, it is "jest a-going to begin" at this moment. In our progress towards the Gate, however, we look in at a few more public-houses. Here is a costermonger's house, where the very trucks and baskets are brought to the bar. Here is that famous hostelry, where is preserved an oil-painting, containing authentic portraits of the three Whitechapel worthies, who once drank one hundred-and-one pots of beer at one sitting. The name of the captain of this gallant band was "Old Fish." Here, again, is a thieves' house—thievish all over, from the squint-eyed landlord to the ruffianly customers. Go in at one door, and go out at another; and don't change more five pound notes at the bar than you can help, my friend. Here are houses with queer signs—the "Grave Maurice," supposed to be a corruption of some dead-and-gone German Landgrave, and "The Blind Beggar," close to Mile End Gate.

Another "gaff" on the right-hand side of the road—but on a grander scale. The Effingham Saloon, with real boxes, a real pit, and a real gallery; dreadfully dirty, and with a dirtier audience. No comic singing, but the drama—the real, legitimate drama. There is a bold bandit, in buff-boots, calling on "yon blew Ev'n to bring-a down-a rewing on ther taraytor's ed." There is nothing new in him, nor in the young lady in pink calico, with her back hair down, expressive of affliction. Nor in the Pavilion Theatre over the way, where "Rugantino the Terrible" is the stock piece, and where there are more buff-boots, rusty broad-swords, calico-skirts, and back hairs.

Shops, Gin-palaces, Saloons—Saloons, Gin-places, Shops; Costermongers, Thieves, and Beggars—Beggars, Thieves, and Costermongers. As we near the Gate, the London Hospital looms heavily on one side, while on the other the bare, bleak walls of Whitechapel Workhouse stretch grimly along, with a woful skirting-board of crouching Irish paupers, who have arrived too late for admission into the Workhouse, and are houseless for the night.

Going along, and still anxious to see what is to be seen, I look, curiously, at the portraits hanging on the walls of the coffee-houses and bar-parlours. The democratic element is not very strong in Whitechapel, it would seem; for the effigies of Her Majesty and Prince Albert are as a hundred to one of the effigies of the Cuffies and Meaghers of the sword. One portrait, though, I see everywhere; its multiplications beating all royal, noble, and democratic portraits hollow, and far outnumbering the Dog Billies, and winners of memorable Derbys. In tavern and taproom, in shop and parlour, I see everywhere the portrait or the bust of Sir Robert Peel.

Mile End Gate at last, and midnight chimes. There is a "cheap-jack," on a rickety platform, and vaunting wares more rickety still, who gets vehemently eloquent as it gets later. But his auditory gradually disperse, and the whole road seems to grow suddenly quiet. Do you know why? The public-houses are closed. The pie-shops, it is true, yet send forth savoury steams; but the rain comes down heavily. Therefore; and as I (and I fear you, too, dear reader) have had enough of Whitechapel for one while; let us jump into this last omnibus bound westwards, reflecting that if we have not discovered the North West Passage, or the source of the Niger, we have beheld a strange country, and some strange phases of life.

from

Saunterings in and About London

Max Schlesinger

SCHLESINGER was a German journalist whose observations of English
life are exceptionally clear, practical, and detailed. His humor is
sometimes unfortunate, and his invention of fictional companions seems
to be a mistaken attempt at sprightliness, but these qualities hardly
interfere with the reportorial value of his work.

English edition by Otto Wenckstern.
London: Nathaniel Cooke, 1853.

Streets and Houses

[3] Every English house has its fence, its iron stockade and its doorway
bridge. To observe the additional fortifications which every Englishman
invents for the greater security of his house is quite amusing. It is exactly
as if Louis Napoleon* was expected to effect a landing daily between luncheon
and dinner, [4] while every individual Englishman is prepared to defend his
household gods to the last drop of porter.

You may see iron railings, massive and high, like unto the columns which
crushed the Philistines in their fall; each bar has its spear-head, and each
spear-head is conscientiously kept in good and sharp condition. The little
bridge which leads to the house-door is frequently shut up; a little door with

* Napoleon III, president and Emperor of France between 1848 and 1871.

sharp spikes protruding from it is prepared to hook the hand of a bold invader. And it is said, that magazines of powder are placed under the bridge for the purpose of blowing up a too pertinacious assailant. This latter rumour I give for what it is worth. It is the assertion of a Frenchman, whom the cleanliness of London drove to despair, and who, in the malice of his heart, got satirical.

A mature consideration of the London houses shows, that the strength of the fortification is in exact proportion to the elegance and value of the house and its contents. The poor are satisfied with a wooden stockade; the rich are safe behind their iron *chevaux de frise*, and in front of palaces, club-houses, and other public buildings, the railings are so high and strong as to engender the belief that the thieves of England go about their business of housebreaking with scaling-ladders, pick-axes, guns, and other formidable implements of destruction. . . .

[5] We cross the threshold of the house.

[6] Sacred silence surrounds us—the silence of peace, of domestic comfort, doubly agreeable after a few hours' walk with the giddy turmoil of street life. And with peace there is cleanliness, that passive virtue, the first the stranger learns to love in the English people, because it is the first which strikes his eye. That the English are capital agriculturists, practical merchants, gallant soldiers, and honest friends, is not written in their faces, any more than the outward aspect of the Germans betrays their straight-forwardness, fitful melancholy, and poetic susceptibility. But cleanliness, as an English national virtue, strikes in modest obstrusiveness [sic] the vision even of the most unobservant stranger.

The small space between the street-door and the stairs, hardly sufficient in length and breadth to deserve the pompous name of a "hall," is usually furnished with a couple of mahogany chairs, or, in wealthier houses, with flower-pots, statuettes, and now and then a sixth or seventh-rate picture. The floor is covered with oil-cloth, and this again is covered with a breadth of carpet. A single glance tells us, that after passing the threshold, we have at once entered the temple of domestic life.

Here are no moist, ill-paved floors, where horses and carts dispute with the passenger the right of way; where you stumble about in some dark corner in search of still darker stairs; where, from the porter's lodge, half a dozen curious eyes watch your unguided movements, while your nostrils are invaded with the smell of onions, as is the case in Paris, and also in Prague and Vienna. Nothing of the kind. The English houses are like chimneys turned inside out; on the outside all is soot and dirt, in the inside everything is clean and bright.

From the hall we make our way to the parlour—the refectory of the house. The parlour is the common sitting-room of the family, the centre-point of the domestic state. It is here that many eat their dinners, and some say their prayers; and in this room does the lady of the house arrange her household affairs and issue her commands. In winter the parlour fire burns from early morn till late at night, and it is into the parlour that the visitor is shewn, unless he happens to call on a reception-day, when the drawing-rooms are thrown open to the friends of the family.

[7] Large folding-doors, which occupy nearly the whole breadth of the back wall, separate the front from the back parlour, and when opened, the two form one large room. The number and the circumstances of the family devote this back parlour either to the purposes of a library for the master, the son, or the daughters of the house, or convert it into a boudoir, office, or breakfast-room. Frequently, it serves no purpose in particular, and all in turn.

These two rooms occupy the whole depth of the house. All the other apartments are above, so that there are from two to four rooms in each story. The chief difference in the domestic apartments in England and Germany consists in this division: in Germany, the members of a family occupy a number of apartments on the same floor or "flat"; in England, they live in a cumulative succession of rooms. In Germany, the dwelling-houses are divided horizontally —here the division is vertical.

Hence it happens, that houses with four rooms communicating with one another are very rare in London, with the exception only of the houses in the very aristocratic quarters. Hence, also, each story has its peculiar destination in the family geographical dictionary. In the first floor are the reception-rooms; in the second the bed-rooms, with their large four-posters and marble-topped wash-stands; in the third story are the nurseries and servants' rooms; and in the fourth, if a fourth there be, you find a couple of low garrets, for the occasional accommodation of some bachelor friend of the family.

London Streets

[12] Holborn is a business street. It has a business character; there is no mistaking it. Shops and plate-glass windows side by side on each hand; costermongers and itinerant vendors all along the pavement; the houses covered with signboards and inscriptions; busy crowds on either side; omnibuses rushing to [13] and fro in the centre of the road, and all around that indescribable bewildering noise of human voices, carriage-wheels, and horses' hoofs, which pervades the leading streets of crowded cities.

Not all the London streets have this business character. They are divided into two classes: into streets where the roast-beef of life is earned, and into streets where the said roast-beef is eaten. No other town presents so strong a contrast between its various quarters. But a few hundred yards from the leading thoroughfares, where hunger or ambition hunt men on, extend for many miles the quiet quarters of comfortable citizens, of wealthy fundholders, and of landed proprietors, who come to town for "the season," and who return to their parks and shooting-grounds as soon as her Majesty has been graciously pleased to prorogue Parliament, and with Parliament the season.

These fashionable quarters are as quiet as our own provincial towns. They have no shops; no omnibuses are allowed to pass through them, and few costermongers or sellers of fruit, onions, oysters, and fish find their way into these regions, for the cheapness of their wares has no attractions for the inhabitants of these streets. These streets, too, are macadamized expressly for the horses and carriages of the aristocracy; such roads are more comfortable for all parties concerned, that is to say, for horses, horsemen, and drivers, and the carriages are, moreover, too light to do much harm to the road. In these streets, too, there are neither counting-houses nor public-houses to disturb the neighbourhood by their daily traffic and nightly revelries. Comfort reigns supreme in the streets and in the interior of the houses. The roadway is lined with pavements of large white beautiful flag-stones, which skirt the area railings; it is covered with gravel, and carefully watered, exactly as the broad paths of our public gardens, to keep down the dust and deaden the rumbling of the carriages and the step of the horses. The horses, too, are of a superior kind, and as different from their poorer brethren, the brewer's, coal-merchant's, and omnibus horses, as the part of the town in which they eat is different from the part in which the latter work.

In the vicinity of the Parks, or in the outskirts of the town, [14] or wheresoever else such quarters have space to extend, you must admire their unrivalled magnificence. From the velvety luscious green, which receives a deeper shade from the dense dark foilage of the English beech-tree, there arise buildings, like palaces, with stone terraces and verandahs, more splendid, more beautiful, and more frequent than in any town on the continent.

An Englishman is easily satisfied with the rough comforts of his place of business. The counting-houses of the greatest bankers; the establishments of the largest trading houses in the city have a gloomy, heavy, and poverty-stricken appearance. But far different is the case with respect to those places where an Englishman proposes to live for himself and for his family.

A wealthy merchant who passes his days in a narrow city street, in a dingy office, on a wooden stool, and at a plain desk, would think it very "ungenteel" if he or his family were to live in a street in which there are shops. And, although it may appear incredible, still it is true, that in the better parts of the town there are many streets shut up with iron gates, which gatekeepers open for the carriages and horses of the residents or their visitors. These gates exclude anything like noise and intrusion. Grocers, fishmongers, bakers, butchers, and all other kitchen-tradesmen occupy, in the fashionable quarters, the nearest lanes and side streets, and many of them live in close vicinity to the mews. For no house, not even the largest, has a carriage-gate; and that we, in Germany, shelter under our roofs our horses, grooms, and all the odours of the stable, appears to the English as strange and mysterious, generally speaking, as our mustachios, and our liberalism in matters of religion. . . .

Vauxhall

[37] The gardens are crowded; dense masses are congregated around a sort of open temple, which at Vauxhall stands *in lieu* of a music-room. The first part of the performance is just over; and a lady, whose voice is rather the worse for wear, and who defies the cool of the evening with bare shoulders and arms, is in the act of being *encored*. She is delighted, and so are the audience. Many years ago this spot witnessed the performances of Grisi, Rubini, Lablache, and other first-class musical celebrities.

The crowd promenade these gardens in all directions. In the background is a gloomy avenue of trees, where loving couples walk, and where the night-air is tinged with the hue of romance. Even the bubbling of a fountain may be heard in the distance. We go in search of the sound; but, alas, we witness nothing save the triumph of the insane activity of the illuminator. A tiny rivulet forces its way through the grass; it is not deep enough to drown a herring, yet it is wide enough and babbling enough to impart an idyllic character to the scene. But how has this interesting little water-course fared under the hands of the illuminator? The wretch has studded its banks with rows of long arrow-headed gas-lights. Not satisfied with [38] lighting up the trees, and walls, and dining-saloons, he must needs meddle with this lilliputian piece of water also. That is *English* taste, which delights in quantities: no Frenchman would ever have done such a thing!

Following the rivulet, we reach the bank of a gas-lit pond, with a gigantic Neptune and eight white sea-horses. To the left of the god opens another gloomy avenue, which leads us straightway to *Fate,* to the hermit, and the temple of Pythia, who, in the guise of a gipsy, reclining on straw under a straw-roofed shed, with a stable lanthorn at her side, is in the habit of reading the most brilliant Future on the palm of your hand, for the ridiculously low price of sixpence only. This is specially English; no house without its fortifications—no open-air amusements without gipsies. The prophetess of Vauxhall is by no means a person of repulsive appearance. You admire in her a comely brown daughter of Israel, with black hair and dark eyes; it is very agreeable to listen to her expounding your fate. She is good-tempered and agreeable, and has a Californian prophecy for all comers. She predicts faithful wives, length of days, a grave in a free soil to every one, even to the German.

The dwelling of the sage hermit is much less primitive, nor are believers permitted to enter it. They must stand on the threshold, from whence they may admire a weird and awful scenery—mountains, precipices and valleys, and the *genius loci,* a large cat with fiery eyes, all charmingly worked in canvas and pasteboard, with a strict and satisfactory regard for the laws of perspective. The old man, with his beard so white and his staff so strong, comes up from the mysterious depth of a pasteboard ravine; he asks a few

questions and disappears again, and in a few minutes the believer receives
his or her Future, carefully copied out on cream-coloured paper, and in verses,
too, with his or her name as an anagram. Of course these papers are all ready
written and prepared by the dozen, and as one lady of our party had the
name of Hedwig—by no means a common name in England—she had to wait
a good long while before she was favoured with a sight of her fate. This, of
course, strengthened her belief in the hermit and the fidelity of her husband.

We, the Pilgrims of Vauxhall, leave the hermit's cell. Our [39] eyes have
become accustomed to the twilight, and as we proceed we behold, in the
background, the tower and battlements of a large and fantastically-built
tower. Can this be Westminster Abbey, or is it a mere optical delusion? Let
us see.

Hark! a gun is fired in the shrubbery. The promenaders, who are familiar
with the place, turn round, and all rush in one direction, sweeping us along
with them. Before we can collect ourselves, we have been pushed forward to
a panoramic stage, on which Nelson, in plaster, is in the act of expiring, while
Wellington, in pasteboard, rides over the battle-field of Waterloo. These two
figures are the worst of their kind; still the public cheer the two national
heroes. No house without its fortifications—no open-air amusements without
gipsies—and no play without the old Admiral and the old General.

Wellington has scarcely triumphed over Napoleon, and silenced the French
batteries, when the cannonade recommences in the shrubbery: one—two
guns! it is the signal for the arena. Unless you purchase a seat in the boxes
or the galleries, you have no chance of seeing the exhibition in the circus, for
the pit, which is gratis, is crowded to suffocation. Englishmen care more for
live horses than they do for pasteboard chargers, fraught though they be with
national reminiscences.

The productions of horsemanship at Vauxhall are exactly on a par with
similar exhibitions on the other side of the Channel. Britons are more at home
on horseback, or on board a ship, than on the strings of the fiddle, or on the
ivory keys of the pianoforte. And thus, then, do the men and women dance
on unsaddled horses, play with balls and knives, and jump through paper and
over boards; half a dozen of old and young clowns distort their joints; a lady
dances on a rope, *à la marionette;* and Miss A., who was idolised at Berlin,
and whom seven officers of the Horse Guards presented with a bracelet, on
which their seven heroic faces were displayed, condescends to produce her
precious bracelet and her precious person in this third-rate circus; and an
American Gusikow makes music on wood, straw, and leather; and the horses
are neighing, and the whips smacking, and the sand is being thrown up, and
the boarding trembles with the tramp of the horses, and there is no end of
cheering; [40] and Miss A. re-appears and curtsies, with the seven gentlemen of the Horse Guards on her arm; and another gun is fired, and the public, leaving the circus, rush madly into the gardens. To the fireworks! they
are the most brilliant exhibition of the evening. The gardens are bathed in
a bluish light, and the many thousand lamps look all pale and ominous. The

gigantic and fantastic city, which before loomed through the twilight of the distant future, burns now in Bengal fire. It is Moscow! it is the Kremlin, and they are burning it! Sounds of music, voices of lamentation, issue from the flames, guns are firing, rockets shoot up and burst with an awful noise, the walls give way—they fall, and from the general destruction issues a young girl, with very thin clothing and very little of it, who makes her escape over a rope at a dizzy height. The exhibition is more awful than agreeable; but the public cheer this, as they do any other neck-or-nothing feat. If the girl were to carry a baby on her perilous way, the cheering would be still greater. . . .

London Thieves and Policemen

[52] The police, whenever and wherever it answers its original purpose, is a most beneficent institution. Its unpopularity in all the states of the Continent is chargeable, not to the principles of the institution, but to their perversion. It is the perversion of the protective force into an instrument of oppression and aggression, which the German hates at home; but he has no aversion to the police as such. Even the maddest of the democratic refugees confess to great love and admiration for the police in England. A man may like his cigar without entertaining a preposterous passion for nicotine.

The policeman, no matter whether in a uniform or in plain clothes, is a soldier of peace—a sentinel on a neutral post, and as such he is as much entitled to respect as the soldier who takes the field against a foreign invader. This is the case in England. The policeman is always ready to give his assistance and friendly advice; the citizen is never brought into an embarrassing and disagreeable contact with the police; and the natural consequence of this state of things is, that the most friendly feelings exist between the policeman and the honest part of the population. Whenever the police have to interfere and want assistance, the inhabitants are ready to support them, for they know that the police never act without good reasons.

The detective police, who act in secret, do not stand on such an intimate footing with the public as the preventive part of the force; but whenever they are in want of immediate assistance for the arrest of an offender, the detective has but to proclaim his functions, and no man, not even the greatest man in the land, would refuse to lend him assistance. In Germany and in France no one will associate with an agent of the secret police, a *mouchard,* or by whatever other name those persons may be called. Every one has an instinctive aversion to [53] coming in contact with this species of animal, for they are traitorous, venomous, and blood-thirsty. And that such is the case, is another proof of the vast superiority of the British institutions over those of the Continent.

That London has not in the fulness of time come to be a vast den of thieves and murderers, is mainly owing to the action of the detective force.

Here, where the worst men of the European and American continents congregate, the functions of a detective are not only laborious but also dangerous. The semi-romantic ferocity of an Italian bandit is sheer good nature, if compared to the savage hardness and villany of a London burglar. The bandit plies his lawless trade in the merry green wood and mossy dell; he confesses to his priest, and receives absolution for any peccadilloes in the way of stabbing he may have happened to commit; on moonlit nights his head rests on the knees of the girl that loves him, in spite of his cruel trade. He is not altogether lost to the gentler feelings of humanity, and, in a great measure, he wants the confounding hardening consciousness of having, by his actions, disgraced himself and his species. But the London robber, like a venomous reptile, has his home in dark holes under ground, in hidden back rooms of dirty houses, and on the gloomy banks of the Thames. He breaks into the houses as a wolf into a sheepfold, and kills those who resist him, and, in many instances, even those who offer no resistance. There is no sun or forest-green for him, no priest gives him absolution, the female that herds with him is, in most cases, even more ferocious and abandoned than himself; and if he be father to a child, he casts it at an early age into the muddy whirlpool of the town, there to beg, to steal, and to perish.

The streets which skirt the banks of the Thames are most horrible. There the policeman does not saunter along on his beat with that easy and comfortable air which distinguishes him in the western parts of the town. Indeed, in many instances, they walk by twos and twos, with dirks under their coats, and rattles to call in the aid of their comrades.

Many policemen and detectives, who, hunting on the track of some crime, have ventured into these dens of infamy have [54] disappeared, and no trace has been left of them. They fell as victims to the vengeance of some desperate criminal whom, perhaps, on a former occasion, they had brought to justice. And it would almost appear to be part of the *haute politique** of the London robbers, that some policeman must be killed from time to time as a warning to his comrades. The guild of assassins, too, have their theory of terrorism.

Another remarkable fact is, that the London policemen, though their duty brings them constantly in contact with the very scum of the earth, contract none of their habits of rudeness, which appear to be an essential portion of the stock-in-trade of the continental police. One should say, that the "force" in England is recruited from a most meritorious class of society, one in which patience, gentleness, and politeness are hereditary.

Look there! A fine strapping fellow crossing the street with a child in his arms! The girl is trembling as an aspen-leaf, for she was just on the point of getting under a wheel. That fine fellow has taken her up; and now you see he crosses again and fetches the little girl's mother, who stands bewildered with the danger, and whom he conducts in safety to the opposite pavement. Who and what is that man? His dress is decent and citizen-like, and yet peculiar;

* A French phrase meaning high diplomacy.

it differs from the dress of ordinary men; coat and trowsers of blue cloth; a number and a letter embroidered on his collar; a striped band and buckle on his arm; a hat with oilskin top, and white gloves—rather a rarity in the dirty atmosphere of London. That man is a policeman, a well got up and improved edition of our own German *Polizeidiener,** those scarecrows with sticks, sabres, and other military acoutrements, standing at the street-corners of German capitals, and spoiling the temper of honest men as well as of thieves.

It is, however, a mistake to believe, as some persons on the continent actually do, that the London police are altogether unarmed and at the mercy of every drunkard. Not only have they, in many instances and quarters, a dirk hidden under their great-coats, but they have also, at all times, a short club-like staff in their pockets. This staff is produced on solemn occasions, for instance, on the occasion of public processions, when every policeman holds his staff in his hand. The staves have of [55] late years been manufactured of gutta percha, and made from this material they are lighter and more durable than wooden staves. In the name of all that is smashing, what a rich full sound does not such a gutta percha club produce when in quick succession it comes down on a human shoulder. That sound is frequently heard by those who, on Saturday or Monday night, perambulate the poorer or more dissolute quarters of the town, when all respect for the constable's staff has been drowned in a deluge of gin. Matters, on such occasions, proceed frequently to the extremity of a duel. The policeman, like any civilian, fights for his skin; he gets a drubbing and returns it with interest. But since his weapon does not give him so manifest an advantage as a sword would, the public consider the *fracas* a fair fight. And after all, the combatants must appear before a magistrate; in the police-court they are on equal terms, and witnesses are heard on either side. There is no prejudice in favour of the policeman.

But stop! Look at the crowd in the street. Two policemen are busy with a poor ragged creature of a woman, whom they carry to a doorway. An accident perhaps? Nothing of the kind. The woman is drunk, and fell down in the road. The policemen are taking her to the station, where she may sleep till she is sober. But it was a strange spectacle to see those two men in smart blue coats and white gloves rescuing the ragged woman from the mire of the street.

Let us go on. At Temple Bar there is a Gordian knot of vehicles of every description. Three drays are jammed into one another. One of the horses has slipped and fallen. The traffic is stopped for a few minutes; and this is a matter of importance at Temple Bar. Just look down Fleet-street—the stoppage extends to Ludgate-hill. But half a dozen policemen appear as if by enchantment. One of them ranges the vehicles that proceed to the city in a line on the left side of the road. A second lends a hand in unravelling the knot of horses. A third takes his position in the next street, and stops the carriages and cabs which, if allowed to proceed, would but contribute their

* The German word for policeman.

CRUCHLEY'S new Plan

1. Regent's Park
2. Clerkenwell
3. Kensington Gardens and Palace
4. Hyde Park
5. Oxford Street

6. Piccadilly
7. Pall Mall
8. St. Giles'
9. Seven Dials
10. Charing Cross
11. Whitehall

12. Westminster Abbey
13. Houses of Parliament
14. Vauxhall Gardens
15. Holborn Hill, Holborn, High Holborn
16. Lincoln's Inn Fields

LONDON improved to 1835

G.F.CRUCHLEY,
LONDON.

quota to the confusion. Two policemen are busy with the horse which [56] lies kicking in the road. They unhook chains and unbuckle straps; get the horse on its legs, and assist the driver in putting him to rights again. They have got dirty all over; and they must, moreover, submit to hear from Mr. Evans, who stands on the pavement dignified, with a broad-brimmed Quaker hat, that they are awkward fellows, and know nothing whatever about the treatment of horses. In another minute, the whole street-traffic is in full force. The crowd vanishes as quickly and silently as it came. The two policemen betake themselves to the next shop, where the apprentice is called upon to brush their clothes.

The continental policeman is the torment of the stranger. The London policeman is the stranger's friend. If you are in search of an acquaintance and only know the street where he lives, apply to the policeman on duty in that street, and he will show you the house, or at least assist you in your search. If you lose your way, turn to the first policeman you meet; he will take charge of you and direct you. If you would ride in an omnibus without being familiar with the goings and comings of those four-wheeled planets, speak to a policeman, and he will keep you by his side until the "bus" you want comes within hailing distance. If you should happen to have an amicable dispute with a cabman—and what stranger can escape that infliction?—you may confidently appeal to the arbitration of a policeman. If, in the course of your peregrinations, you come to a steam-boat wharf or a railway-station, or a theatre or some other public institution, and if you are at a loss how to proceed, pray pour your sorrows into the sympathetic ear of the policeman. He will direct yourself and baggage; in a theatre, he will assist you in the purchase of a ticket, or at least tell you where to apply and how to proceed. The London policeman is almost always kind and serviceable. . . .

The Metropolis "en Negligée"

[71] Early in the morning, before the chimneys of the houses and factories, of the railway-engines and steamers, have had time to fill the air with smoke, London presents a peculiar spectacle. It looks clean. The houses have a pleasing appearance; the morning sun gilds the muddy pool of the Thames; the arches and pillars of the bridges look lighter and less awkward than in the daytime, and the public in the street, too, are very different from the passengers that crowd them at a later hour.

Slowly, and with a hollow, rumbling sound do the sweeping-machines travel down the street in files of twos and threes to take off every particle of dust and offal. The market-gardener's carts and waggons come next; they proceed at a brisk trot to arrive in time for the early purchasers. After them, the coal-waggons and brewer's drays, which only at certain hours are permitted to unload in the principal streets of the city. At the same time, the light, two-wheeled carts of the butchers, fish-mongers, and hotel-keepers, rattle along at a slapping pace; for their owners—sharp men of business—would be the first in the market to choose the best and purchase at a low price. Here and there a trap is opened in the pavement, and dirty men ascend from the regions below; they are workmen, to whose care is committed the city under-ground, which they build, repair, and keep in good order. Damaged gas and water-pipes, too, are being repaired, and the workmen make all possible haste to replace the paving-stones and leave the road in a passable condition. For the sun mounts in the sky and their time is up. They return to their lairs and go to sleep just as the rest of the town awakens to the labours of the day.

Besides these, there are a great many other classes whose avocations compel them to take to the street by break of day. At a very early hour they appear singly or in small knots, with long, white clay pipes in their mouths; as the day advances, they come in troops, marching to their work in docks and ware-houses. Ill-tempered looking, sleepy-faced barmen take down the shutters of the gin-shops; cabs, loaded with portmanteaus and band-boxes, hasten to deposit their occupants at the various railway-stations; horsemen gallop along, eager for an early country-ride; from minute to minute there is an increase of life [72] and activity. At length the shops, the windows and doors of houses are opened; omnibuses come in from the suburbs and land their living freight in the heart of the city; the pavements are crowded with busy people, and the road is literally crowded with vehicles of every description. It is day and the hour is 10 A.M.

Long before this, hundreds of high chimney-towers have belched forth their volumes of thick black smoke, and that smoke obscures the horizon with long streaks of black smut, and mixes and becomes more dense as the millions of chimneys on the house-tops contribute their quota, until a dusky atmos-phere is formed, which intercepts the rays of the sun. Such is London by day. That is the enormous city with her deep grey robe of smoke and fog, which she spins afresh every morning, and silently unravels during the hours of the night, that she may, as Penelope of old, keep idlers and courtiers away from her gates. . . .

London Parks and People

[104] The English are in many respects like our own good honest peasants. So long as the latter keep to their ploughs, they are most amiable and respect-able; but if you find them in town, and induce them to put on fashionable clothes, you may rely on it that thus affected they will give you plenty of kicks. Let an Englishman make a park, and his production will be admirable; but if you wish for an entrance into a park, you had better not apply to him. Fortunately Hyde Park is much larger than its two splendid portals. There is plenty of room to lose them from your sight; and there are a great many agreeable scenes which will banish them from your memory. Passing through the Marble-arch to those regions where the Exhibition building stands, we

cross a meadow large enough to induce us to believe that we are far away
from London. In the west, the ground rises in gentle hills with picturesque
groups of trees on their summits and in the valleys; here and there an old
tufted oak, with its gnarled branches boldly stretched out; the grass is fresh
and green, though all the passengers walk on it. It is green up to the very
trunks of the trees, whose shade is generally injurious to vegetation; it is
green throughout the winter and through the summer months, though there
is not a drop of rain for many weeks, for the mild and moist atmosphere
nourishes it and favours the growth of ivy which clusters round any tree too
old to resist its approaches. Thus does Hyde Park extend far to the west and
the south, until it finds its limits in bricks and mortar. A slight blue mist
hangs on the distant trees; and through the mist down in the south there are
church towers looming in the far distance like the battlements of turretted
castles [105] in the midst of romantic forests. The trees recede; a small lake
comes in view, it is an artificial extension of the Serpentine,* which has the
honor of seeing the elegance of London riding and driving on its banks. Early
in the morning the lake is plebeian. The children of the neighbourhood swim
their boats on it; apprentices on their way to work make desperate casts for
some half-starved gudgeon; the ducks come forward in dirty morning wrap-
pers. Nursery-maids with babies innumerable take walks by order; and at a
very early hour a great many plebeians have the impertinence to bathe in the
little lake. But to-day the park and the river are in true aristocratic splendour; here and there, there is indeed some stray nursery-maid walking on the
grass, and some little tub of a boat with a ragged sail floating on the lake;
there is also a group of anglers demonstrating to one another with great
patience that the fish wont bite to-day, but all along the banks of the river
far down to the end of the park and up to the majestic shades of Kensington
gardens there is an interminable throng of horses and carriages. Those who
have seen the Prater of Vienna in the first weeks of May will be rather disappointed with the aspect of the drive in Hyde Park, where the upper classes
of London congregate in the evening between five and seven o'clock, partly
to take the air, and partly because it is considered fashionable to see now and
then in order to be seen. Extravagant turn-outs and liveries, such as the
Viennese produce with great ostentation, are not to be found in London.
The English aristocracy like to make an impression by the simplicity and
solidity of their appearance; and the metropolis is the last of all places where
they would wish to excite attention by a dashing and extravagant exterior.
They have not the least desire either to dazzle or to awe the tradespeople or
to make them envious. They are too sure of their position to be tempted to
advertise it: whoever wants this assurance cannot pretend to belong to the
aristocracy. By far more interesting, and indeed unrivalled, is Rotten-row, the
long broad road for horsemen, where, on fine summer evenings, all the youth,
beauty, celebrity, and wealth of London may be seen on horse-back.

Hundreds of equestrians, ladies and gentlemen, gallop to and [106] fro.

* Formed from a neighboring river.

How fresh and rosy these English girls are! How firmly they sit! What splendid forms and expressive features! Free, fresh, bold, and natural. The blue veil flutters, and so does the riding-habit; a word to the horse and movement of the bridle, and they gallop on, nodding to friends to the right and left, the happiness of youth expressed in face and form, and no idea, no thought, for the thousand sorrows of this earth. A man of a harmless and merry mind may pass a happy summer's evening in looking at this the most splendid of all female cavalcades; but he who has become conscious of those all-pervading sufferings of humanity which, felt through thousands of years, denied through thousands of years, and asserted only within the last few years by the millions of our earth—he who has pressed this thorny knowledge of the world to his heart, let him avoid this spot of happiness-breathing splendour, lest the thorns wound him more severely still. Then comes an old man, with his horse walking at a slow pace, his low hat pushed back that the white hair on his temples may have the benefit of the breeze. His head bent forward, the bridle dangling in a hand weak with age, the splendour of the eyes half-dimmed, his cheeks sunken, wrinkles round his mouth and on his forehead, his aquiline nose bony and protruding; who does not know him? His horse walks gently on the sand; every one takes off his hat; the young horse-women get out of his way; and the Duke smiles to the right and to the left. Few persons can boast of so happy a youth as this old man's age. He turns round the corner; the long broad row becomes still more crowded; large groups of ten or twenty move up and down; fast riding is quite out of the question, when all of a sudden a couple come forward at a quick pace. There is room for them and their horses in the midst of Rotten-row, however full it may be, for every one is eager to make way for them: it is the Queen and her husband, without martial pomp and splendour, without a single naked sword within sight. The crowd closes in behind her; the young women appear excited; the old men smile with great glee at seeing their Queen in such good health. Dandies in marvellous trowsers, incredible waistcoats, and stunning ties, put up their glasses; the anglers on the lake crowd to one side in order to see the Queen; the nursery-[107] maids, the babies, and the boys with their hoops come up to the railings; the grass plots, where just now large groups of people sat chatting, are left vacant, and the shades of the evening are over the park. The sun is going down behind the trees; its parting rays rest on the Crystal Palace with a purple and golden glare, whose reflection falls on Rotten-row and its horse-men.

In a very short time this spot will be empty. . . .

The Clubs

. . . [114] Pall Mall is one of the most splendid streets in London; its splendour is chiefly owing to the club houses. There are, [115] in this street, the Oxford and Cambridge Club, the Army and Navy Club, the Carlton, the

Reform, the Travellers', and the Athenæum. Besides these, there are in London a large number of club-houses, of which it may generally be said, that their chief end and aim is to procure a comfortable home by means of association, in as cheap and perfect a manner as possible.

But the words, "as cheap and perfect as possible," convey quite a different idea to the German to what they do to the Englishman. A short explanation may not, perhaps, be out of place at this point.

A younger son of an old house, with an income of, say from two to four hundred pounds, cannot live, and do as others do, within the limits of that income. He can neither take and furnish a house, nor can he keep a retinue of servants or give dinners to his friends. The club is his home, and stands him in the place of an establishment. At the club, spacious and splendidly furnished saloons are at his disposal; there is a library, a reading-room, baths, and dressing-rooms. At the club he finds all the last new works and periodicals; a crowd of servants attend upon him; and the cooking is irreproachable. The expenses of the establishment are defrayed by the annual contributions and the entrance fees. But, of course, neither the annual contributions nor the entrance-fees, pay for the dinners and suppers, the wines and cigars, of the members. Members do dine at the clubs: indeed, the providing of dinners is among the leading objects of these establishments, and the dinners are good and cheap, compared to the extortionate prices of the London hotels. The club provides everything, and gives it at cost price; a member of a good club pays five shillings for a dinner, which in an hotel would be charged, at least, four times that sum.

The *habitués* of the London Clubs would be shocked if they were asked to pass their hours and half-hours in our German coffee and reading-rooms; and, on the other hand, persons accustomed to the bee-hive life of Vienna coffee-houses consider the London Clubs as dull though handsome edifices. Lordly halls, [116] splendid carpets, sofas, arm-chairs, strong, soft, and roomy, in which a man might dream away his life; writing and reading-rooms tranquil enough to suit a poet, and yet grand, imposing, aristocratic; doors covered with cloth to prevent the noise of their opening and shutting, and their brass handles resplendent as the purest gold; enormous fire-places surrounded by slabs of the whitest marble; the furniture of mahogany and palisander; the staircases broad and imposing as in the *palazzos* of Rome; the kitchens *chefs d'oeuvre* of modern architecture; bath and dressing-rooms got up with all the requirements of modern luxury; in short, the whole house full of comfortable splendour and substantial wealth. All this astonishes but does not dazzle one, because here prevails that grand substantial taste in domestic arrangements and furniture, in which the English surpass all other nations, and which it is most difficult to imitate, because it is most expensive.

The influence which club-life exercises on the character of Englishmen is still an open question among them. The majority of the fairer portion of Her Majesty's subjects hate and detest the clubs most cordially. Mrs. Grundy* is

* A well-known personification of prudery.

loud in her complaints, that all that lounging, gossiping, and smoking deprives those "brutes of men" of the delight they would otherwise take in her intellectual society, and that club dinners make men such epicures, they actually turn up their noses at cold mutton. And even when at home, Mr. Grundy is always dull, and goes about sulking with Mrs. Grundy. To be sure, all he wants is to pick a quarrel, and go and spend his evening in that "horrid club." But there are some women who presume to differ from the views of this admirable type of old English matrons. They are fond of clubs, and hold a man all the more fitted for the fetters of matrimony after yawning away a couple of years in one of these British monasteries. The club-men, say these ladies, make capital husbands; for the regulations of the club-houses admit of no domestic vices, and these regulations are enforced with such severity, that a woman's rule appears gentle ever afterwards. . . .

On the Thames

. . . [138] The further we go down the river, the more closely packed are the vessels on either side. For above two miles the broad Thames is wofully narrow; and the steamers, which run up and down must just pick their way through as best they can. Accidents will happen; and the man at the wheel must keep a sharp look out. Those who never sailed on the Thames, have no idea of the number of black funnelled monsters, yclept steamers, which continually whisk past one another. There is one just now steering right down upon us; within another second our sides must be stove in. Well done! She has turned aside, and rushes past. But scarcely is the danger over, when another monster of the deep comes paddling on; and a large schooner is wedging its way between us and the said monster of the deep; and on our right there is an awkward Dutchman, swinging round on her anchor; and on our left, there is a lubber of a collier, with her gun-wales just sticking out of the water; and there, goodness gracious! there it is—a very nut-shell of a boat, and two women in it, passing close under our bows. I really dont know why we did not upset them, and why the others did not run into us. That nut-shell of a boat had a narrow escape among the steamers, [139] and these women were fully aware of it; and there is no end of accidents, and yet those people *will* row across the river.

It is a perfect blessing that the English know better than anybody else how to steer a boat under difficulties. Look at that man at the wheel! Immoveable, with his head bent forward, his eyes directed to the ship's course, his hands ready to turn the wheel: that fellow knows what steering on the Thames is! To all appearance, it is not near so difficult as rope-dancing, but I say it's worse than rope-dancing; it requires the most consummate address. And then there's the responsibility! The sailors of all nations stand in great awe of the London Thames. They navigate their vessels to the East Indies; they weather the storms of the Cape, and think nothing of its blowing "big

guns;" but none of them would undertake to steer a vessel from Blackwall
to London-bridge. "It's too crowded for us," they say; "and the little nut-
shells of steamers are enough to make an honest sailor giddy; and the river
is so narrow. If you fancy you are clear of all difficulties and can go on,
there's sure to be some impertinent boat in your way. Turn to the right! Why
there's not room for a starved herring to float!"

And the old steersman descends from his high place, and resigns his functions to the Thames pilot. If he is a conceited blockhead, let him try—that's
all. But if the vessel comes to harm, the insurance is lost; for the under-
writers at Lloyd's will not be responsible for any damage done in the pool,
unless the wheel is in the hands of a regular pilot. And they are right, for
with all the difficulties and dangers there are few accidents.

Let us then, trusting to the skill of that particular steersman who guides
our own destinies and those of our boat, look at the scenery around. A forest
of masts looms through the perennial fog; the banks of the river are lined with
warehouses; some old and dilapidated, while others are new, solid, and strong.
A stray flag fluttering in the evening breeze, a sailor hanging on the spars and
chewing tobacco, a monkey of a boy sky-larking on the topmost cross-trees
of an Indiaman*—these are some of the sights of the lower Thames. Let us
now look at the party on board our own vessel; for, after all, we ought to
know the people who [140] are in the same boat with us, and who, in case of
an accident would share our watery grave.

The boat is full. A first-class ticket to Gravesend costs nine-pence, and the
society is of a mixed description—of course. But it is one of the peculiarities
of England, that a "mixed society" does not by any means present so striking an appearance as in Germany or France. It is not easy to look *into*
people; and as for their exterior, their walk, manners, dress, and conduct,
there is even among the poorer classes, a strong flavour of the "gentleman."
The French blouse, or the German "kittel," † have no existence in this country; the black silk hat is the only headdress which Englishmen tolerate. A
man in a black dress coat, hat, and white cravat, hurrying through London
streets early in the morning, is not, as a raw German would fancy, a professor
going to his lecture-room, or an *attaché* on the track of some diplomatic
mystery. No; in the pocket of that man, if you were to pick it, you would
find a soap-box, strop, and razor—he is a barber. Or, as the case may be, a
man-milliner, or waiter, or tailor, or shoe-maker. Many an omnibus driver sits
on the box in a white cravat. In Paris, they say, with a black dress-coat and
affability, you find your way into the most fashionable drawing-rooms. Men
in black dress-coats descend now and then into London sewers, and that, too,
without being in the least affable.

The women of England, too, do not betray their social position by their
dress. Coloured silks, black velvets, silk or straw bonnets with botanical ornaments, are worn by a lady's maid, as well as by the lady. Possibly, the maid's

* A ship travelling the route to India.
† German; a smock frock.

dress may be less costly; the lady, too, may sweep her flounces with a distinguished air: there may be some difference or other, but who can see all and know all by just looking at people?

See, for instance, that lovely face under a grey bonnet—there! to the left of the cabin-stairs. She has just risen from her seat. What a slender, graceful figure! Pray dont look at her feet. What ease, what decency in her every movement; and how grandly, yet how confidently, does she take the arm of her companion! By Jove, he has got a black dress-coat, and a white [141] tie! A handsome couple! He is well-shaven, has fine thin lips, with that peculiar, lurking smile of superiority, which the most good-natured Englishmen can scarcely divest themselves of; his auburn hair is splendidly got up; his dress is of superfine cloth; his linen is unexceptionable; he has a gold chain dangling on his waistcoat, and dazzling all beholders. That man, for one, is a gentleman!

"He is nothing of the kind," says Dr. Keif; "he does not pay his tailor's bill. He is a journeyman tailor, and the coat I wear is the work of his hands; it is a capital coat, and I will thank him for making it." Saying which, the Doctor made his way to the young couple, and forthwith shook hands with them.

"They are as good as betrothed," said the Doctor, on his return. "Going for a day's pleasure to Greenwich; honest, decent people those. That's what I like in English prudery, that it cares for trifles only. Take it all in all, and you will find that the state of affairs is more satisfactory here than it is in Germany. That girl's father and mother—honest and decent people, I tell you—have no objection to her gadding about for whole days, and half the nights, too, under the protection of her sweetheart. They walk in the park, sit under the trees, talk of love, marriage, household affairs, Morrison's pills,* and other interesting subjects; and while they talk, they eat cold beef and hot mustard. And the result is, an honest marriage, without dishonourable antecedents. In Germany, such excursions would be suspicious in the extreme. Where's the prudery, I should like to know. Well, well," said the Doctor, shaking his head, "it's the nature of the people."

"And of the tie," said Mr. Baxter. "A white tie, and a black dress coat, kill all rakishness and scampishness, even in the most talented individuals. Choke a man with a white tie, squeeze him tight in a black coat, and he must needs be prudent, calculating, and respectable. He can't help it. It's for that very reason I have exacted from my son, at Heidelberg, a vow that he will eschew white ties and black coats, at least, until he is married."

Getting Around London

[155] The necessity of expeditious and cheap locomotion in the streets of London has called forth a variety of methods of travelling. The cheapest,

* See footnote, page 60.

simplest, oldest, and most natural of them is *walking*. In the narrow and crowded streets of the City, where conveyances make but little progress, this method is certainly the safest, and, withal, the most expeditious. Strangers in London are not fond of walking, they are bewildered by the crowd, and frightened at the crossings; they complain of the brutal conduct of the English, who elbow their way along the pavement without considering that people who hurry on, on some important business or other, cannot possibly stop to discuss each kick or push they give or receive. A Londoner jostles you in the street, without ever dreaming of asking your pardon; he will run against you, and make you revolve on your own axis, without so much as looking round to see how you feel after the shock; he will put his foot upon a lady's foot or dress, exactly [156] as if such foot or dress were integral parts of the pavement, which ought to be trodden upon; but if he runs you down, if he breaks your ribs, or knocks out your front teeth, he will show some slight compunction, and as he hurries off, the Londoner has actually been known to turn back and beg your pardon.

Of course all this is very unpleasant to the stranger, and the more delicate among the English themselves do not like it. None but men of business care to walk through the City at business hours; but if, either from choice or necessity, you find your way into those crowded quarters, you had better walk with your eyes wide open. Don't stop on the pavement, move on as fast you can, and do as the others do, that is to say, struggle on as best you may, and push forward without any false modesty. The passengers in London streets are hardened; they give and receive kicks and pushes with equal equanimity.

Much less excusable is the kicking and pushing of the English public at their theatres, museums, railway stations, and other places of public resort. Nothing but an introduction to every individual man and woman in the three kingdoms will save you from being, on such occasions, pushed back by them. You have not been introduced to them; you are a stranger to them, and there is no reason why they should consult your convenience. The fact is, the English are bears in all places, except in their own houses; and only those who make their acquaintance in their dens, know how amiable, kind, and mannerly they really are. . . .

[158] "Live and learn," ought to be the motto of the student of London cab-ology. No mortal could ever boast of having mastered the subject. There is no want of police regulations, and of patriots to enforce them; but still the cabmen form a class of British subjects, who, for all they are labelled, booked, and registered, move within a sphere of their own, beyond the pale of the law. The Commissioners of Police have drawn up most elaborate regulations concerning cabs; they have clearly defined what a cab ought to be, but the London cabs are exactly what they ought not to be. The faults of these four-wheeled instruments of torture can never sufficiently be complained of. Not only do they shorten the honest old English mile; but they bear a strong family-likeness to the Berlin droshkies. If the horse is wanted,

it is sure to be eating; if the cabby is wanted, he is equally sure to be drinking. If you would put the window down, you cannot move it; if it is down, and you would put it up, you find that the glass is broken. The straw-covered bottom of the cab has many crevices, which let in wind and dust; the seats feel as if they were stuffed with broken stones; the check-string is always broken; the door won't shut; or if shut, it won't open: in short (we make no mention of the horse), to discover the faults of a London cab is easy; to point out its good qualities is, what I for one, have never been able to achieve.

Whenever a stranger is bold enough to hail a cab, not one, but half a dozen come at once, obedient to his call; and the eagerness the drivers display is truly touching. They secure their whips, descend from their high places, and surround the stranger with many a wink and many a chuckle, to learn what he wants, and to "make *game* of him."

Supposing the stranger speaks the English language fluently [159] enough to make himself understood, of course he will name the place to which he wishes to go, and ask what they will take him for. He may rely on it, that of any conclave of cabmen, each one will demand, at least, double the amount of his legal fare. He demurs to the proposal, whereupon the six cabmen mount their boxes forthwith, return to their stand in the middle of the road, and indulge in jocular remarks on "foreigners," and "Frenchmen" in general. Blessed is that foreigner, if his studies of the English language have been confined to Byron, Thackeray, and Macaulay, for in that case he remains in happy ignorance of all the "good things" that are said at his expense. The retreat, however, was merely a feint; a few skirmishers advance again, and waylay the stranger. Again, and again, do they inquire, "what he will give?" They turn up the whites of their eyes, shrug their shoulders, make offers confidently, and decline propositions scornfully, and go on haggling and demonstrating until one of them comes to terms, and drives off with the victim.

But is there no legal scale of fares? Of course there is, but with the enormous extent of London it was impossible to establish a general fare for each "course" according to the cab regulations of the German, French, and Italian towns. A certain sum, say one shilling for each drive, would have wronged either the passenger or the driver. To get rid of the dilemma the fare was fixed at eight-pence per mile. But who can tell how many miles he has gone in a cab? A stranger of course cannot be expected to possess an intimate knowledge of places and distances. An old Londoner only may venture to engage in a topographic and geometrical disputation with a cabman, for gentlemen of this class are not generally flattering in their expressions or conciliating in their arguments; and the cheapest way of terminating the dispute is to pay and have done with the man. As a matter of principle the cabman is never satisfied with his legal fare; even those who know the town, and all its ways, must at times appeal to the intervention of a policeman or give their address to the driver, not, indeed, for the purpose of fighting a duel with him, but that he may, if he choose, apply to the magistrate for protection. But it is a remarkable fact, that [160] the cabmen of London are by no means eager to adopt the latter expedient.

The Hansom Cabs,* which of late years have been exported to Paris and Vienna, are generally in a better condition than the four-wheeled vehicles; but their drivers are to the full as exacting and impertinent as their humbler brethren of the whip. To do them justice, if they are exorbitant in their demands, they at least are satisfactory in their performance. They go at a dashing pace whenever they have an open space before them, and they are most skillful in winding and edging their light vehicles through the most formidable knots of waggons and carriages. The "Hansom" man is more genteel and gifted than the vulgar race of cabmen; he is altogether smarter (in more than one sense) and more dashing, daring, and reckless.

When cabby returns to his stand, he drops the reins, chats with his comrades, recounts his adventures, and "fights his battles o'er again," or he lights his pipe and disappears for a while in the mysterious recesses of a pothouse. His horse and carriage are meanwhile left to the care of an unaccountable being, who on such occasions pops out from some hiding-place, wall-niche, or cellar. This creature appears generally in the shape of a dirty, ricketty, toothless, grey-haired man; he is a *servus servorum*,† the slave of the cabmen, commonly described as a "waterman." For it was he who originally supplied the water for the washing of the vehicles. In the course of time, however, his functions have extended, and the waterman is now all in all to the cab-stand. He cleans the cabs, minds the horses, attends to the orders of passengers, opens and shuts the doors, and fetches and carries to the cabstand generally tobacco, pipes, beer, gin, *billets-doux,* and other articles of common consumption and luxury; in consideration for which services, he is entitled to the gratuity of one penny on account of each "fare"; and he manages to get another penny from the "fare" as a reward for the alacrity and politeness with which he opens the door. But further particulars of this mysterious old man we are unable to give. No one knows where he lives; no one, not even Mr. Mayhew, has as yet been able to ascertain where and at what hours he takes his meals. At two o'clock in the morning he may be seen busy with his [161] pails, and at five or six o'clock you may still observe him at his post, leaning against the area railings of some familiar public-house. But the early career of the man, his deeds and misdeeds, joys and sufferings, before he settled down as waterman to a cab-stand—these matters are a secret of the Guild, and one which is most rigorously preserved. Poor, toothless, old man! The penny we give thee will surely find its way to the gin-shop, but can we be obdurate enough to refuse giving it, since a couple of those coins will procure for thee an hour's oblivion?

We turn to the omnibuses, the principal and most popular means of locomotion in London. And here we beg to inform our German friends, that those

---

* Low, light, two-wheeled carriages.
† Latin, meaning "a slave of slaves."

classes of English society whose members are never on any account seen at the Italian Opera, and who consume beer in preference to wine, and brandy in preference to beer, affect a sort of pity, not unmixed with contempt, for those who go the full length of saying "Omnibus." The English generally affect abbreviations; and the word "bus" is rapidly working its way into general acceptation, exactly as in the case of the word "cab," which is after all but an abbreviation of "cabriolet."

Among the middle classes of London, the omnibus stands immediately after air, tea, and flannel, in the list of the necessaries of life. A Londoner generally manages to get on without the sun; water he drinks only in case of serious illness, and even then it is qualified with "the ghost of a drop of spirits." Certain other articles of common use and consumption on the Continent, such as passports, vintage-feasts, expulsion by means of the police, *cafés,* cheap social amusements, are entirely unknown to the citizens of London. But the Omnibus is a necessity; the Londoner cannot get on without it; and the stranger, too, unless he be very rich, has a legitimate interest in the omnibus, whose value he is soon taught to appreciate.

The outward appearance of the London omnibus, as compared to similar vehicles on the Continent, is very prepossessing. Whether it be painted red as the Saints' days in the Almanack, or blue as a Bavarian soldier, or green as the trees in summer, it is always neat and clean. The horses are strong and elegant; the driver is an adept in his art; the conductor is active, quick [162] as thought, and untiring as the *perpetuum mobile.* But all this cannot, I know, convey an idea of "life in an omnibus." We had better hail one and enter it, and as our road lies to the West, we look out for a "Bayswater."

We are at the Whitechapel toll-gate, a good distance to the East of the Bank. From this point, a great many omnibuses run to the West; and among the number is the particular class of Bayswater omnibuses one of which we have entered. It is almost empty, the only passengers being two women, who have secured the worst seats in the furthermost corners, probably because they are afraid of the draught from the door. The omnibus is standing idly at the door of a public-house, its usual starting-place. The driver and conductor have been bawling and jumping about, especially the latter, and they are now intent upon "refreshing" themselves. The horses look a little the worse for the many journeys they have made since the morning. Never mind! this omnibus will do as well as any other, and we prepare to secure places on the outside. . . .

[163] While we have been indulging in these reflections, the number of passengers has increased. There is a woman with a little boy, and that boy *will* not sit decently, but insists on kneeling on the seat, that he may look out of the window. An old gentleman has taken his seat near the door; he is a prim old man, with a black coat and a white cravat. There is also a young girl, a very neat one too, with a small bundle. Possibly she intends calling on some friends on the other side of the town; she proposes to pass the night there, and has taken her measures accordingly. A short visit certainly

is not worth the trouble of a long omnibus journey. Thus there are already six inside passengers, for the little boy, who is not a child in arms, is a "passenger," and his fare must be paid as such. The box-seat, too, has been taken by two young men; one of them smokes, and the other, exactly as if he had been at home, reads the police reports in to-day's *"Times."*

Stop! another passenger! a man with an opera-hat, a blue, white-spotted cravat, with a corresponding display of very clean shirt-collar, coat of dark green cloth, trousers and waistcoat of [164] no particular colour; his boots are well polished, his chin is cleanly shaved; his whiskers are of respectable and modest dimensions. There is a proud consciousness in the man's face; an easy, familiar carelessness in his movements as he ascends. He takes his seat on the box, and looks to the right and left with a strange mixture of *hauteur* and condescension, as much as to say: "You may keep your hats on, gentlemen." He produces a pair of stout yellow gloves; he seizes the reins and the whip—by Jove! it's the driver of the omnibus!

Immediately after him there emerges from the depths of the public-house another individual, whose bearing is less proud. He is thin, shabbily dressed, and his hands are without gloves. It is the conductor. He counts the inside passengers, looks in every direction to find an additional "fare," and takes his position on the back-board. "All right!" the driver moves the reins; the horses raise their heads; and the omnibus proceeds on its journey.

The street is broad. There is plenty of room for half a dozen vehicles, and there are not many foot-passengers to engage the conductor's attention. He is at liberty to play some fantastic tricks to vary the monotony of his existence; he jumps down from his board and up again; he runs by the side of the omnibus to rest his legs, for even running is a recreation compared to standing on that board. He makes a descent upon the pavement, lays hands on the maid of all work that is just going home from the butcher's, and invites her to take a seat in the "bus." He spies an elderly lady waiting at the street-corner; he knows at once that she is waiting for an omnibus, but that she cannot muster resolution to hail one. He addresses and secures her. Another unprotected female is caught soon after, then a boy, and after him another woman. Our majestic coachman is meanwhile quite as active as his colleague. He is never silent, and shouts his "Bank! Bank! Charing-cross!" at every individual passenger on the pavement. Any spare moments he may snatch from this occupation are devoted to his horses. He touches them up with the end of his whip, and exhorts them to courage and perseverance by means of that peculiar sound which holds the middle between a hiss and a groan, and which none but the drivers of London omnibuses can produce.

[165] In this manner we have come near the crowded streets of the city. The seat at our back is now occupied by two Irish labourers, smoking clay-pipes, and disputing in the richest of brogues, which is better, Romanism without whiskey, or Protestantism with the desirable addition of that favourite stimulant. There is room for two more passengers inside and for three outside.

Our progress through the city is slow. There are vehicles before us, behind us, and on either side. We are pulling up and turning aside at every step. At the Mansion-house we stop for a second or two, just to breathe the horses and take in passengers. This is the heart of the city, and, therefore, a general station for those who wish to get into or out of an omnibus. These vehicles proceed at a slow pace, and take up passengers, but they are compelled to proceed by the policeman on duty, who has strict instructions to prevent those stoppages which would invariably result from a congregation of omnibuses in this crowded locality.

Our particular omnibus gives the policeman no trouble, for it is full, inside and out, and this important fact having been notified to the driver, the reins are drawn tight, the whip is laid on the horses' backs, and we rush into the middle of crowded Cheapside. Three tons, that is to say, 60 cwt., is the weight of a London omnibus when full, and with these 60 cwts. at their backs, the two horses will run about a dozen English miles without the use of the whip, cheered only now and then by the driver's hiss. And with all that they are smooth and round and in good condition; they are not near so heavy as those heavy horses of Norman build which go their weary pace with the Paris omnibuses, nor are they such wretched catlike creatures as the majority of the horses which serve a similar purpose in Germany. Their harness is clean; on the continent it might pass for elegant. Although fiery when in motion, they never lay aside that gentleness of temper which is peculiar to the English horses. A child might guide them; they obey even the slightest movement of the reins; nay, more, an old omnibus-horse understands the signals and shouts of the conductor. It trots off the moment he gives that stunning [166] blow on the roof of the omnibus, which, in the jargon of London conductors, means: "Go on if you please;" and the word "stop" will arrest it in the sharpest trot.

But for the training and the natural sagacity of those animals, it would be impossible for so many omnibuses to proceed through the crowded city streets at the pace they do, without an extensive smashing of carriages, and a great sacrifice of human life resulting therefrom. We communicated our impressions on this subject to the omnibus driver, and were much pleased to find our opinion corroborated by the authority of that dignitary. . . .

Drury-Lane

[266] In the Strand, just opposite to majestic Somerset-House, and half-hidden by the railings of the church-yard, which encroaches upon the natural dimensions of the street, there is a narrow passage, which turns up into Drury-lane. That lane, though of unequal breadth, is always narrow, and numberless are the blind alleys, courts, and passages on either side. The first and second floors of the high and narrow houses, shelter evidently a class of small tradesmen and mechanics, who in other countries would pass as "re-

spectable," while here they work for the merest necessaries of life, and, like their customers, live from hand to mouth. A few of them are usurers, preying [267] upon poverty, coining gold from its vices and morbid longings. As for the garrets of those houses, we would not for the world answer for the comfort of their inhabitants. All the lower floors are let out as shops, in which are displayed dingy dresses and articles of female ornament, coarse eatables, cheap and nasty literature, shockingly illustrated; thick-soled shoes, old clothes, awful cigars—all at very low prices. But the gin-palaces are the lions of Drury-lane; they stand in conspicuous positions, at the corners and crossings of the various intersecting streets. They may be seen from afar, and are lighthouses which guide the thirsty "sweater" on the road to ruin. For they are resplendent with plate glass and gilt cornices, and a variety of many-coloured inscriptions. One of the windows displays the portrait of the "NORFOLK GIANT," who acts as barman to this particular house; the walls of another establishment inform you, in green letters, that here they sell "THE ONLY REAL BRANDY IN LONDON," and a set of scarlet letters announces to the world, that in this house they sell "THE FAMOUS CORDIAL MEDICATED GIN, WHICH IS SO STRONGLY RECOMMENDED BY THE FACULTY." Cream Gin, Honey Gin, Sparkling Ale, Genuine Porter, and other words calculated utterly to confound a tee-totaller, are painted up in conspicuous characters, even so that they cover the door-posts. It is a remarkable fact, that the houses which are most splendid from without, appear most dismal and comfortless from within. The landlord is locked up behind his "bar," a snug place enough, with painted casks and a fire and an arm-chair; but the guests stand in front of the bar in a narrow dirty place, exposed to the draught of the door, which is continually opening and shutting. Now and then an old barrel, flung in a corner, serves as a seat. But nevertheless the "palace" is always crowded with guests, who, standing, staggering, crouching, or lying down, groaning, and cursing, drink and forget.

On sober working-days, and in tolerable weather, there is nothing to strike the uninitiated in Drury-lane. Many a capital of a small German country is worse paved and lighted. Nor is misery so conspicuous and staring in this quarter as in Spitalfields, St. Giles', Saffron-hill, and other "back-slums" of London. But at certain bestial periods, misery oozes out of all its pores [268] like Mississipi mud. Saturday and Monday nights, and Sunday after Churchtime, those are the times in which Drury-lane appears in full characteristic glory. A Sunday-afternoon in Drury-lane is enough to make the cheerfullest splenetic. For to the poor labourer the Lord's day is a day of penance or dissipation. The cotton-frock and fustian-jacket are scared away from the churches and the parks by their respectful awe of rich toilettes and splendid liveries. For the poor man of England is ashamed of his rags; he has no idea of arranging them into a graceful *draperie* in the manner of the Spanish or Italian Lazarone,* who devoutly believes that begging is an honest trade. Even the lowest among the low in England are proud enough to avoid the

* An Italian term for a beggar.

society of a higher *caste,* though that superiority consist but in half a degree. They consort with persons of their own stamp, among whom they may walk with their heads erect. Church and park have moreover no charm for the blunted senses of the overworked and under-fed artizan. He is too weak and fatigued to think of an excursion into the country. Steamers, omnibuses, or the rail, are too expensive. His church, his park, his club, his theatre, his place of refuge from the smell of the sewers that infect his dwelling—his sole place of relaxation—is the gin-palace.

To provide against the Sunday, he takes a supply of fire-water on Saturday evening when he has received his week's wages, for with the stroke of twelve the sabbath shuts the door of all public-houses, and on Sunday-morning the beer or brandy paradise must not open before one o'clock in the afternoon, to be closed again from three to five. Hence that unsacred stillness which weighs down upon Drury-lane on Sunday-mornings. The majority of the inhabitants sleep away their intoxication or *ennui.* Old time-worn maudlinness reigns supreme in the few faces which peer from the half-opened street-doors; maudlinness pervades the half-sleepy groups which surround the public-house at noon to be ready for its opening; chronic maudlinness pervades the atmosphere. And if a stray ray of light break through the clouds, it falls upon the frowsy loungers and the dim window-panes in a strange manner, as though it had no business there.

[269] It is Saturday-night, and the orgies of Drury-lane have commenced. . . .

A dense fog, with a deep red colouring, from the reflection of numberless gas-jets, and the pavement flooded with mud; a fitful illumination according to the strength of the gas, which flares forth in long jets from the butchers' shops, while the less illumined parts are lost in gloomy twilight. If your nerves are delicate, you had better not pass too close by the gin-shops, for as the door opens—and those doors are always opening—you are overwhelmed with the pestilential fumes of gin. The pavements are crowded. Slatternly servants with baskets hurry to the butchers and grocers, and the haunters of the coffee-houses of Drury-lane elbow their way through the very midst of the population—the *sweepings* of humanity. A wicked word this, but the only one fit for these forms of woe and livid faces, in which hunger contends with thirst, and vice with disease.

What subjects for Hogarth on the narrow space of a couple of flag-stones! How ravenous the craving which flashes from the eyes of that grey-haired woman, as she drags a slight, yellow-haired girl—perhaps her own child—to the gin-shop! The little girl follows in a dumb wooden way; but her small slight hand is shut with an anxious grasp, as though she feared to lose her weekly earnings—the wages, perhaps, of hard work, or still harder beggary. She stumbles at the threshold, and almost falls over a couple of children that are crouching on the ground, shivering with cold, and waiting for their father within. The father comes, staggering and kicking the air, with manifest danger to his equilibrium, and cursing awfully. The kick was meant for his wife, a thin woman, with hollow yellow cheeks, whose long serpent-like curls are covered with an old silk bonnet, while her stockingless feet are contained in large slippers. She counts five copper pence in her bony hand, looks at her drunken husband, and at the fatal door, and at the costermonger's cart in the [270] middle of the street; and she counts her pence, and recounts them, and cannot come to the end of them, though they are but five. The large oysters in the dirty cart, too, excite her appetite. Which is it to be? the public-house or a lot of oysters? "Penny a lot, oysters!" shouts the man, as he moves his cart forward. A dozen greedy eyes watch his movements.

Similar groups are met with at every step. At the door of almost every gin-shop you see drunken women, many of them with children in their arms; and wherever you go, amidst the confused noise and murmur of many voices, you hear distinctly the most awful oaths. . . .

from

English Traits

Ralph Waldo Emerson

EMERSON WROTE *English Traits* as a series of essays in 1856, after having visited England in 1832-33 and in 1847. He met many English men of letters and became a life-long friend of Thomas Carlyle. Emerson was the most prominent American writer of his day, certainly the one most respected by the British public, and a central figure in the group of authors who called themselves the Transcendental Club. Originally a Unitarian minister, he resigned soon after beginning his ministry, and devoted himself to writing and lecturing. *English Traits* shows that Emerson was less interested in everyday facts about England than in observations that would lead him to valuable generalizations and fundamental truths.

The Complete Works of Ralph Waldo Emerson,
vol. V, Concord edition. Boston and New York:
Houghton Mifflin Company, 1903.

CHAPTER VI, Manners.

[102] I find the Englishman to be him of all men who stands firmest in his shoes. They have in themselves what they value in their horses,—mettle and bottom.* On the day of my arrival at Liverpool, a gentleman, in describing

* Stamina or determination.

to me the Lord Lieutenant of Ireland, happened to say, "Lord Clarendon has pluck like a cock and will fight till he dies;" and what I heard first I heard last, and the one thing the English value is *pluck*. The word is not beautiful, but on the quality they signify by it the nation is unanimous. The cabmen have it; the merchants have it; the bishops have it; the women have it; the journals have it;—the Times newspaper they say is the pluckiest thing in England, and Sydney Smith had made it a proverb that Lord John Russell, the minister, would take the command of the Channel fleet to-morrow.*

They require you to dare to be of your own opinion, and they hate the practical cowards who cannot in affairs answer directly yes or no. They dare to displease, nay, they will let you break all [103] the commandments, if you do it natively and with spirit. You must be somebody; then you may do this or that, as you will.

Machinery has been applied to all work, and carried to such perfection that little is left for the men but to mind the engines and feed the furnaces. But the machines require punctual service, and as they never tire, they prove too much for their tenders. Mines, forges, mills, breweries, railroads, steam-pump, steam-plough, drill of regiments, drill of police, rule of court and shop-rule have operated to give a mechanical regularity to all the habit and action of men. A terrible machine has possessed itself of the ground, the air, the men and women, and hardly even thought is free.

The mechanical might and organization requires in the people constitution and answering spirits; and he who goes among them must have some weight of metal. At last, you take your hint from the fury of life you find, and say, one thing is plain, this is no country for fainthearted people: don't creep about diffidently; make up your mind; take your own course, and you shall find respect and furtherance.

It requires, men say, a good constitution to travel in Spain. I say as much of England, for [104] other cause, simply on account of the vigor and brawn of the people. Nothing but the most serious business could give one any counterweight to these Baresarks,† though they were only to order eggs and muffins for their breakfast. The Englishman speaks with all his body. His elocution is stomachic,—as the American's is labial. The Englishman is very petulant and precise about his accommodation at inns and on the roads; a quiddle‡ about his toast and his chop and every species of convenience, and loud and pungent in his expressions of impatience at any neglect. His vivacity betrays itself at all points, in his manners, in his respiration, and the inarticulate noises he makes in clearing the throat;—all significant of burly strength. He has stamina; he can take the initiative in emergencies. He has that

---

* Sydney Smith (1771-1845) was a clergyman, essayist and wit who often wrote for the *Edinburgh Review*. Lord John Russell (1792-1878) was a Parliamentarian and liberal reformer who helped to draft and pass the important Reform Bill of 1832.
† Wild Norse warriors.
‡ A fastidious person.

aplomb which results from a good adjustment of the moral and physical nature and the obedience of all the powers to the will; as if the axes of his eyes were united to his backbone, and only moved with the trunk.

This vigor appears in the incuriosity and stony neglect, each of every other. Each man walks, eats, drinks, shaves, dresses, gesticulates, and, in every manner acts and suffers without reference to the bystanders, in his own fashion, only careful [105] not to interfere with them or annoy them; not that he is trained to neglect the eyes of his neighbors,—he is really occupied with his own affair and does not think of them. Every man in this polished country consults only his convenience, as much as a solitary pioneer in Wisconsin. I know not where any personal eccentricity is so freely allowed, and no man gives himself any concern with it. An Englishman walks in a pouring rain, swinging his closed umbrella like a walking-stick; wears a wig, or a shawl, or a saddle, or stands on his head, and no remark is made. And as he has been doing this for several generations, it is now in the blood.

In short, every one of these islanders is an island himself, safe, tranquil, incommunicable. In a company of strangers you would think him deaf; his eyes never wander from his table and newspaper. He is never betrayed into any curiosity or unbecoming emotion. They have all been trained in one severe school of manners, and never put off the harness. He does not give his hand. He does not let you meet his eye. It is almost an affront to look a man in the face without being introduced. In mixed or in select companies they do not introduce persons; so that a presentation is a circumstance as valid as [106] a contract. Introductions are sacraments. He withholds his name. At the hotel, he is hardly willing to whisper it to the clerk at the book-office. If he give you his private address on a card, it is like an avowal of friendship; and his bearing, on being introduced, is cold, even though he is seeking your acquaintance and is studying how he shall serve you.

It was an odd proof of this impressive energy, that in my lectures I hesitated to read and threw out for its impertinence many a disparaging phrase which I had been accustomed to spin, about poor, thin, unable mortals;—so much had the fine physique and the personal vigor of this robust race worked on my imagination.

I happened to arrive in England at the moment of a commercial crisis. But it was evident that let who will fail, England will not. These people have sat here a thousand years, and here will continue to sit. They will not break up, or arrive at any desperate revolution, like their neighbors; for they have as much energy, as much continence of character as they ever had. The power and possession which surround them are their own creation, and they exert the same commanding industry at this moment.

They are positive, methodical, cleanly and [107] formal, loving routine and conventional ways; loving truth and religion, to be sure, but inexorable on points of form. All the world praises the comfort and private appointments of an English inn, and of English households. You are sure of neatness and of personal decorum. A Frenchman may possibly be clean; an Englishman is conscientiously clean. A certain order and complete propriety is found in his dress and in his belongings.

Born in a harsh and wet climate, which keeps him in doors whenever he is at rest, and being of an affectionate and loyal temper, he dearly loves his house. If he is rich, he buys a demesne and builds a hall; if he is in middle condition, he spares no expense on his house. Without, it is all planted; within, it is wainscoted, carved, curtained, hung with pictures and filled with good furniture. 'Tis a passion which survives all others, to deck and improve it. Hither he brings all that is rare and costly, and with the national tendency to sit fast in the same spot for many generations, it comes to be, in the course of time, a museum of heirlooms, gifts and trophies of the adventures and exploits of the family. He is very fond of silver plate, and though he have no gallery of portraits of his ancestors, [108] he has of their punch-bowls and porringers. Incredible amounts of plate are found in good houses, and the poorest have some spoon or saucepan, gift of a godmother, saved out of better times.

An English family consists of a few persons, who, from youth to age, are found revolving within a few feet of each other, as if tied by some invisible ligature, tense as that cartilage which we have seen attaching the two Siamese. England produces under favorable conditions of ease and culture the finest women in the world. And as the men are affectionate and true-hearted, the women inspire and refine them. Nothing can be more delicate without being fantastical, nothing more firm and based in nature and sentiment than the courtship and mutual carriage of the sexes. The song of 1596 says, "The wife of every Englishman is counted blest." The sentiment of Imogen in Cymbeline is copied from English nature; and not less the Portia of Brutus, the Kate Percy and the Desdemona.* The romance does not exceed the height of noble passion in Mrs. Lucy Hutchinson,† or in Lady Russell, or even as one discerns through the plain prose of Pepys's Diary, the sacred habit of an English wife. Sir Samuel Romilly‡ could not bear the [109] death of his wife. Every class has its noble and tender examples.

Domesticity is the taproot which enables the nation to branch wide and high. The motive and end of their trade and empire is to guard the independence and privacy of their homes. Nothing so much marks their manners as the concentration on their household ties. This domesticity is carried into court and camp. Wellington governed India and Spain and his own troops, and fought battles, like a good family-man, paid his debts, and though gen-

---

* Imogen, Portia, Kate Percy, and Desdemona are women who appear in Shakespeare's plays.

† Mrs. Lucy Hutchinson, born in 1620, the wife of Colonel John Hutchinson, one of the judges who sentenced King Charles I to death during the Puritan Revolution, was a learned lady known for her biography of her husband.

‡ Sir Samuel Romilly (1757-1818), a legal reformer who succeeded in having criminal laws made more humane.

eral of an army in Spain, could not stir abroad for fear of public creditors. This taste for house and parish merits has of course its doting and foolish side. Mr. Cobbett attributes the huge popularity of Perceval, prime minister in 1810, to the fact that he was wont to go to church every Sunday, with a large quarto gilt prayer-book under one arm, his wife hanging on the other, and followed by a long brood of children.

They keep their old customs, costumes, and pomps, their wig and mace, sceptre and crown. The Middle Ages still lurk in the streets of London. The Knights of the Bath take oath to defend injured ladies; the gold-stick-in-waiting survives. They repeated the ceremonies of the [110] eleventh century in the coronation of the present Queen. A hereditary tenure is natural to them. Offices, farms, trades and traditions descend so. Their leases run for a hundred and a thousand years. Terms of service and partnership are life-long, or are inherited. "Holdship has been with me," said Lord Eldon, "eight-and-twenty years, knows all my business and books." Antiquity of usage is sanction enough. Wordsworth says of the small freeholders of Westmoreland, "Many of these humble sons of the hills had a consciousness that the land which they tilled had for more than five hundred years been possessed by men of the same name and blood." The ship-carpenter in the public yards, my lord's gardener and porter, have been there for more than a hundred years, grandfather, father, and son.

The English power resides also in their dislike of change. They have diffi-culty in bringing their reason to act, and on all occasions use their memory first. As soon as they have rid themselves of some grievance and settled the better practice, they make haste to fix it as a finality, and never wish to hear of alteration more.

Every Englishman is an embryonic chancellor: his instinct is to search for a precedent. The favorite phrase of their law is, "a custom [111] whereof the memory of man runneth not back to the contrary." The barons say, "*Nolumus mutari;*" * and the cockneys stifle the curiosity of the foreigner on the reason of any practice with "Lord, sir, it was always so." They hate innovation. Bacon told them, Time was the right reformer; Chatham, that "confidence was a plant of slow growth;" Canning, to "advance with the times;" and Wellington, that "habit was ten times nature." All their states-men learn the irresistibility of the tide of custom, and have invented many fine phrases to cover this slowness of perception and prehensility of tail.

A sea-shell should be the crest of England, not only because it represents a power built on the waves, but also the hard finish of the men. The English-man is finished like a cowry or a murex. After the spire and the spines are formed, or with the formation, a juice exudes and a hard enamel varnishes every part. The keeping of the proprieties is as indispensable as clean linen. No merit quite countervails the want of this whilst this sometimes stands in lieu of all. " 'Tis in bad taste," is the most formidable word an Englishman

* "We do not wish to change."

can pronounce. But this japan* costs them dear. There is a prose in certain Englishmen which exceeds in wooden deadness all rivalry [112] with other countrymen. There is a knell in the conceit and externality of their voice, which seems to say, *Leave all hope behind*. In this Gibraltar of propriety, mediocrity gets entrenched and consolidated and founded in adamant. An Englishman of fashion is like one of those souvenirs, bound in gold vellum, enriched with delicate engravings on thick hot-pressed paper, fit for the hands of ladies and princes, but with nothing in it worth reading or remembering.

A severe decorum rules the court and the cottage. When Thalberg the pianist was one evening performing before the Queen at Windsor, in a private party, the Queen accompanied him with her voice. The circumstance took air, and all England shuddered from sea to sea. The indecorum was never repeated. Cold, repressive manners prevail. No enthusiasm is permitted except at the opera. They avoid every thing marked. They require a tone of voice that excites no attention in the room. Sir Philip Sidney is one of the patron saints of England, of whom Wotton said, "His wit was the measure of congruity."

Pretension and vaporing are once for all distasteful. They keep to the other extreme of low tone in dress and manners. They avoid pretension [113] and go right to the heart of the thing. They hate nonsense, sentimentalism and high-flown expression; they use a studied plainness. Even Brummel,† their fop, was marked by the severest simplicity in dress. They value themselves on the absence of every thing theatrical in the public business, and on conciseness and going to the point, in private affairs.

In an aristocratical country like England, not the Trial by Jury, but the dinner, is the capital institution. It is the mode of doing honor to a stranger, to invite him to eat,—and has been for many hundred years. "And they think," says the Venetian traveller of 1500, "no greater honor can be conferred or received, than to invite others to eat with them, or to be invited themselves, and they would sooner give five or six ducats to provide an entertainment for a person, than a groat to assist him in any distress." It is reserved to the end of the day, the family-hour being generally six, in London, and if any company is expected, one or two hours later. Every one dresses for dinner, in his own house, or in another man's. The guests are expected to arrive within half an hour of the time fixed by card of invitation, and nothing but death or mutilation is permitted to detain them. The English dinner is precisely [114] the model on which our own are constructed in the Atlantic cities. The company sit one or two hours before the ladies leave the table. The gentlemen remain over their wine an hour longer, and rejoin the ladies in the drawing-room and take coffee. The dress-dinner generates a talent of table-talk which reaches great perfection: the stories are so good that one

---

* A hard varnish.
† George Bryan Brummel (1778-1840), the famous dandy, known as "Beau Brummel."

is sure they must have been often told before, to have got such happy turns. Hither come all manner of clever projects, bits of popular science, of practical intervention, of miscellaneous humor; political, literary and personal news; railroads, horses, diamonds, agriculture, horticulture, pisciculture and wine.

English stories, *bon-mots* and the recorded table-talk of their wits, are as good as the best of the French. In America, we are apt scholars, but have not yet attained the same perfection: for the range of nations from which London draws, and the steep contrasts of condition, create the picturesque in society, as broken country makes picturesque landscape; whilst our prevailing equality makes a prairie tameness: and secondly, because the usage of a dress-dinner every day at dark has a tendency to hive and produce to advantage every thing good. Much [115] attrition has worn every sentence into a bullet. Also one meets now and then with polished men who know every thing, have tried every thing, and can do every thing, and are quite superior to letters and science. What could they not, if only they would?

from

A Frenchman Among the Victorians

Francis Wey

FRANCIS WEY, born in 1812, was an important educational official, president of the Société des Gens de Lettres, an art critic, a philologist, and a frequent contributor to French periodicals. His book, *Les Anglais Chez Eux*, was written after 1856, and was the result of a number of visits to England spread over at least a decade. As might be expected of a sensitive and well-educated French observer, Wey was extremely critical of English art, entertainment, and food. However, he was deeply impressed by the luxury of the clubs, and actually enjoyed the enforced inactivity and dullness of the notorious English Sunday.

Trans. from the French by Valerie Pirie.
New Haven, Conn.: Yale University Press, 1936.
Reprinted by permission of Sidgwick & Jackson Ltd.

Tavern Fare

. . . [37] After visiting Whitehall, we returned to the hotel, where a plentiful dinner awaited us, and, to dispose of the evening, the least weary among us started out to visit some taverns. London is really a city for the married. Home life here must have very real charms, for the bachelor is not catered for at all. Public-houses are most uncomfortable and very poorly stocked. If you go into a coffee-house you will only find tea or coffee there, as they are not licensed to sell any other drinks. There are places where one drinks without eating, others where one eats without drinking. In some oyster bars you find fish but [38] no meat. The larger taverns are better provided with food: one can dine there, but for supper about midnight is the time when they are most popular.

The saloons are usually on the first floor of the building, and the entrance money is one shilling, in exchange for which you are given some small refreshment. The tables, covered with oilcloth or leather, are placed against the wall and partitioned off, in cubicles. The Englishman likes to be isolated, he wants privacy even in public. Tea is drunk, or boiling grog, ale, inky-coloured porter or strong beer. Brandy is a favourite beverage and often served in tumblers. The room is plain, people do not go there to be amused, and drinking is a serious business. The more liquor they absorb the quieter they become, and if occasionally a less morose drinker breaks into a tipsy song, the oppressive silence soon reduces him to muteness again. This is how most Londoners who cannot afford to belong to clubs spend their evenings; and at midnight they reel homewards. Could anything be more tedious?

At the end of the room on a raised platform three gentlemen sit at a table. They are [39] correctly dressed in black swallow-tail coats and white ties. Suddenly one of them hits the table with an auctioneer's hammer. Dead silence follows—and to the accompaniment of a piano our three gentlemen, as serious as Anglican ministers, start singing, sometimes alone, sometimes in chorus, sentimental ballads, or Anglo-Italian tunes which have the greatest success judging by the unstinted applause they elicit. As the English have the faculty of enjoying the same thing indefinitely, this entertainment lasts for hours.

This description applies to all taverns of the Strand or round Covent Garden. Others have unfortunately installed mechanical organs which grind away unceasingly. In some you might find a theatre with clowns and buffoons acting serious plays, even Shakespeare. This genius has remained so popular with the people that they are careful in the lowest ale-houses to announce the performances as "conforming to the original text."

Shakespeare's plays are also billed at the Haymarket; but the upper classes do not patronise their national theatre, which will soon be bankrupt no doubt. They swarm to the [40] Italian operas which are given on the same nights to full houses.

About midnight, the crowd of pleasure-seekers leaves the public gardens, the theatres, the open-air dancing places, and surges into the none-too-respectable Piccadilly saloons. They may also find vulgar amusements in the streets, or they invade the oyster bars, where they feed till morning. At daybreak policemen gather up from the pavement drunkards of both sexes, alas! and of all conditions.

I do not know if the English ever rest; but London never sleeps. Yet the day is busy enough. At all hours workshops are full and the resorts of idlers overflow. Although the town has a population of almost three million souls, one cannot account for the numbers of people about. The streets are seething with traffic, entire populations are floating on the Thames, the parks are strewn with loafers, monuments with sightseers, the gardens and pleasances of the neighbourhood are overrun with trippers, and the bustle never decreases during the whole week. They eat at all hours, everywhere and unceasingly. Their cast-iron digestive organs enable them to withstand and even thrive upon [41] an alimentary diet which would more than satisfy the appetite of wolves. The fare of a delicate, ethereal girl would easily still the inner cravings of two Parisian bargees.* However rigid English prudery may be in the home circle, it is shocked by nothing in the street, where licentiousness runs riot. This apparent inconsistency is the result of the Englishman's ingrained regard for individual liberty.

London Clubs

. . . [50] No stranger could possibly gain admittance into a club without being introduced by a member, and these impregnable fortresses play a most important part in an Englishman's life. [51] The general idea on which club life is based is the facilitating of intercourse between people of the same opinions or calling. There are aristocratic clubs, military clubs, clubs for university men or scholars, such as the Oxford and Cambridge, commercial clubs, etc., without counting the political ones. It is not an easy thing to be elected to the most exclusive clubs, and a membership confers such an enviable notoriety that one has seen most distinguished, well-bred people wait patiently even ten years for such an honour to be conferred on them.

The Reform Club to which I was bidden is one of the most splendid of these establishments and cannot be outdone by any other in point of luxury and comfort. The members belong to the highest circles of the industrial and financial worlds.

The building alone cost three millions, but Pall Mall is lined with these sumptuous palaces, and it is only one of many.

The Reform Club is a majestic building, practically square and reminiscent of the Farnese Palace in Rome. It is two floors high with nine windows along the frontage and eight on the sides. A porter sits at a desk in the lobby to [52] answer visitors' questions and probably to see that none but members penetrate within its imposing portals. The interior hall is surrounded by colonnades supporting a large gallery. The floor is tessellated in imitation of Roman mosaic. The pillars are made of stucco of the colour of Siennese marble; the dome which lights the hall is of diapered flint glass and is supported by twenty Ionic columns; their red porphyry basements breaking the line of a stone balustrade rest on the gallery, which is reached by a broad white marble stairway. This gallery, where one can stroll as in a covered cloister, is fitted with easy chairs, mirrors, pictures and a thick carpet. It is a kind of general sitting-room from which you can observe the hall below into which visitors are ushered. A drawing-room so large that it must be intended

* Bargemen.

for dancing, a card-room, reading-room and private reception-rooms open into this gallery, as do also the two important libraries; the one containing literary works, the other legal and political ones. There are two librarians on the staff of the club. On the upper floor there are a considerable number of bedrooms. London is so vast, time so precious, that large sums of money are spent on saving minutes. [58] If a member happens to have business appointments for the next morning, or expects to be kept late in the evening, instead of going home he brings or sends his things to the club and spends the night there.

Every bedroom has a recess fitted with a white marble basin into which through two taps hot and cold water can be poured at any time. Soaps, unguents, perfumes, essences, toilet articles; a complete array of them is to be found there, as well as highly trained valets always in readiness to dress or shave one. If a member merely wants to change his clothes, he can do so just as conveniently on the ground floor and thus avoid the fatigue of climbing the stairs. Even well-appointed bathrooms are to be found there.

In the basement are the kitchens, planned by the famous French *chef,* Alexis Soyer; there one can see roasting, in front of a wall of fire five feet high, enormous sections of beef, sheep cut in half and long chaplets of fowls. A double screen enables the cooks, by taking an occasional peep, to keep an eye on the roast without being themselves grilled alive. In another room fitted with a gigantic baking oven all the pastry is made. Further along are the dairy, the stillroom,* the [54] larder, where pieces of meat ready cut are placed in enormous chests on beds of ice that drain off into zinc receptacles. Fish is kept in the same way. Everything is clean, even luxurious, and the kitchen utensils are resplendent.

Having been shown all these marvels by Mr. P., who was delighted at my unfeigned admiration, we went into the coffee-room, a large high room giving on to a charming garden. Twenty servants in dress clothes wait on a number of small tables noiselessly and with extreme promptitude. They tread with felt soles on the thick pile of expensive carpets; plates and dishes, instead of being piled up on top of one another, are brought and removed singly. The sound of footsteps, creaky shoes, the clatter of crockery and knives and forks are vexations unknown to the fortunate mortals who dine in clubs. This quietude may account for the excessive complacency of their digestions!

The rules of the club do not allow a member to treat a guest without also inviting a member. As on that day my host had invited two guests, two fellow-members had been included in the party. One of them was an officer in the Queen's Guards. Before the Crimean War, English soldiers could be [55] discerned by the softness of their voice, and the modesty of their bearing, studied good manners, and the ease with which they avoided any roughness which might be reminiscent of the barracks. As, besides, these officers travel widely during their leave, and have been quartered all over the globe,

* A store-room for cakes, preserves and other delicacies, sometimes used for the preparation of tea or coffee.

they are capable of talking on other than military subjects. Never have I met a man with more charming manners than this officer. There is nothing surprising in the fact, as Commissions in the British Army are expensive to purchase and are only granted to the well-bred. The Army, therefore, is an aristocratic corps, and the towns where the best regiments are quartered are much sought after, and have a great reputation for distinction and elegance. . . .

English Food

[58] So many people have asked me what the food is like in England that I must treat the subject as sufficiently interesting not to be omitted. The most usual method at the dinner-table up to five or six years ago was for the dishes to be placed in front of the host and for him to carve for his family and guests. The fashion nowadays is to wait *à la Russe;* it is a complicated ceremonial and tends to make meals more formal.

The fundamental part of an English dinner is the fish and the roast, the rest is accessory. The size of these two dishes is of the greatest importance. The fish comes first. For an honoured guest there is a salmon or a sturgeon of at least one yard in length, served with a variety of sauces, mostly full of strong condiments which English people much appreciate. Their flavour as I can best describe it is that of fireworks which have been thoughtfully set alight in readiness for [59] swallowing. Then come entrées—supposedly French—consisting of over-cooked game, high fowl or heavy pastry. The roast, proportionate to the number and quality of the guests, is worthy of Homeric times. Luxury consists in presenting simultaneously several dishes of fish or of roast meats. *Hors d'œuvres* are numerous and sweets strange; a very usual one is a sort of cake with sour herbs; or more popular still, the stewed stems of the rhubarb plant whose medicinal properties are well known; yet these prudish people openly advertise the defects of their most private internal economy by their shameless partiality for this amazing fare! Salad is served on a dish. It mostly consists of a lettuce just cut in two. I have seen it eaten dry with the fingers, and just dipped in salt. Vegetables are simply boiled in water and handed round with the meat. With dessert enormous cheeses, of Cheshire or Stilton, make their appearance, accompanied by boats full of butter. Fruit follows, melon being classed in this category, after which everything is removed from the table, even the cloth, and fresh glasses and wine are brought in. Only wine is privileged to be placed on the table—for beer and ale there is a special ritual. A servant presents you with [60] an empty salver, and unless you have been warned of this custom beforehand, you are naturally much taken aback. Let me tell you that you are expected to place your glass on it. The servant having filled it at the sideboard will return it to you, still on its salver, and so his hands will not have come into contact with your glass, which would be against English ideas of hygiene and propriety. At the Reform Club wine is drunk in the old-fashioned English way. Sherry, port and claret precede champagne, but are served continuously through the meal. Spiced wine is a specialty of the club, and this is how it is prepared. A bottle of sherry is poured into a deep pitcher which is placed in an ice pail. One adds a little maidenhair fern, a cup of green tea, a glass of soda water, some powdered cinnamon, cloves and lemon peel. If the weather is hot a few pieces of ice are also put in. This ice, crystal clear and of the greatest purity, is brought specially for the Reform Club from some far-distant place in America, as nowhere else can the like of it be found. This mixture, though very potent, has a fine flavour and promotes the appetite. Made with sherry it is called *sangris,* and with claret *sangorum.*

[61] To give you an idea of the luxury of these clubs you must know that their carpets and beautiful hand-woven table-linen are made specially for them from special designs, which are their private property, and bear the club's name woven into the texture. The silver and china have also been made for the exclusive use of the club, which owns all the original models. It is easy to surmise the enormous outlay such luxury must entail. After dinner we passed through a gorgeous reception-room, bright with gilding and paintings, to ensconce ourselves in a smaller room. A number of these "boudoirs" are necessary, as the Englishman is so discreet that if he sees three or four men in one room he will hesitate even to go through it; curiosity and indiscretion are here the greatest of crimes.

Time flies in the company of men who have learned much by experience and little in books; who have travelled widely and noticed a great deal; have no wish to dazzle you by exaggerated statements, and who listen even better than they talk. Mr. Paton entertained us with accounts of his travels, and seemed to take a great interest in my impressions of London and its inhabitants. He was not peculiar in that, for I have found all [62] Englishmen anxious to hear a Frenchman's opinion of them and ingenuously pleased when it is flattering.

There is nothing more different from an Englishman at home than an Englishman abroad, and on the last are founded most of the prejudices which we lose when we cross the Channel. Their conversation is more restricted than ours, for they do not embark on topics they are ignorant of, nor start an argument on insufficient or superficial knowledge. They confine themselves to their own subjects, even in social intercourse. It gives one great satisfaction to gain their approval, because one feels their esteem is worth having, and the more your acquaintance with them ripens, the more attentions they have for you. They only put themselves out for people they respect, and never respect those they do not know. With us it is exactly the contrary.

Most French travellers have deplored the lack of amenities to be found by foreigners in London. There are none of those cheerful, brilliantly lit *cafés* in which to meet, where one can read the papers, have a game of cards, or exchange the day's gossip of an evening; none of those splendid restaurants where the fashionable young [68] bloods congregate. And the result is that tourists return to France vexed, and grumbling that the English people are bears. Would it not be more sensible to try and discover the cause of the great difference which exists in that respect between London and Paris?

Sixty clubs, analogous to the one I have just described, and harbouring practically the entire male element of the upper classes, in palaces where luxury and comfort are of the most lavish description, would leave scant patronage for good *cafés* and *restaurants*. Clubs take the place of them all with advantage. They are a perfect substitute for the *café*, the reading-room and the restaurant. Therefore, far from being deprived by the rigidity of decorum from the amenities of French life, the Englishman has improved on them. He enjoys and concentrates them under one roof. That is why the spurious luxury of our public establishments does not impress him; he finds it gaudy, and the animation and allurements of female society seem to him a poor exchange for the quiet, the comfort, the large scale on which every-thing is conducted in his club. . . .

London Omnibuses and the West End

. . . [69] We had heard so much about the London omnibuses, with their velvet upholstery and veneered panelling, that we were anxious to see these wonderful conveyances. So our amazement was great on boarding one in the Strand to find it narrow, rickety, jolting, dusty and extremely dirty. The only advantage of these vehicles is that they are closed by a door. The conductor stands outside on a small footboard, [70] incessantly hailing the passers-by. The custom, anyhow, is never to go inside an omnibus, even when it rains, if there is an inch of space unoccupied outside; women, children, even old people, fight to gain access to the top. A T-shaped wooden bench divides the coach in its entire length. If all the seats are occupied people stand between the legs of those who are seated. It was not till we had reached St. Paul's that the conductor asked us for our fares in a detached indolent manner that must have been habitual as it appeared to surprise no one. We were soon in the *City*, which designation has a mysterious vagueness for all foreigners. There seems to be no relation whatever between its material and its moral frontiers, for the world divides London into two sections—the West End and the City—and yet the City itself seems roughly located between Temple Bar and Cheapside with St. Paul's as its centre. The West End comprises the districts where the genteel reside or those inhabited by either the aristocracy or the artistic and financial world.

Every man living on his income or exercising one of the learned profes-sions has his abode in the West End: if not he loses caste. No one [71] would dare to confess that he lives outside that hallowed area, nor in that case could he ever induce any fashionable visitors to call on him. Retired tradesmen would have intercourse with their equals, but well-bred persons would live in utter solitude.

There are two kinds of aristocracies in London, the aristocracy of birth and the aristocracy of wealth. The possessors of those immense fortunes amassed by their commercial ancestors call themselves proudly *merchant-princes*. These two classes live segregated, hostile and irreconcilable, unless some ruined Lord Squanderfield decides to repair his battered fortunes by marrying some plebeian maiden mounted on such a pyramid of gold that he can almost consider her his equal. Such alliances are the theme of most English novels. Neither of these social circles, whether their standing is due to birth or riches, would dream of setting foot in the City. I would wager that London contains 100,000 women who have never gone further down the Strand than Somerset House; on the other hand, there are certainly as many cooped up in the City who have never ventured as far as Regent Street. But, as my reader, I trust, is more inquisitive than [72] these unconcerned City dwellers, we will indulge in a ramble along this wonderful thoroughfare.

As wide as our boulevards, as lively as our Rue de la Paix, and beginning likewise at the base of a monumental column, Regent Street from Pall Mall to Park Crescent is fully two miles long. It is the only spot, outside the park, where society people are certain to meet, as smart women would never dream of shopping elsewhere. This main artery of the West End displays therefore all the tempting treasures of luxury trades.

Towards four o'clock, starting from Regent's Quadrant and to right and left in Oxford Street, the crowd surges this way and that; carriages stand in groups in front of Swan and Edgar's silk shop, or at Allison's, where the latest fashions and materials are displayed. Buzzing round the carriages are innumerable horsemen, gentlemen wishing to pay their respects to the ladies, and even fair equestrians returning from their ride in the park. The pavements are swarming with pedestrians, idlers, or shoppers bent on a visit to the gunmaker, the haberdasher's or the jeweller's.

Artists settle down for a talk in the picture shops, music lovers meet in the premises of Messrs. Cramer and Beales.

[73] Beyond Langham Place there are no shops. With Portland Place we reach a residential and stately vicinity.

Regent Street is a precious observatory; it is only there that rank and fashion can be studied at close quarters in a public place and in morning clothes. In spite of the throng the predominance of the upper classes gives the crush an appearance of orderly confusion not devoid of a certain dignity. Only here could you find the fashionable world so perfectly at home in the middle of the street.

The Docks

. . . [103] The Tower is an interesting monument, but the English with their mania for spurious restoring have completely altered its character. The old towers alone now bear witness to its original aspect.

But there is no disappointment awaiting one in London where active, modern life is concerned. The Tower no longer stands guard over the City, which relies on a more modern, more peaceable and superior power to ensure its security. Only a few feet away are the docks where the opulent fleets of this modern Tyre are anchored. The nearest are St. Katherine's, next to this the London Docks, and a bit further on are the immense docks of the East India Co., the splendour of which has spelt our ruin.

These gigantic works date from the beginning of the century, and St. Katherine's was only opened in 1828. They are fine, square, [104] inner harbours, navigable three hours before high tide. It is there that ships are loaded and unloaded. Under the spacious warehouses are vaults built on piles, underground storehouses, running the whole length of the docks to the extent of five or six miles. The tobacco dock alone has an area of more than an acre. There are cellars where can easily be stored 70,000 pipes* of rum or wine. The West India Docks cost 35 millions and were financed by public subscription. The fortunate shareholders are much to be envied.

These strange precincts are prodigiously alive. One would think that to amass such quantities of provisions, the fecundity of the whole earth must have been exhausted. There are places where you literally sink ankle-deep into sugar, and the honey-like smell of the molasses at such a degree of concentration seizes you by the throat. Further on there are preserved fruits, spices galore, log-wood in sufficient quantity to dye the lake of Geneva red, spirits and cottons, perfumes and evil-smelling drugs. The nose here comes into its own! It is titillated by surprises and sensations of all sorts.

This commercial cave of Aladdin gives one an [105] idea of the splendour and the preponderating wealth of this nation. Monstrous octopus whose tentacles reach out and drain the substance of the whole world!

One of the most curious sights, and I should think a unique one, in the world, is the "Queen's Pipe." It is an immense furnace in which are burnt all the goods that would not fetch enough money to cover the sum imposed on them for duty. The English have the reputation of being wasteful, but such a holocaust to the god of thriftlessness is unbelievable if one has not witnessed it. Night and day this roaring fire is kept supplied with thousands of pounds' worth of merchandise—fabrics of all sorts, cigars by the ton, hams enough to feed a regiment, jewelry, watches, every conceivable kind of thing is reduced to ashes in the "Queen's Pipe." I am told that not long ago 45,000

* Cylindrical storage vessels of wood or metal.

pairs of French gloves were burnt here, and on another occasion 900 legs of smoked mutton shipped from Australia! As to wine and spirits, they are poured into the Thames, at least so they say! . . .

A French Group at the Theatre:
The Streets at Night

[109] "To-night—Special Performance." Such is the usual heading of the play bill posted on Her Majesty's Theatre. The flimsiest pretext is sufficient for an English manager to break out into huge lettering on enormous posters. On this occasion Shakespeare's *Tempest* was announced, set to music by Scribe and Halévy. Such illustrious collaborators were sufficient to attract the least curious, as the united efforts of England's most famous dramatist and our masters of comic opera could scarcely fail to provide a most exceptional entertainment. The French expedition, therefore, all agog at the expected treat, sat down to an early dinner, and on the guide's suggestion retired to attend to their "toilette." As all the seats were booked in advance for this much-advertised performance, [110] I had to join the caravan, for which the management had reserved a certain number of tickets. I arrived punctually in the hall of the hotel at the appointed time and found it in a state of pandemonium. The great majority of my compatriots had considered that the brushing of one sleeve with the other and the dusting of their shoes with a handkerchief was a perfectly adequate preparation for the evening's solemnity, and were protesting violently on being informed that morning dress was prohibited in the theatre and that only black evening clothes were admissible. Many Parisians are convinced that outside Paris the whole world is provincial, they had therefore brought with them garments suitable only for a fishing expedition or a tramp in country lanes. Black trousers had to be borrowed from whoever possessed them, frock coats turned in on the sides and stitched back to look like dress coats; the whole hotel seemed transformed into a theatrical dressing-room.

"Can you imagine," said a gentleman to me, "how people can come to London in such toggery? I never move without clothes for all circumstances." He really was beautifully turned out. He wore immaculate butter-coloured [111] gloves, a magnificent blue silk waistcoat upon which fell the ends of a fawn-coloured cravat with large orange spots, and he was freshly shaved. But the guide catching sight of him just then made a gesture of despair.

"Ah, mon Dieu! Monsieur will be refused admission!" he wailed. "Black and white is the only wear allowed."

"I wonder they don't insist on a décolleté, or kilts, while they are about it," grumbled our crestfallen dandy. Meanwhile he had been stripped of his resplendent waistcoat; his elegant tie had been exchanged for a white linen handkerchief fastened at the back and his coat buttoned up to the chin.

The caravan, now sufficiently decorous to pass muster, presented a most burlesque appearance. We started off, the worst scarecrows hoping to escape notice by huddling in the centre of the group and making themselves as small and inconspicuous as possible. Although we each had our ticket, and had paid as much as thirteen francs for these seats in the pit, we were made to queue up at the corner of the Haymarket, the subscribers to the boxes and stalls being alone allowed direct access to the house. We had [112] been waiting for an hour at least, when a sudden movement of oscillation in the ranks was immediately followed by a hail of blows, elbow play and general scramble, irrespective of the age or sex of the victims. This is the mode of entrance to a theatre practised generally by the natives of this island! But the mêlée having started like Waterloo ended like Austerlitz. No sooner had we recovered from the first shock of surprise than our military training asserted itself. Of one accord we rallied and formed a compact group admirably cohesive, and having returned blow for blow we carried all before us and burst into the house followed by cries of "French dogs" and other imprecations which we did not resent as we did not understand them! We imagined we had satisfied all requirements of etiquette in regard to our attire, but we were rudely disillusioned. A kind of Master of Ceremonies inspected us and found plenty of cause for objections. The green fringe of a cravat had to be tucked away, a grey hat deposited in the cloakroom. Coloured gloves were removed and their owners left bare-handed. Even the ladies were subjected to much ignominy—one of them having to part with a pink taffetas bonnet trimmed with [113] rows of lace of which she was particularly proud. The functionary removed it delicately and handed it to an attendant with the phlegmatic indifference which is accounted civility over here. The poor lady was so flustered she did not realise that the lining of her hat had remained on her head and presented the ludicrous and pathetic spectacle of a flower shorn of its petals.

When I had recovered my breath and equanimity I looked round me with interest, as Her Majesty's Theatre is very fashionable. The auditorium is built in the Italian style and decorated in the English taste. It is very high and honeycombed with small boxes, much too enclosed and gloomy looking. Women are sunk up to the neck in those 200 cubicles all alike with no relief whatever in the decoration. The house is painted a dirty buff, with chocolate-coloured medallions, adorned with measly Pompeian figures to enliven it. The boxes have blue hangings and yellow curtains.

As a rule, the taste in this country tends to an inordinate preference for light colours. They are averse to shadows, living as they do under an opaque and cloudy sky. Their houses have enormous windows and often glass roofs, so as to [114] admit a flood of light. They have even invented the *bow window* which allows the light to penetrate from three different sides at once. Some streets, especially in Brighton, are entirely built on this principle, and viewed in profile look like a succession of glass turrets. This fondness for light and glaring colours explains their predilection for water colours, but tends to make their oil painting look like aquarella. The works of their artists

are livid, discordant, glassy and badly lighted, for the effect of light is obtained by contrast from the solidity of the shadows. These drawbacks are
even more noticeable in scenic decorations, which are washed out, lack depth
and tire the eyes. The result is that the actors' features are indistinguishable,
nor can one have a clear view of the occupants of the boxes, whose heads
merge into the semitones of the background.

The orchestra began to play and the chorus soon joined in. As the volume
of sound grew and filled the house, I became uncomfortably aware that something was wrong. The instruments sounded out of tune, added to which I
thought the people behind me had joined in the singing, half a bar behind
time. I soon realised, [115] however, that Her Majesty's Theatre possessed
an echo that would make the fortune of any grotto! No one but ourselves
seemed to notice it, which gives the measure of the musical sensibility of an
English audience.

The passages to the boxes are dark and unfrequented during the intervals,
the lobby is merely a large colonnaded hall with a few divans, where the only
sounds to be heard are the clatter of tea cups and the hissing of kettles. The
need of foregathering to talk and exchange impressions does not exist here as
it does in Latin countries. A few visits, however, are paid to the boxes which
bear the full names and titles of the occupants on the doors.

The right thing to do here is to leave the play before the end, and never
was I more willing to conform to custom. On my way home I was accosted by
a beggar woman wearing sordid rags and a rakish hat. I was foolish enough
to give her a small coin, and so she followed me whining for more, first on
one side, then on the other, till having exhausted every dodge I could think
of to escape from her importunities, I started to shout and gesticulate at
her and brandish my stick with such gusto that I managed to discourage
[116] her at last. Begging in London reaches alarming proportions. There
are 15,000 professional beggars, a large percentage of whom are Irish. You
cannot take a step without encountering these wretched creatures, so appalling in the exhibition they make of their squalor and destitution that one
does not know what feeling moves one most, pity or disgust. As a general
rule the working-classes are filthy beyond description. Their clothes are posi-
tively caked with a layer of shining grime so thick that it is solid. Hands and
faces are a revolting sight. This class is evidently utterly demoralised by
misfortune. It is a remarkable thing that one never sees a Jew amongst all
these beggars. The Jewish community have their own philanthropic institutions and their organisation must be very efficient.

Notwithstanding this appalling state of things, it is only fair to say that
charity is established here on a grand scale, and that new asylums and
shelters are continually being opened for the relief of distress. How then can
one explain such a state of things? It must be that in modern social organisation public prosperity can only be obtained by certain classes at the price
of cruel compensations in others.

[117] What intensifies the outward aspect of this destitution is the system

of devoting whole streets, in fact whole districts, to the housing of the work-ing-classes. There, without supervision, and by instinct of imitation, idleness begets slovenliness, dirt spreads and becomes contagious. Starving creatures wallow in the mire and sink to the lowest depths of debauch. The solidarity of indecency makes its manifestations more apparent. There is no good ex-ample given them, no decent neighbourhood to compel them to restraint. Their cynicism has therefore free rein. If one wants to create the ideal of filth, physical degradation and moral bestiality, one cannot do better than crowd the dregs of the population in those hovels which form the slums.

Another factor which contributes largely to maintain this state of pauper-ism is the excessive abuse, among the lower classes, of alcoholic drinks. Gin is responsible for much of its misery.

It is truly a horrible and revolting sight to witness, especially on a Satur-day night, the ghastly scenes enacted at the door of public-houses in the City, or the South Lambeth and Surrey districts. Drunken women by the hundred [118] lie about higgledy-piggledy in the mud, hollow-eyed and purple-cheeked, their ragged clothing plastered with muck. Occasionally they will stagger up to fight, and woe betide any unfortunate woman who approaches the door to try and drag her husband away from one of these dens, as the harpies will set upon her for a certainty. It is heartrending to see these poor creatures weak with hunger beating a hasty retreat with their frightened and starving offspring clinging to their skirts. I am told that they are often reduced to selling their hair to buy a crust of bread. . . .

Shopping in London

. . . [144] The detached attitude of shopkeepers in London is amazing. As everybody here carries a walking-stick I thought I would like to buy one. I therefore strolled down Fleet Street, scanning the bundles placed outside the shop doors. Having seen one I rather fancied I went in and asked to look at it. On closer inspection it disappointed me, so putting it down on the counter, I uttered with true British laconicism the one word *"No."* To my great surprise the salesman, instead of bringing me any others, quietly returned to his desk, taking no further notice of me, and I left the shop without his making the slightest attempt to detain me.

In London, shopkeepers do not extol their [145] wares, they seem quite indifferent as to whether you make or do not make a purchase; but the town is full of flower girls, and they, on the other hand, are most importunate. For twopence I bought a bunch of lovely moss roses incredibly fresh and fragrant. The next item on my list was a pair of gloves. I had the greatest difficulty in getting the assistant to show me more than two fingers of each glove, as though displaying the entire article was beneath his dignity. The cashier took my money with the attitude of a man receiving a subscription for some charitable purpose, and my parcel was handed to me by the shopman with a benevolent expression as though he were making me a small gift. Sometimes even, they seem so averse to parting with their goods that you feel you are depriving them of cherished possessions. I felt this so acutely at a haberdasher's, who had done his best to conceal from me all the articles I wanted, that in a spirit of atonement I presented my bunch of roses to his charming daughter. This small act of courtesy met with the greatest success and quite dispelled his look of grievance and my embarrassment.

It is not advisable to bargain in London shops [146] as we do in Paris. The assistant thinks at first that you have misunderstood him, but when he realises what you are driving at he stiffens visibly like a man of honour to whom one has made a shady proposal. He gives you to understand, politely but plainly, that his prices being equitable, cannot be reduced. His resolute bearing is so unmistakable that only a fool would insist. Hawkers, dealers in booths or stalls, or small nondescript shops are the only tradespeople that you can drive a bargain with. In fact the higher the commercial class the more conscientious is the price quoted.

To make a last experiment on the subject of the tradesman's attitude towards the customer, I went one day to a shop at the corner of Ludgate Hill where the finest and most expensive cachemires and Chinese silks are to be found. It had been raining all the morning that peculiar sooty liquid special to London. I had therefore put on my oldest and shabbiest clothes. I wore no gloves, my overcoat was threadbare, out of shape and bespattered with mud. To complete the turnout I wore a cheap grey felt hat, which had it been brand new would still have been quite out of place in London. I felt confident that in [147] such a guise the result of my experiment would be really conclusive.

A smart barouche and pair stood waiting at the door. I pushed my way past a couple of supercilious-looking footmen and sauntered into the shop, my hands behind my back. Having examined various rolls of Irish poplin, I looked round for a salesman. Immediately a dapper young man stepped forward and stood awaiting my pleasure. I asked him to show me an emerald green Indian cachemire shawl worth about £100. He evinced no surprise whatever, merely waved me towards the counter to which he followed me. I caught sight of myself in a mirror, my appearance was really shocking. He produced the shawl, which I examined; then I asked for others, blue, red, etc. They were all fine expensive specimens which in Paris would never have been shown to a man dressed as I was. When I had turned the whole shop out I declared with perfect composure that I would think it over. The salesman accompanied me to the door, towards which I moved without haste, glancing to right and left in a leisurely fashion. He held the door open for me, bowed respectfully, and closed it on me with utter placidity. . . .

The London Parks

. . . [161] In summer there are four parks open to the public in London. The Green Park and St. James' Park are the recreation grounds of the middle classes who, having to go on foot and not disposing of much leisure, cannot go further afield. Wealthy people owning carriages patronise Regent's Park and Hyde Park. In each of these pleasure grounds there are certain alleys in which it is the accepted thing to leave your conveyance and take a stroll—in Regent's Park they are the botanical or zoological gardens—in Hyde Park, Kensington Gardens and the Serpentine.

These broad open spaces that take about an hour to drive through seem the borderland between town and country, and one is amazed on reaching their extreme limits to find oneself hemmed in again by more houses and more streets! The gigantic proportions of London are almost impossible to grasp. This capital, already [162] four times as large as Paris, is increased every year by more than 2,000 houses.

The fashionable residential quarters have no shops; in these vicinities as well as in those inhabited by the middle classes each family lives in its own house. The great majority of dwellers in the West End are *"carriage folk,"* which presupposes an income of from two to three thousand a year. There are 80,000 private carriages in London, one can therefore surmise that between the hours of four and six every day at least 40,000 of them are being driven about the streets or parks. The usual itinerary is the following— proceeding along Regent Street through Portland Place they drive up Regent's Park hill as far as the Zoo or the Botanical Gardens. Then about five o'clock they start off again, and following Oxford Street enter Hyde Park by Cumberland Gate. There they join the press of carriages and riders crowding in hundreds about Kensington Gardens. Innumerable women saunter round on the lawns in the shade of magnificent trees while the military bands play. It is a unique and wonderful sight, and I had the luck to see it on one occasion in particularly agreeable and unusual circumstances.

[163] On a certain Tuesday, which is one of the two fashionable days for Hyde Park, having called at a house where I had been asked to dinner, my appearance was hailed as providential. Mrs. B. it seemed was not well, and her husband, a magistrate who took his duties seriously, was too busy to accompany his daughter to the Kensington parade. I was wondering what was expected of me in the contingency, when a servant announced that the carriage was at the door. Mr. B. immediately rose, I did the same, and bowing to my hostess followed him out. The hall door being open I caught sight of Miss B. already seated in a well-appointed barouche. Mr. B. escorted me to it, I got in, the door was banged and off we went! Before I could realise what had happened I found myself on the way to Hyde Park *en tête à tête* with Miss B.!

Unexpected situations certainly have their attractions but also their embarrassments. Considering how very pretty my companion was, my position was indeed a strange one. I soon recognised, however, that I alone thought it unusual, and I made superhuman efforts to *anglicise* myself sufficiently to regain my [164] composure. I appeal to my compatriots! It is a situation so utterly outside the average Frenchman's experience that it would have taken any one of them aback! I have been told since then that the old-fashioned freedom of intercourse between the sexes is going out in England, and that French habits of *chaperonage* are now gaining ground. It would certainly have been unscrupulous of me to take advantage of a position of trust, but I was relieved to find that our conversation would not have to be conducted on too conventional a line. We were soon discussing sentimental subjects in an impersonal manner as is the custom over here. It is the recognised privilege of young ladies who having to find their own husbands must be given some means of getting into contact with the opposite sex. In France we find husbands for our daughters; here they have to do so for themselves. This distinction has far-reaching effects and is the reason for the fundamental disparity in our social customs. Having entered Hyde Park, our carriage took its place in the rolling stream of vehicles. The riding tracks were crowded with equestrians galloping in company with their friends on soil as carefully tended as in a circus ring. Sometimes [165] a squadron of *amazones*, their skirts trailing to the ground, their veils floating behind them, cantered past us, a perfect vision of grace and charm. It was difficult to know what one admired most, their litheness, ease and daring or the beauty of their mounts.

The carriage was going at a foot's pace towards Kensington Gardens when a young man rode up to the door, and after bowing to Miss B., accompanied us for a few moments. He then took his leave, a trifle regretfully I thought, but anxious not to intrude no doubt; from his respectful attitude and Miss B.'s easy manner I surmised a possible *fiancé*. Nevertheless he left us without showing any signs of resentment at my presence, having, in fact, scarcely bestowed a glance on me. The carriage drew up by the Serpentine, upon which a quantity of small boats were sailing. We alighted, Miss B. accepted my proffered arm and we mingled with the crowd. I have been told that forty to fifty thousand people gather in Hyde Park on the days when the bands are playing—it would be difficult to find a better chance of observing the different elements which compose smart society.

Two to three thousand women thronged the [166] lawns under the shade of the splendid limes, oaks and beeches, which not being shorn of their lower branches as they are in France, grow very low and thick. Parties in groups sat together on chairs or squatted on the grass. A flock of sheep, fatter than any sheep I had ever seen in my life, grazed peacefully, and cows ruminated with philosophical indifference in the midst of the gathering. The London butchers own numerous flocks and grazing rights even in the royal precincts, and these animals fulfil the double purpose of fattening themselves and fertilising the land.

It is a unique experience, in the very heart of a large city, to embrace at a glance pompous equipages with powdered attendants and magnificent horses and rustic herds of cows, sheep and goats with elegant women trailing silks and laces among them.

From five to six is the smart time in Kensington Gardens, and the predilection for light colours so noticeable in England gives dresses a very festive air. A great deal of white is worn. It is a tremendous luxury, as this smoky atmosphere turns it grey in a few hours. Taste has improved enormously of late. It is not unusual to meet [167] women very well dressed, in spite of the bold flights of fancy they indulge in where contrast of colours is concerned, and which is their stumbling-block. They also have a habit of puffing out their skirts from waist to hem by means of whalebone or even wire hoops. These skirts swing about like bells and give their wearers a jerky gait which is not graceful.

There is no exaggeration in the much vaunted beauty of English women. Mahomed's paradise must be full of them. I gazed right and left bewildered with admiration, and pleasantly conscious meanwhile that the lady I was escorting more than held her own. In contrast to the young men's modest and reserved mien, the young ladies are very self-assured, though their expression is yielding. Their fine eyes look straight at the men, who pass them by with lowered lids, apparently quite indifferent to their charms.

"What has struck you most in London?" Miss B. asked me.

"The coldness of your compatriots towards the fair sex and the warmth of their passion for horses," I replied.

Around the bandstands five or six hundred [168] ladies on horseback were gathered, with a few young horsemen fluttering about. As soon as the music ceased they all scampered away, to return as soon as the next piece began. Riding is the most popular pastime. One can see octogenarians, children of ten, mothers of families with their numerous progeny, all trotting along on well-bred horses alarmingly fresh and spirited. Round a bend we met one of Miss B.'s aunts, greetings were exchanged, I was introduced, bowed, and we moved on. I was amazed that such near relations should not immediately foregather and remain in company; however, the indifference of English people to family ties has its advantages, especially as the aunt had terribly long teeth, and I was quite content to prolong the *tête-à-tête*, which lasted till Miss B. eventually put me down at my hotel. . . .

Cremorne

. . . [173] Cremorne, I must tell you, is a pleasure resort with a lake and beautiful gardens, and is immensely popular. This establishment is situated exactly opposite its rival, Vauxhall, on the other side of the river. The company there is very mixed: students and shop girls, soldiers and civilians, dissipated young bloods, paterfamilias with their better halves, schoolboys and children's nurses; Cremorne welcomes them all. It is not an edifying place, but, as I have said before, Londoners leave their prudery at home.

Cremorne, like Vauxhall and other such places, offers a variety of attractions. One moves on methodically from the one to the other at the sound of a large bell which a man rings as he leads the way, the crowd trotting along behind him. We trotted with the herd and Lionel continued to evade me.

"Let us listen to the music," he suggested. [174] As soon as the quavering melody had dissolved: "Quick to the theatre or we won't get a seat!" he cried. And we had to gallop after the bellman, be jostled by the crowd, and sit through a farce acted by pierrots, harlequins, policemen and field-marshals. There were waterfalls, snow-capped mountains and polar bears in white cotton trousers. The actors oozed sentiment, the actresses danced, the chorus bellowed. As a conclusion the devil appeared in pink tights with gilded horns —he went through various transformations and ended up as an attorney. It was all an incomprehensible jumble. As we left the theatre I perseveringly attempted to engage Lionel's attention, but the cursèd bell-ringer drowned my voice and we were carried along by the human stream. We found ourselves in a large room, the centre of which had been roped off. In this enclosure was a small man alert and thin, rolling niggerish black eyes and waving a pair of hairy hands, each one clasping a small wooden hammer. In front of this repulsive creature was a table covered with bricks of varying sizes placed on a wire frame. The hubbub ceased suddenly and we were given a real Anglo-Saxon treat. The man hit a brick [175] with one of the hammers and it gave out the sound that you expect from a breaking tile. After this prelude, his little hammers seemed to go mad, flying from brick to brick with incredible rapidity, and from a certain rhythm in his movements one realised that he meant to convey a musical impression. One must really be born and bred in the British Isles to listen patiently to such harmonious strains! A few moments later the bricks were discarded for wooden cylinders and the arid melody began afresh, still drier but more complicated. This *concerto* of demented nuts dancing in a bag roused the wildest enthusiasm among the audience. Liszt would have had a poor reception had he been billed to play after this prince of British melody.

"Now," said Lionel. "Let us have some ginger-beer."

In a Chinese bandstand an orchestra struck up a schottische. A minute later the carefully levelled open space was filled with couples and the surrounding tables with onlookers. We took our seats and the waiter uncorked a couple of oval-shaped bottles and poured us out a frothy sparkling liquid which might have been lemonade had it not tasted of pepper and pimentos. This [176] fashionable refreshment sets the roof of your mouth on fire, and while I still gasped for breath, Lionel seized the hand of a young person of doubtful morality and flung himself with entire abandon into a Bacchanalian rendering of the polka. People dance here with their hips and their shoulders, seeming to have little control over their legs. They have no ear for time. Frivolous young things improvise all sorts of indecorous antics. This, however, does not seem in any way to interfere with the staid enjoyment of the numerous middle-aged couples who placidly saunter round, occasionally colliding with one or another of the boisterous merry-makers. Nobody here takes the slightest notice of his neighbour's doings. . . .

Francophobia at the Lyceum:
Christmas Pantomime at the Surrey Theatre

. . . [213] I remember once being present at a revue where each character stood for one of the chief events of the year. France was represented by a milliner, for before Malakoff * the only field of glory we were allowed was the one of fashion. Britannia as Minerva was equipped with helmet and lance. John Bull, the citizen-king, with a baggy check coat, a congested, drunken countenance, wore a tinsel crown and held a sceptre. He had a large lion's tail fastened to the seat of his trousers, which being set in motion by some mechanism, stood straight up as a sign of anger or pride, or whenever he turned his back on the public. This trivial buffoonery never failed to let loose a perfect storm of hilarity. When this grotesque creature approached the actress impersonating France with jokes which we guessed from their success to be obscene, my friends gave signs of unequivocal discontent, but fortunately the action was so disconnected and impossible to follow that their attention soon wandered. Our nation was so abused in this play that the public kept turning [214] round to see what effect it was having on the "Frenchies." Happily, most of the allusions were entirely lost on us, but when John Bull started to thrash Marianne† we got up and left with quiet dignity. Jeered at on the stage, derided in the audience, the French tourist in those days expiated the weakness of his Government.

That evening had left such a disagreeable impression on my mind that I was anxious to obliterate it by witnessing a Christmas pantomime under more auspicious circumstances.

During the last week of the year all the smaller theatres get up one of those extravaganzas which constitute Londoners' only amusement during those festive days. Society goes to them on the sly, and it is the general subject of conversation for a month at least. A good pantomime epitomises the events and ideas of the moment. It must be up to date, scourge the people's bugbear and flatter its idol. It has full licence to be coarse and would be disappointing if it were not. The Princess' and the Surrey Theatres have had the greatest successes for this Christmas season of 1856. The first with *Harlequin,* the second with *The Prince of Pearls.* Although in the first-

---

* Site of a French victory in the Crimean War.
† A feminine figure personifying France.

mentioned the meeting on [215] the stage of Henry VIII and Cardinal Wolsey with the characters of the *Gazza Ladra* rather tickled me, and, although the scenery was charming and the ballet dancers a treat to behold, yet I will confine myself to a description of *The Prince of Pearls,* which was perhaps the greater success of the two.

The managers, Messrs. Shepherd and Creswick, are evidently quite aware of their supremacy as proved by the self-sufficiency of their posters. Their announcement contains the following gems:

"The Pantomime at the Surrey Theatre is the best in London, it has been got up regardless of cost . . . specialists of every category have been consulted, archæologists, zoologists, phrenologists and physiologists. The supernatural parts have been treated with circumspection—our witches are really *old*. Our fairies just sufficiently so to exhibit limbs, eyes, wings and smiles fit to turn the heads of all young mortals who behold them. . . . The comic parts will keep the public in such roars of laughter that if their buttons do not fly off their seams will surely burst, etc."

I must admit that the case was barely overstated.

The play opens in the den of three witches, [216] by *a remarkably savage scene*. But the various incidents of the drama are less *savage* than one might have feared from such an ominous beginning. From the cavern we are wafted to the Prince's Palace, where twenty-four oysters disgorge twenty-four pearls in the guise of twenty-four alluring dancers. And so all along graceful fantasy will be interwoven with the ugliness of brutal parody which is the main subject of the entertainment. This parody is composed of a medley of various dramas, *Jane Shore*, Shakespeare's *Richard III* and Delavigne's *Enfants d'Edouard*. Enormous cardboard heads conceal the actors', who wear historical costumes cleverly exaggerated. No words can give a correct idea of the cunning hideosity of those masks, scientifically moulded, as the management proclaims, with the aid of a phrenologist. The melancholy of Hastings, the brutality of Tyrrel, the sufferings of Jane Shore, the sensuality of the Archbishop of Canterbury, are wonderfully imprinted on those pasteboard countenances.* But the palm must go to Richard III for the ease with which he carries his hump and his buffoon-like ferocity. Gloucester is a hybrid figure, half ogre, half mountebank, seasoning his cruelty with mock [217] gallantry. To emphasize this trait he never appears on the stage without a quizzing glass.† Richard III, Henry VIII and Charles I are the three kings most familiar to the London cockneys. In this country blood keeps the memory green.

When Gloucester visits the little princes in the tower they are dressed in

---

* The play dealt with the crimes of Richard III. Jane Shore had been the mistress of Edward IV, Richard's predecessor on the throne, and William, Baron Hastings was a member of his court. Sir James Tyrrel was a follower of Richard's who is supposed to have killed the two sons of Edward, "the princes in the tower." Jane Shore, Hastings and Tyrrel were all executed by Richard III.

† A monocle.

nightshirts and velvet caps, and are wearing the ribbon and star of St. George. He makes them eat boiling pap with a large wooden spoon with which he raps them on the nose—to the public's huge delight. Now and then there is a break in the farce and the spectator is transported to the ethereal regions of unreality—where fairies and genii float in landscapes of gold, crystal and diamonds. And so one moves alternately from dreams of bliss to the horror of nightmares. But that is not all. Each one of these historical impersonations plays a dual rôle; so that at a given moment the most unexpected transformations take place. Conquerors and conquered, executioners and victims cast off their dramatic garb and take part in a dishevelled Bacchanalia. The plaintive Jane Shore is now Columbine, Richard III a clown, Hastings Harlequin, and the murdered princes [218] pantaloons. All the characters join in a rough-and-tumble, and the pantomime commences in real earnest. Blows are freely exchanged with any available instruments, the actors kick, laugh, yell, jest, roar and rollick in an indescribable pandemonium. Thereupon mock policemen intervene and are roughly handled by the actors. Meanwhile the background representing the different London districts moves slowly past. Then comes a scene of political satire. The General Staff of the British Army drag themselves in on crutches; Cobden* and his adherents are flogged like schoolboys; food adulterers are belaboured by the people.

Suddenly the scene changes to a market-place and is swarming with live chickens, turkeys, pigeons, ducks. They squawk with fright and many of them jump or fly among the audience; a general uproar ensues, while on the stage sheep and calves have made their appearance and a pig is having its tail twisted and squealing the house down. How would it be possible to describe such a hurly-burly of an entertainment which lasts three hours without a break; which is acted with such rapidity that notices have to be posted up to explain the acts, and which [219] brings into contact Cobden, Richard III, Columbine, Hastings, Lord Raglan,† the Prince of Pearls, Admiral Napier, the Queen of Grapes, the Emperor of the French and Queen Victoria.

England's ally has not been forgotten. Four men stagger in with a large bale of goods on which is written *French divertissement*. With a touch of his wand Harlequin has wrought a miracle. The bale opens and disgorges a tower bearing the name of Malakoff printed across a tricolour flag, and out of this tower steps a mameluke of three years old representing Turkey liberated. The orchestra play *Partant pour la Syrie* and the audience yells *hurrah!* I must be even more sensitively patriotic than I realised, for my heart was thumping and I had an overwhelming impulse, which fortunately I was able to repress, to kiss every pretty English girl in the theatre. Mean-

---

* Richard Cobden (1804-1865), a merchant, economist and Member of Parliament who advocated free trade.
† Commander of British troops in the Crimean War.

while Admiral Napier had appeared in full-dress uniform, ordered a few Cossacks to be put in irons, shaken the editor of the *Times* by the hand, been chaired, then discarding his uniform danced a frantic jig with Harlequin. It all ended by a scene in an enchanted island lit by multi-coloured Roman candles. From the centre rose an enormous spray [220] of flowers, supporting the figures of Queen Victoria and Napoleon III standing hand-in-hand. These parts were taken by small children in consideration of the demands of perspective. The Prince of Pearls and the Queen of Grapes crowned them with laurel wreaths, the young ladies of the ballet grouped themselves around with their legs in the air, Columbine and the clown fell on their knees, Richard III's soldiers presented arms and the curtain fell to the majestic strains of *God Save the Queen*.

No words can express the animation, the gaiety, the boldness, the madness, the incoherence, the coarseness, the splendour, the whimsical poetry and the brutality of these Christmas pantomimes. Their greatest charm is their unexpectedness and diversity. At the Princess's Theatre I saw a whole militia composed of ostriches ten feet high. At the Surrey, Gloucester's soldiers, most beautifully and correctly dressed, wore leopard's heads. It would be impossible to imagine entertainments better calculated to cheer the spirits and divert the eyes. . . .

English Sundays

. . . [251] As a general rule the salutary side of the English Sunday is overlooked, and only its drawbacks, which are more apparent, taken into account. That is why French people who come over here in a holiday spirit, unable to adapt themselves to the quietude of which they feel no need, are loud in their abuse of such an institution, and exaggerate its severities. Many of my compatriots, for instance, believe that one would be heavily fined for playing any musical instrument, even in one's own home. Alas! No. The laws of the country are not as beneficent as all that, and one can perform a cornet solo or practise scales on the piano without incurring any penalty. There are also absurd tales about having to fast all day unless one has laid in stores of food on the Saturday. It is all nonsense. Bakers, pork butchers, tobacconists, oyster rooms, taverns, pastrycooks keep their shops open all the morning till eleven o'clock. They are then closed, as it is the time for religious services, and everybody is supposed to go to church. At one o'clock the shutters are taken down. From three to five they close again, after which time all eating and drinking houses are open as usual.

[252] But not till midnight does London really reawaken. Then the dancing saloons and all-night haunts turn on their lights, burst into noisy music, and revelry is let loose once more. All public establishments are closed on Sundays: museums, galleries, theatres—even the churches at times when

a service is not actually taking place. The day is devoted in proportionate shares to God and one's family. Therefore English people stay at home or go for a walk, as carriages are not taken out. The well-to-do mostly desert London on the Saturday evening, going to the country or to some seaside place. The motive of this custom is equality. The *Methodists* insist that servants, museum attendants, actors, etc., should be enabled to rest as well as employers, sightseers and theatre-goers. There are even houses, I am told, where the dining-room table is laid on the Saturday night and not cleared till the Monday. If the closing of shops is a legal measure, it has only been adopted to pacify the unchristianlike resentment of pious tradesmen who could not bear to feel that their religious fervour was enriching their less God-fearing competitors.

In spite of all preconceived notions, I much [253] enjoyed English Sundays. Worn out with activity and work (for during six weeks I never slept more than four hours out of twenty-four) I felt an all-pervading satisfaction at having time which I was forced to waste, and at being protected from any duty, pleasure or study. I seemed to feel that the general inaction contributed to my own relaxation. The incredible stillness soothed my nerves and I drifted into a state of dreamy vagueness as though I had been drugged. The fact that 200,000 factory chimneys have ceased belching out clouds of smoke allows the atmosphere to clear. It is to the inviolability of the Sabbath that Londoners owe the knowledge that the sky is sometimes blue. Fifteen years ago taverns and all drinking haunts were open all day. It is only since then that the law has enforced the closing of these places during two hours morning and afternoon. In this country, where drunkenness is rampant, it was inevitable that the workman, used to a hard day's work, and faced with twenty-four hours' idleness which he did not know how to employ, should find his way to the drinking bar. Feeling rich with his week's pay in his pocket, he drank persistently till he had spent it all. On Sunday night, sick [254] and penniless, he returned to his starving family. To-day this same workman digests from eleven to one what he has imbibed in the morning, his wife takes advantage of the closing of the bars to get him home, and may with luck prevent him from returning there in the afternoon. In any case there is a chance of something being saved of his week's earnings. Four hours' reflection are as salutary to the stomach as to the head. It is a well-known thing that the drunkard will imbibe unceasingly if left to himself, but an interval of two hours during which he has been interrupted will often turn him against further potations. And so the regulations about taverns, like the laws of Moses, give to temporal interests the consecration of religious institutions; this constitutes the genius of legislation!

During the last fourteen years it is undeniable that intemperance has been greatly reduced and that street brawls are not so common. But these improvements do not prevent occasional lapses, as I saw one day outside a gin-house in Whitechapel two fine fellows throw off their coats and have a savage set-to. The hitting was terrific, though I am convinced it conformed to all the rules of boxing. Each blow sounded like [255] a rock dropping on to a bed of clay. One nose was turned into red-currant jelly, an eye suddenly went black and purple, but further damage was prevented by the arrival of a policeman who arrested the champions. Not so long ago boxing was all the rage, taverns warmly encouraged the sport; but there were so many casualties that these exhibitions were forbidden. The British bull-dog must be getting soft! . . .

from

Notes on England

Hippolyte Taine

HIPPOLYTE TAINE (1828-1893), the French critic and historian, is best known in English-speaking countries for his History of English Literature (1863). However, he wrote books and articles on many other subjects, including French literature, art, psychology, and history. He was a leading intellectual figure of his time, particularly well known for advocating the application of scientific principles to literary and artistic questions, and for his own methodical analyses and presentations. He visited England in 1858 and 1871, and published his *Notes sur l'Angleterre* in 1872.

Translated by W. F. Rae. New York: Holt and Williams, 1872.

I, Boulogne to London Bridge.

[3] . . . Conversation with an Englishman of the middle class, son of a merchant, I should suppose; he does not know French, German, or Italian; he is not altogether a gentleman. Twenty-five years of age; sneering, decided, incisive face; he has made, for his amusement and instruction, a trip lasting twelve months, and is returning from India and from Australia. Forty thousand miles in all. He says, "To understand the people, they must be seen." He is from Liverpool. A family that does not keep a carriage may live comfortably there upon three or four hundred pounds sterling. One must

marry, that is a matter of course; he hopes to be married before two or three years are over. It is better, however, to remain a bachelor, if one does not meet the person with whom one desires to pass one's whole life. "But one always meets with her; the only thing is not to let the chance slip." He has met the proper person more than once when quite a young man; but then he was not rich enough; at present, being "independent," he will try again. A dowry is unnecessary. It is natural, and even pleasant, to undertake the charge of a portionless wife and of a family. "If your wife is good, and you love her, she is well worth that."

It is clear to me that their happiness consists in being at home at six in the evening, with a pleasing, attached wife, having four or five children on their knees, and respectful domestics. In the boat there is a family of four children, of whom the eldest is four and a half, and the mother twenty-three or twenty-four. At the [4] sea-side, on the beach, I have often seen entire broods, the father of the family at their head; it is not rare to meet with children who mount in steps from the baby at the breast up to the girl of eighteen. The parents do not feel themselves either over-burdened or embarrassed. According to this Englishman, they owe nothing but education to their children; the daughters marry without a dowry, the sons shift for themselves. I know a solicitor who makes much money and spends it all, except £300 or £400 a year, with which he insures his life in the names of his children; at each new arrival, there is a fresh policy of £2,000, payable to the child at its father's death. In this way the child is provided for, and besides commerce, industry supplies him with a quantity of outlets which are denied to a young Frenchman.

Of all the countries this Englishman has seen, England is the most moral. Still, in his opinion, the national evil is "the absence of morality." In consequence he judges France after the English fashion. "The women are badly brought up there, do not read the Bible, are too fond of balls, occupy themselves wholly with dress. The men frequent cafés and keep mistresses, hence so many unfortunate households. This is the result not of race, but of education. French women in England, seriously brought up in English fashion, make very good wives here." "Is everything good in your country?" "No; the national and horrible vice is drunkenness. A man who earns 20s. a week drinks ten of them. Add to this improvidence, stoppage of work, and poverty." "But in cases of distress you have the poor-houses, the workhouses?" "They will not go to them, they prefer to fast, to die of hunger." "Why?" "For [5] three reasons. Because they wish to drink at their ease. Because they hate being shut up. Because there are formalities; they must prove that they belong to the parish, but the most of them do not know where they were born, or find it too difficult to procure the necessary papers." He is a talkative fellow devoid of affected seriousness. Two other Englishmen with whom I conversed in the boat are like unto him. I have always found this disposition among the English; probably if they have the contrary reputation, it is because when in a foreign country and obliged to speak another language, they are silent through bashfulness, and keep watch in order not to commit themselves. Speak English imperfectly with a bad accent, they are no longer uneasy, they feel themselves your superiors. If you put a question to them politely, gently, or ask them to do you a small service, they are complying and even officious. I discovered this twenty times last year in London and everywhere else.

Other figures in the boat. Two young couples who remain on deck covered with wrappings under umbrellas. A long downpour has begun; they remain seated; in the end they were drenched like ducks. This was in order that husband and wife should not be separated by going below to the cabins. Another young wife suffered much from sea-sickness; her husband, who had the look of a merchant's clerk, took her in his arms, supported, tried to read to her, tended her with a freedom and expression of infinite tenderness. Two young girls of fifteen and sixteen, who speak German and French exceedingly well and without accent, large restless eyes, large white teeth; they chatter and laugh with perfect unconstraint, with admirable petulance of friendly gaiety; not the [6] slightest trace of coquetry, none of our nice little tricks which have been learned and done on purpose; they never think about the onlookers. A lady of forty in spectacles beside her husband, in a worn-out dress, with relics of feminine ornaments, extraordinary teeth in the style of tusks, very serious and most ludicrous; a Frenchwoman, even middle-aged, never forgets to adjust herself—to arrange her dress. Patience and phlegm of a tall dry Englishman, who has not moved from the seat, has taken but a single turn, who has spoken to no one, who suffices to himself. As a contrast, three Frenchmen, who put random questions, make haphazard assertions, grow impatient, gesticulate, and make puns or something akin to them, appeared to me pleasant fellows.

Gradually the clouds have disappeared and the sky is radiant. Right and left we pass small country houses, pretty, clean, and freshly painted. Green grass is seen appearing at the horizon, here and there large trees well-placed and well-grouped. Gravesend on the left heaps its brown houses around a blueish steeple. Vessels, warehouses, increase in number. One feels that one is approaching a great city. The small landing-stages project fifty paces into the river over the shining mud which the fallen tide leaves dry. Every quarter of an hour, the imprint and the presence of man, the power by which he has transformed nature, become more visible; docks, magazines, shipbuilding and caulking yards, stocks, habitable houses, prepared materials, accumulated merchandise; to the right is seen the skeleton of an iron church which is being prepared here for erection in India. Astonishment ends by turning into bewilderment. From Greenwich, the river is nothing but a street a [7] mile broad and upwards, where ships ascend and descend between two rows of buildings, interminable rows of a dull red, in brick or tiles, bordered with great piles stuck in the mud for mooring vessels, which come here to unload or to load. Ever new magazines for copper, stone, coal, cordage, and the rest; bales are always being piled up, sacks being hoisted, barrels being rolled, cranes are creeking, capstans sounding. The sea reaches London by the river; it is an inland port; New York, Melbourne, Canton, Calcutta, are in direct connection with this place. But that which carries the impression to its height, is the sight of the canals through which the docks communicate with the sea; they form cross-streets, and they are streets for ships; one suddenly perceives a line of them which is endless; from Greenwich Park where I ascended last year, the horizon is bounded with masts and ropes. The incalculable indistinct rigging stretches a spiders'-web in a circle at the side of the sky. This is certainly one of the great spectacles of our planet; to see a similar conglomeration of erections, of men, of vessels, and of business, it would be necessary to go to China.

However, on the river to the west rises an inextricable forest of yards, of masts, of rigging: these are the vessels which arrive, depart or anchor, in the first place in groups, then in long rows, then in a continuous heap, crowded together, massed against the chimneys of houses and the pulleys of warehouses, with all the tackle of incessant, regular, gigantic labour. A foggy smoke penetrated with light envelops them; the sun there sifts its golden rain, and the brackish, tawny, half-green, half-violet water, balances in its undulations striking and strange reflections. It might [8] be said this was the heavy and smoky air of a large hothouse. Nothing is natural here, everything is transformed, artificially wrought from the toil of man, up to the light and the air. But the hugeness of the conglomeration and of the human creation hinders us from thinking about this deformity and this artifice; for want of pure and healthy beauty, the swarming and grandiose life remains; the shimmering of embrowned waves, the scattering of the light imprisoned in vapour, the soft whitish or pink tints which cover these vastnesses, diffuse a sort of grace over the prodigious city, having the effect of a smile upon the face of a shaggy and blackened Cyclop.

II, Sunday in London. The Streets and Parks.

[9] Sunday in London in the rain: the shops are shut, the streets almost deserted; the aspect is that of an immense and a well-ordered cemetery. The few passers-by under their umbrellas, in the desert of squares and streets, have the look of uneasy spirits who have risen from their graves; it is appalling.

I had no conception of such a spectacle, which is said to be frequent in London. The rain is small, compact, pitiless; looking at it one can see no reason why it should not continue to the end of all things; one's feet churn water, there is water everywhere, filthy water impregnated with an odour of soot. A yellow, dense fog fills the air, sweeps down to the ground; at thirty paces a house, a steam-boat appear as spots upon blotting-paper. After an hour's walk in the Strand especially, and in the rest of the City, one has the spleen, one meditates suicide. The lofty lines of fronts are of sombre brick, the exudations being encrusted with fog and soot. Monotony and silence; yet the inscriptions on metal or marble speak and tell of the absent master, as in a large manufactory of bone-black closed on account of a death.

[10] A frightful thing is the huge palace in the Strand, which is called Somerset House. Massive and heavy piece of architecture, of which the hollows are inked, the porticoes blackened with soot, where, in the cavity of the empty court, is a sham fountain without water, pools of water on the pavement, long rows of closed windows—what can they possibly do in these catacombs? It seems as if the livid and sooty fog had even befouled the verdure of the parks. But what most offends the eyes are the colonnades, peristyles, Grecian ornaments, mouldings, and wreaths of the houses, all bathed in soot; poor antique architecture—what is it doing in such a climate? The flutings and columns in front of the British Museum are begrimed as if liquid mud had been poured over them. St. Paul's, a kind of Pantheon, has two ranges of columns, the lower range is entirely black, the upper range, recently scraped, is still white, but the white is offensive, coal smoke has already plastered it with its leprosy.

These spots are melancholy, being the decay of the stone. And these nude statues in memory of Greece! Wellington as a fighting hero, naked under the dripping trees of the park! That hideous Nelson, stuck on his column with a coil of rope in the form of a pig-tail, like a rat impaled on the top of a pole! Every form, every classical idea is contrary to nature here. A swamp like this is a place of exile for the arts of antiquity. When the Romans disembarked here they must have thought themselves in Homer's hell, in the land of the Cimmerians. The vast space which, in the south, stretches between the earth and the sky, cannot be discovered by the eye; there is no air; there is nothing but liquid fog; in this pale smoke objects are [11] but fading phantoms, Nature has the look of a bad drawing in charcoal which some one has rubbed with his sleeve. . . .

[16] The population numbers three millions and a quarter; that makes twelve cities like Marseilles, ten cities like Lyons, two cities like Paris put together; but words upon paper are no substitutes for the sensation of the eyes. It is necessary to take a cab several days in succession, and proceed straight on towards the south, the north, the east, and the west, during a whole morning, as far as the uncertain limits where houses grow scanty and the country begins.

Enormous, enormous—this is the word which always recurs. Moreover, all is rich and well ordered; consequently, they must think us neglected and poor. Paris is mediocre compared with these squares, these crescents, these circles and rows of monumental buildings of massive stone, with porticoes, with sculptured fronts, these spacious streets; there are sixty of them as vast as the Rue de la Paix; assuredly Napoleon III. demolished and rebuilt Paris only because he had lived in London. In the Strand, in Piccadilly, in Regent Street, in the neighbourhood of London Bridge, in twenty places, there is a bustling crowd, a surging traffic, an amount of obstruction which our busiest and most frequented boulevard cannot parallel. Everything is on a large scale here; the clubs are palaces, the hotels are monuments; the river is an arm of the sea; [17] the cabs go twice as fast; the boatmen and the omnibus-conductors condense a sentence into a word; words and gestures are economised; actions and time are turned to the utmost possible account; the human being produces and expends twice as much as among us.

From London Bridge to Hampton Court are eight miles, that is, nearly three leagues of buildings. After the streets and quarters erected together, as one piece, by wholesale, like a hive after a model, come the countless pleasure retreats, cottages surrounded with verdure and trees in all styles— Gothic, Grecian, Byzantine, Italian, of the Middle Age, or the Revival, with every mixture and every shade of style, generally in lines or clusters of five, ten, twenty of the same sort, apparently the handiwork of the same builder, like so many specimens of the same vase or the same bronze. They deal in houses as we deal in Parisian articles. What a multitude of well-to-do, comfortable, and rich existences! One divines accumulated gains, a wealthy and spending middle-class quite different from ours, so pinched, so straitened. The most humble, in brown brick, are pretty by dint of tidiness; the window panes sparkle like mirrors; there is nearly always a green and flowery patch; the front is covered with ivy, honeysuckle, and nasturtiums.

The entire circumference of Hyde Park is covered with houses of this sort, but finer, and these in the midst of London retain a country look; each stands detached in its square of turf and shrubs, has two stories in the most perfect order and condition, a portico, a bell for the tradespeople, a bell for the visitors, a basement for the kitchen and the servants, with a flight of steps for the service; very few mouldings and ornaments; no outside sun-shutters; large, clear windows, [18] which let in plenty of light; flowers on the sills and at the portico; stables in a mews apart, in order that their odours and sight may be kept at a distance; all the external surface covered with white, shining, and varnished stucco; not a speck of mud or dust; the trees, the turf, the flowers, the servants prepared as if for an exhibition of prize products. How well one can picture the inhabitant after seeing his shell! In the first place, it is the Teuton who loves Nature, and who needs a reminder of the country; next, it is the Englishman who wishes to be by himself in his staircase as in his room, who could not endure the promiscuous existence of our huge Parisian cages, and who, even in London, plans his house as a small castle, independent and enclosed. Besides, he is simple, and does not desire external display; on the other hand, he is exacting in the matter of condition and comfort, and separates his life from that of his inferiors. The number of such houses at the West-end is astonishing! The rent is nearly £500; from five to seven servants are kept; the master expends from twelve to twenty-four hundred pounds a year. There are ten of these fortunes and these lives in England to every one in France.

The impression is the same when visiting the parks; the taste, the area are quite different from what is the case among us. St. James's Park is a genuine piece of country, and of English country; huge old trees, real meadows, a large pond peopled with ducks and waterfowl; cows and sheep, in an enclosed space, feed on the grass, which is always fresh. There are even sheep in the narrow green border that surrounds Westminster Abbey; these people love the country in their hearts. It is sufficient to read their literature [19] from Chaucer to Shakespeare, from Thomson to Wordsworth and Shelley, to find proofs of this. What a contrast to the Tuileries, the Champs Elysée, the Luxembourg! As a rule, the French garden, that of Louis XIV., is a room or gallery in the open air, wherein to walk and converse in company; in the English garden, such as they have invented and propagated, one is better alone; the eyes and the mind converse with natural things. We have arranged a park on this model in the Bois de Boulogne; but we have committed the blunder of placing therein a group of rocks and waterfalls; the artifice is discovered at a glance, and offends; English eyes would have felt it.

Regent's Park is larger than the Jardin des Plantes and the Luxembourg put together. I have often remarked that our life seems to them cooped up, confined; they need air and space more than we do; Englishmen whom I knew in Paris left their windows open all night; thus arises their longing for motion, their horse and foot races in the country. Stendhal justly said that a young English girl walks a greater distance in a week than a young Roman girl in a year; the Northern man, of athletic temperament, has a need of free respiration and of exercise. This park is in a retired neighbourhood; one hears no longer the rolling of carriages, and one forgets London; it is a solitude. The sun shines, but the air is always charged with damp clouds, floating watering-pots which dissolve in rain every quarter of an hour. The vast watery meadows have a charming softness, and the green branches drip with monotonous sound upon the still water of the ponds. I enter a hothouse where there are splendid orchids, some having the rich velvet of the iris, others a fresh colour of that inexpressible, delicious, mingled [20] tint transfused with light like palpitating living flesh, a woman's breast; the hand desires yet dreads to press it; alongside, palm-trees raise their stems in a tepid atmosphere. A strange thing to us is that there are no keepers; admission is free, and no damage is done; I can understand that they must ridicule our establishments and public festivals, with their accompaniments of municipal guards. It is the same at the railway stations: every one is free to move about, to stand on the side of the line, to come and meet his friends at the carriage door; they are surprised and annoyed to see us caged in our waiting-rooms, enclosed, led like sheep, and always under the eye or the hand of an official.

I returned on foot to Piccadilly; again the London weather begins—the small and constant rain, the dissolving mud. F., who has spent the winter here, says that there is little snow, not more than in the centre of France; but, on the other hand, there is perpetual fog, rain nearly every day, and the most execrable muddy streets for pedestrians. As evidences, look at the foot coverings and the feet of the ladies. Their boots are as large as those of gentlemen, their feet are those of watermen, and their gait is in keeping. My question continually recurs, How do the English spend their leisure hours, among others, their Sunday? They have the Club and often wine. F., in his club, had a neighbour who, in the reading-room, drank a large glass of wine, then went to sleep, drank a second half an hour afterwards and went to sleep again, and so on in succession without ever saying a word. Another of great wealth, a leading merchant, and who has sixteen gardeners at his country seat, is occupied all day with his business, returns home in the evening, speaks but [21] seldom, lives like an automaton among his children; his daughter amuses herself by travelling about the entire year with a governess; in the family circle he merely finds the money—this is a common trait of the English character, deficiency in expansion and in amiability.

From Regent's Park to Piccadilly the spacious and interminable streets have a funereal aspect; the roadway is of black macadam; the rows of buildings, of the same cast, consist of blackened brick, where the window-panes shine with dark reflections; each house is separated from the street by railings and an area. There are few shops, not a single pretty one, no large plateglass windows and engravings; that would be too dismal for us; nothing to attract and gladden the eyes; lounging is impossible; it is necessary to do one's work at home, or to take one's umbrella and go to business or to one's society.

Hyde Park is the largest of them all, with its small rivulet, its wide greensward, its sheep, its shady walks, resembling a pleasure park suddenly transported to the centre of a capital. About two o'clock the principal alley is a riding-ground; there are ten times more gentlemen and twenty times more ladies on horseback than in the Bois de Boulogne on its most frequented days; little girls and boys of eight ride on ponies by the side of their father; I have seen ample and worthy matrons trotting along. This is one of their luxuries. Add to it that of having servants. For instance, a family of three persons which I visited keeps seven servants and three horses. The mother and daughter gallop in the park daily; they often pay visits on horseback; they economise in other things—in theatre-going, for example; they go but seldom to the theatre, [22] and when they do it is to a box which has been presented to them. This vigorous exercise appears indispensable for health; young girls and ladies come here even when it rains. To keep three horses and a carriage costs nearly £200 a year. Looking at this crowd of persons on horseback one comes to the same conclusion as after seeing the houses and the staff of servants. The wealthy class is much more numerous in England than in France. Another index is the outlay in linen, clothes, gloves, and dresses always new. The climate dirties everything rapidly; they must be continually renovated. In every newspaper I find the addresses of dealers who come to the house and buy slightly soiled clothes; the obligation of a gentleman is to be always irreproachably well dressed; his coat when shabby is handed over to a man of the lower class, ends in rags on the back of a beggar, and thus marks the social rank of its possessor. Nowhere else is the disparity of conditions so clearly written in the externals of men. Imagine the evening dress of a man of fashion or the rose-coloured bonnet of a lady; you will find the former again on a miserable wretch squatting on one of the stairs of the Thames, and the latter at Shadwell on the head of an old woman groping amidst rubbish.

From five to seven o'clock is the review of ladies' dresses. Beauty and ornamentation abound, but taste is wanting. The colours are outrageously crude and the forms ungraceful; crinolines too distended and badly distended, in geometrical cones or bunched, green flounces, embroideries, flowered dresses, quantities of floating gauze, packets of falling or frizzed hair; crowning this display tiny embroidered and imperceptible bonnets. The bonnets are too much [23] adorned, the hair, too shiny, presses closely on the temples; the small mantle or casaque falls formless to the lower part of the back, the petticoat expands prodigiously, and all the scaffolding badly joined, badly arranged, variegated and laboured, cries and protests with all its gaudy and overdone colours. In the sunshine, especially, at Hampton Court the day before yesterday, amongst the shopkeepers' wives, the absurdity was at its height; there were many violet dresses, one being of a wild violet clasped round the waist with a golden band, which would have made a painter cry out. I said to a lady, "The toilette is more showy among you than in France." "But my dresses come from Paris!" I carefully refrained from replying, "But you selected them. . . ."

III, St. James's Park, Richmond, the Docks, and East-End.

[25] I have paid many visits, and taken several walks. The things which please me most are the trees. Every day, after leaving the Athenaeum, I go and sit for an hour in St. James's Park; the lake shines softly beneath its misty covering, while the dense foliage bends over the still waters. The rounded trees, the great green domes make a kind of architecture far more delicate than the other. The eye reposes itself upon these softened forms, upon these subdued tones. These are beauties, but tender and touching, those of foggy countries, of Holland. Yesterday, at eight o'clock in the evening, although the weather was fine, everything seen from the Suspension Bridge appeared vapoury; the last rays disappeared in whitish smoke; on the right, the remains of redness; over the Thames, and in the rest of the sky a pale slate tint. There are tones like these in the landscapes of Rembrandt, in the twilights of Van der Neer; the bathed light, the air charged with vapour, the insensible and continuous changes of the vast exhalation which softens, imparts a bluish tint to, and dims the [26] contours, the whole producing the impression of a great life, vague, diffused, and melancholy—the life of a humid country. . . .

[27] . . . Hampton Court is a large garden in the French style, laid out in the time of William III. Our style was then the reigning one in Europe. Yet English taste is discoverable here also: the borders have been planted with standard rosebushes, and these, closely trained along the slight espaliers, form columns of flowers. Ducks, swans swim in all the pieces of water; water-lilies unfold their velvet stars. The old trees are propped up by iron rods. When they die, in order that they may not be wholly lost, the remainder of their trunks are converted into a kind of huge urn. Clearly, they are cared for and they are loved. There are no fences. I noticed young boarding-school girls walking and playing on the grass, but they never pluck a flower. The following notice suffices to protect the garden:—"It is hoped that the public will abstain from destroying that which is cultivated for the public gratification." I have seen families of common people taking their dinners on the greensward of Hyde Park; they neither tore up nor spoilt anything. This is perfect; the aim of every society is [29] that each one should be always his own constable, and end by not having any other.

My English friends confirm what I had guessed about the large number and the vastness of the private fortunes. "Take a cab from Sydenham; for five miles you will pass houses which indicate an annual outlay of £1,500 and upwards." According to the official statistics of 1841, there are one million of servants to sixteen millions of inhabitants. The liberal professions are much better remunerated than on the Continent. I know a musician at Leipzig of first-class talent; he receives 3s. a lesson at the Academy of Leipzig, 6s. in the city, and one guinea in London. The visit of a doctor who is not celebrated costs 4s. or 9s. in Paris, and a guinea here. With us a professor at the College of France receives £300, at the Sorbonne £480, at the School of Medicine £400. A professor at Oxford, a head of a house, has often from £1,000 to £3,000. Tennyson, who writes little, is said to make £5,000 a year. The Head Master of Eton has a salary of £6,080, of Harrow £6,280, of Rugby £2,960; many of the masters in these establishments have salaries from £1,200 to £1,240—one of them at Harrow has £2,220. The Bishop of London has £10,000 a year, the Archbishop of York has £15,000. An article is paid for at the rate of £8 the sheet in the *Revue des Deux Mondes*, and £20 in the English Quarterlies. The *Times* has paid £100 for a certain article. Thackeray, the novelist, has made £160 in twenty-four hours through the medium of two lectures, the one being delivered in Brighton, the other in London; from the magazine to which he contributed his novels he received £2,000 a year, and £10 a page in addition; this magazine had 100,000 subscribers; [30] he estimated his own yearly earnings at £4,800. It must be understood that I put on one side the enormous fortunes made in manufactures, those of the nobility, the profit or revenues of £200,000 yearly; their outlay is proportionate. A young engineer, a younger son, and who was obliged to make his fortune, said to me one day, "With £8,000 yearly one is not wealthy in England, one is merely very comfortably off." Another, who spends his summers in the country, added, "look at the

family circles of our farmers; their daughters learn French and to play on
the piano; they dress splendidly." The rule is to make much and to spend
much: an Englishman does not put anything aside, does not think of the
future, at the most he insures his life; in this he is the reverse of a Frenchman, who is saving and abstemious.

Whence comes all this money, and how is it distributed? I shall endeavour
to procure the statistics; meantime, let us examine one of the great reservoirs
whence gold flows through the people of all conditions, and over the whole
country—the Docks of London.

I always find that London resembles ancient Rome as Paris resembles
ancient Athens. This modern Rome, how heavily must it weigh, like the
other, upon the labouring class! For every monstrous erection, Babylon,
Egypt, imperial Rome, indicates an accumulation of efforts, an excess of
fatigue. I have never seen a great city, whether a capital or place of manufactures, without thinking of the nations which have vanished from around
the Mediterranean under the pressure of the Roman machine. It is true that
to-day there are no more slaves before the law; yet frequently man is a
slave in fact, and by the constraint of his condition.

[31] These docks are prodigious, overpowering; there are six of them
each of which is a vast port, and accommodates a multitude of three-masted
vessels. There are ships everywhere, and ships upon ships in rows, show
their heads and their swelling bosoms, like beautiful fish, under their cuirass
of copper. One of them has arrived from Australia, and is of 2,500 tons
burden, others are 3,000 tons and upwards; some of them hail from all parts
of the world, this is the trysting-place of the globe. For the most part they
are magnificent. Seen from the keel they are leviathans, and they are slender
and as elegant as swans. A merchant who is here superintending the arrival
of spices from Java, and the transhipment of ice from Norway, tells me that
about 40,000 vessels enter every year, and that on an average, there are from
5,000 to 6,000 in the docks or the river at one time.

In the wine quarter the cellars contain 30,000 barrels of port. A crane dis-
charges them. They seem to move of their own accord. When brought on a
little wheeled truck, they slide down an incline to their places, almost without labour. The machines work so well that they appear to be living auxil-
iaries, voluntary slaves. Note that bridge; it weighs a hundred tons; yet one
man moves it by means of a screw-jack. There is a quarter for groceries, a
quarter for skins and leather, a quarter for tallow. The cellars and the warehouses are colossal. Under their arch, equal to that of a large bridge, one
beholds the peopled and profound obscurity recede far away. Rembrandt
would have found ready-made pictures in their mysterious distances, in the
flickering blackness of their choked-up air-holes, in these infinite receptacles
where a hive of men is moving about. They [32] roll the casks without
confusion and with calmness. One hears the voices of clerks calling out the
numbers. In the middle of the cellar a foreman, seated at a small table,
makes entries or looks on. The masters, who are grave, and in black hats,

walk about superintending in silence. Yet around the capstans are creaking, and sailors in boats are scraping or scrubbing their ship. Thus occupied in their working coats, with their serious air, their phlegmatic or wearied faces, they form a pleasing sight; one feels that they are in their right places, every living being, animal or man, is beautiful in his proper place.

I was smoking, seated on a bale, when a man passing along said, without stopping, "Five shillings fine." "Is it forbidden then?" "Yes." Nothing more. There is no better way of working or making others work than to be sparing in gestures or words. At Hyde Park Corner there are two policemen whom I have frequently watched for a considerable time; they never speak; if there be a block of vehicles, they raise their arm to stop a coachman, and lower it as a sign that he may drive on: the coachman instantly and silently obeys. Our steward on board the steamboat, many servants, and merchants whom I have seen, do likewise; when, in giving orders and executing them, chattering, exclamations, tokens of impatience, fumbling, and disorder are thus suppressed, the command and the performance gear into each other as quickly and as surely as two wheels.

At the end of an hour the mind feels itself overstocked; it is requisite to permit the images to group and to arrange themselves. I was at the corner of Shadwell Basin and I gazed upon the slate-coloured river before me shining and exhaling mist; the [33] northern bank winds and bounds the horizon with its blackish fringe mottled with red; a few vessels descend with the supple and slow movement of a sea-bird; their sombre hulls and brown sails balance themselves upon the water which shimmers. To north and south a mass of ships raise their crowded masts. The silence is almost complete; one hears but the strokes of distant hammers, the vague tinkle of a bell, and the fluttering of birds in the trees. A Dutch painter, Van der Heyden, Backhuysen, would have taken pleasure in beholding this plain of water, the distant tones of brick and tar, this uncertain horizon where stretch the sleeping clouds. I have seen nothing more picturesque in London. The rest is too scrubbed and varnished, or too bustling and too foul.

Shadwell, one of the poor neighbourhoods, is close at hand; by the vastness of its distress, and by its extent, it is in keeping with the hugeness and the wealth of London. I have seen the bad quarters of Marseilles, of Antwerp, of Paris, they do not come near to it. Low houses, poor streets of brick under red-tiled roofs cross each other in every direction, and lead down with a dismal look to the river. Beggars, thieves, harlots, the latter especially, crowd Shadwell Street. One hears a grating music in the spirit cellars; sometimes it is a negro who handles the violin; through the open windows one perceives unmade beds, women dancing. Thrice in ten minutes I saw crowds collected at the doors; fights were going on, chiefly fights between women; one of them, her face bleeding, tears in her eyes, drunk, shouted with a sharp and harsh voice, and wished to fling herself upon a man. The bystanders laughed; the noise caused the adjacent lanes to be emptied of their occupants; ragged, poor children, [34] harlots—it was like a human sewer suddenly discharging its contents. Some of them have a relic of neatness, a new garment, but the greater number are in filthy and unseemly tatters. Figure to yourself what a lady's bonnet may become after passing during three or four years from head to head, having been crushed against walls, having had blows from fists; for they receive them. I noticed blackened eyes, bandaged noses, bloody cheek-bones. The women gesticulate with extraordinary vehemence; but most horrible of all is their shrill, acute, cracked voice, resembling that of an ailing screech-owl.

From the time of leaving the Tunnel, street boys abound—bare-footed, dirty, and turning wheels in order to get alms. On the stairs leading to the Thames they swarm, more pale-faced, more deformed, more repulsive than the scum of Paris; without question, the climate is worse, and the gin more deadly. Near them, leaning against the greasy walls, or inert on the steps, are men in astounding rags; it is impossible to imagine before seeing them how many layers of dirt an overcoat or a pair of trousers could hold; they dream or dose open-mouthed, their faces are begrimed, dull, and sometimes streaked with red lines. It is in these localities that families have been discovered with no other bed than a heap of soot; they had slept there during several months. For a creature so wasted and jaded there is but one refuge—drunkenness. "Not drink!" said a desperate character at an inquest. "It were better then to die at once."

A trader said to me, "Look after your pockets, sir," and a policeman warned me not to enter certain lanes.

I walked through some of the broader ones; all the houses, except one or two, are evidently inhabited by [35] harlots. Other small streets, dusty courts, reeking with a smell of rotten rags, are draped with tattered clothes and linen hung up to dry. Children swarm. In a moment, in a narrow court, I saw fourteen or fifteen around me—dirty, barefooted, the little sister carrying a sucking child in her arms, the year-old nursling whose whitish head had no hair. Nothing is more lugubrious than these white bodies, that pale flaxen hair, these flabby cheeks encrusted with old dirt. They press together, they point out the gentleman with curious and eager gestures. The motionless mothers, with an exhausted air, look out at the door. One observes the narrow lodging, sometimes the single room, wherein they are all huddled in the foul air. The houses are most frequently one-storied, low, narrow—a den in which to sleep and die. What a place of residence in winter, when, during weeks of continuous rain and fog, the windows are shut! And in order that this brood may not die of hunger, it is necessary that the father should not drink, should never be idle, should never be sick.

Here and there is a dust-heap. Women are labouring to pick out what is valuable from it. One, old and withered, had a short pipe in her mouth. They stand up amidst the muck to look at me; brutalised, disquieting faces of female Yahoos; perhaps this pipe and a glass of gin is the last idea which floats in their idiotic brain. Should we find there anything else than the instincts and the appetites of a savage and of a beast of burden? A miserable black cat, lean, lame, startled, watches them timidly out of the corner of its eye, and furtively searches in a heap of rubbish. It was possibly right in feeling uneasy. The old woman, muttering, followed it with a look as wild as its own. [36] She seemed to think that two pounds weight of meat were there.

I recall the alleys which run into Oxford Street, stifling lanes, encrusted with human exhalations; troops of pale children nestling on the muddy stairs; the seats on London Bridge, where families, huddled together with drooping heads, shiver through the night; particularly the Haymarket and the Strand in the evening. Every hundred steps one jostles twenty harlots; some of them ask for a glass of gin; others say, "Sir, it is to pay my lodging." This is not debauchery which flaunts itself, but destitution—and such destitution! The deplorable procession in the shade of the monumental streets is sickening; it seems to me a march of the dead. That is a plague-spot—the real plague-spot of English society.

VII, English Marriages and Married Women

[94] A conversation with several Englishmen about marriage; they have lived abroad, and I think them impartial; besides, their statements agree. A young English girl will not marry unless through inclination; she weaves a romance for herself, and this dream forms part of her pride, of her chastity; thus many, and of exalted character, think they have fallen short should they marry without experiencing the enthusiasm suited to an absolute preference. To marry is to abandon oneself wholly and for ever. Witness, with regard to this deep sentiment, the novels by ladies—above all, "John Halifax, Gentleman," and others by the same authoress.* These are the theories of a pure, exclusive mind, which seems to have traversed the whole world without receiving, I will not say a stain, but the shadow of one.

In this romance of the heart, the young girl continues English, that is to say, positive and practical. She does not dream of outpourings, of sentimental walks, hand-in-hand in the moonlight, but of her share in an undertaking. She wishes to be the helper, the useful partner of her husband in his long journeys, in his difficult enterprises, in all his affairs whether [95] wearying or dangerous. Such, for example, were Mrs. Livingstone and Lady Baker;† the one traversed Africa from side to side; the other went to the sources of the Nile, and narrowly escaped dying in consequence. I have seen an English Bishop of a large island, a country of beasts and cannibals; his poor wife carried on her countenance the marks of that terrible climate. A young

* This was Dinah Marie Mulock (1826-1887), whose novels were idealized portrayals of middle-class life.
† The second wife of Sir Samuel Baker, a famous traveller, hunter and explorer, accompanied him most of the way on a three-year expedition up the Nile between 1861 and 1865. She was not an Englishwoman, but a Hungarian.

girl of the neighbourhood, rich and of good family, is at this moment making her preparations, packing up her piano, &c.; the gentleman she is about to marry will take her to Australia; she will return once only in five or six years to kiss her old parents. Another young lady of twenty-four, very weak and delicate; her husband is in the Punjab (£6,000 of salary, £1,200 for the expenses of his establishment); she has been for two years in Europe with an affection of the throat, which will return as soon as she returns to India; four young children; they are sent to Europe before they are two years old; the Indian climate kills them; there are here entire boarding schools recruited by these little Anglo-Indians. Very often a lady, daughter of a marquis or baronet, having a dowry of £3,000 or £3,250, marries a simple gentleman, and descends of her own free will from a state of fortune, of comfort, of society, into a lower or much inferior grade. She accustoms herself to this. The reverse of the medal is the fishery for husbands. Worldly and vulgar characters do not fail in this respect; certain young girls use and abuse their freedom in order to settle themselves well. A young man, rich and noble, is much run after. Being too well received, flattered, tempted, provoked, he becomes suspicious and remains on his guard. This is not the case in France; the young girls are too closely [96] watched to make the first advance; there the game never becomes the sportsman. Commonly, the dowries are very small. I have been told of several families in which the eldest son has one or two hundred thousand pounds sterling; the daughters receive from three to five thousand. However, in order to marry, it is necessary that they should feel a passion. Many do not marry in consequence of a thwarted inclination, and continue to live with their eldest brother. Every Englishman has a bit of romance in his heart with regard to marriage; he pictures a home with the wife of his choice, domestic talk, children; there his little universe is enclosed, all his own; so long as he does not have it he is dissatisfied, being in this matter the reverse of a Frenchman, to whom marriage is generally an end, a makeshift. Frequently he is obliged to wait, especially if a younger son, because he has not sufficient as yet wherewith to maintain his wife. He goes to India, to Australia, labours with all his might, returns, and marries; here the passions are tenacious and deep. When an Englishman is in love, one of my entertainers said to me, he is capable of anything. Thackeray has very well marked the intensity and the persistence of this sentiment in his portrait of Major Dobbin, the lover of Amelia, in "Vanity Fair"; he waits fifteen years without hope, because for him there is but one woman in the world. This causes silent rendings of the heart and long inner tragedies. Numbers of young men experience it; and the protracted chastity, the habits of taciturn concentration, a capacity for emotion greater and less scattered than among us, carries their passions to the extreme. Frequently it ends in nothing, because they are not beloved or because the disparity of rank is [97] too great, or because they have not money enough wherewith to maintain a family—a very costly thing here. Then they become half insane; travel to distract their minds, proceed to the ends of the earth. One who was mentioned to me, very distinguished, was supplanted by a titled rival; during two years apprehensions were felt for his reason. He went to China and to Australia; at present he occupies a high post, he has been made a baronet, he presides over important business, but he is unmarried; from time to time he steals off, makes a journey on foot, in order to be alone and not to have any one to converse with.

I have previously noted that young people see and associate together in perfect freedom, without being watched, they can thus study and understand each other as much as they please; for four months, for five months and more, they ride on horseback and chat together during several successive seasons in the country. When the young man has made up his mind it is to the young girl that he addresses himself first, asking the consent of the parents in the second place; this is the opposite of the French custom, where the man would consider it indelicate to utter a single clear or vague phrase to the young girl before having spoken to her parents. In this matter the English find fault with us, ridicule our marriages summarily settled before a lawyer. Yet C———, who is English, and knows France well, allows that their love-matches end more than once in discord and our marriages of arrangement in concord. The wife's dowry is nearly always placed in the hands of trustees, who take charge of it on their own responsibility, handing over the interest only to the family; in general this income is the wife's pin-money: with it [98] she must dress herself and dress her children. The fortune becomes thus a kind of dotal or paraphernalia fund, secured against the accidents which may happen to the husband. This precaution is taken, because, according to law, all the wife's property is engulfed in that of the husband; without this clause, she would enter the married state deprived of all share in the common fund; she can hold nothing in her own right; she is a simple infant in presence of her husband. Such is one of the reasons inducing Mr. J. Stuart Mill * to protest so vigorously against the subjection of women. In fact they are kept in subjection here by the law, religion, manners, and much more closely so than among us. The husband is their lord, and very often he accepts the title seriously; as the wife brings but little money into the establishment, and as her small share remains apart, he thinks himself authorised to say nothing to her about his concerns. Sometimes she is unacquainted with what he does, how he makes the money which he acquires; he gives so much monthly for the household expenses, and renders no account of the rest. Whether he speculates, builds, sells, or buys, is none of her business: frequently ruin arrives without her being able to foresee it. She is merely a housekeeper; she must not busy herself about anything save her household and her children. Most frequently she contents herself with that part; owing to her conscience and education she is gentle and submissive. Nevertheless, on the avowal of my friends, this inequality has grave inconveniences; the husband is often a despot, and should he die, the wife,

* John Stuart Mill (1806-1873), English essayist and political liberal, who advocated women's rights.

kept all her life in ignorance and dependence, is not capable, as with us, of clearing up the affairs, of governing the children, of replacing the head of the family. . . .

[106] . . . The person to whom one presents a letter of introduction does not consider himself quits by an invitation to dinner; he gives you information, acts as your guide, traces out your plan, charges himself with occupying and amusing you, takes you to his Club, introduces you to his friends, takes you to his [107] parents, introduces you to his set of acquaintances, invites you to visit him at his country house, and gives you other letters of introduction when you take your departure; you end by saying to him, "This is too much; I shall never be able to make a return in Paris for what you have done for me here." The like reception is met with among those to whom you have been introduced in the second place, and the same in succession; sometimes, after an hour's conversation, the gentleman whom you see for the first time books you to come and spend a week at his country seat. Should you go, you will be treated as a member of the family. Still more striking is the opening of the heart; frequently at the end of one or two days a gentleman does not hesitate to tell you about his private affairs. I requested information concerning domestic matters. Sometimes my host, in order to be precise, told me the amount of his income, of his expenses, the amount of his rent, the history of his fortune, of his family, of his marriage, a quantity of minor domestic and personal facts. Persons in society are more reticent in France.

We seek for the causes of this difference; the following is a summary of them:—The Englishman is hospitable; 1st. On account of weariness: most of the persons in society live in the country for eight months of the year; sometimes at a distance from a town, and very solitarily; they have need of conversation, new ideas. 2nd. As an effect of social customs; in London they scarcely speak; they live moving about; they remain too short a time, sometimes less than three months; there is too great a crowd, and too much to do; the country-house is the true drawing-room, the place for associating together. [108] 3rd. As an effect of domestic habits; many children, many servants; in a well-appointed great house order and a certain reserve are indispensable; the habitual stoicism of characters and manners operates in the same sense. Then, the presence of a stranger does not have the result, as among us, of interrupting acquaintanceship, stopping the general impulse, the gaiety, the chit-chat, compelling people to be on their guard, to restrain their familiarity and heedlessness. There is only another chair filled at table, in the drawing-room, nothing more; the tone has not changed. 4th. By the arrangement for comfort and the service: the organisation is perfect, and the machine in order; the domestics are punctual, the rooms ready, the hours fixed; there is nothing to undo or do over again; nor, above all, is there any makeshift required to entertain a visitor. 5th. By kindliness, humanity, and even by conscience; to be useful is a duty, and a foreigner is so thoroughly lost, so little at his ease in the new country where he has landed! He ought to be helped.

VIII, English Households.

[109] This leads to a consideration of the interiors. Rule and discipline are more strongly felt therein than among us. In this department, as in the others, the meshes of the social net-work are loosened in France and tightly drawn in England.

I have three households in view; in the one are seven domestics, cook and scullery maid, two housemaids, lady's maid, coachman, valet; in the second, fifteen; in the third, eighteen. A man servant has from £40 to £50 wages, and, if he be on board wages, which is common enough in London, twelve shillings a week are added for his board. Each has his post rigorously defined. The work is divided, no one either trespasses on, or trusts to another. For example, in the last of the houses which I have just cited, there is a special man for sweeping, carrying coal, lighting and keeping up the fires. There are two classes of servants, the lower and the upper, the latter are responsible and transmit the master's orders; at their head is the butler for the men, and the head lady's maid for the women; if a groom should appear with a dirty coat, his master says nothing to him, but reprimands the butler. These [110] upper servants are a species of sergeants, who have an opinion and the authority of their position: defined distribution of employment, hierarchy of powers constitute the leading traits of a workable organisation. And the latter traits complete the former. These servants stand on their dignity; they will enter none but a respectable mansion. S——, requiring to add a housemaid to his staff, thought of a country girl, who, not having been married, had a child; but before taking her, he placed the matter before his servants. They consulted together, and, owing to the good character given of her, admitted the poor girl among them. Generally their manners are correct, though many are young, unmarried, and under the same roof; in S——'s whole life but one accident had happened in his house. On the other hand they do their work conscientiously, with perfect punctuality and regularity, at the appointed time, without fail; they have a watchword which they obey to the letter. However, it appears as if the machine works of its own accord; the masters have scarcely any need to interfere; on this head S—— maintains again that at bottom, in an Englishman, there is the sense of duty, that this sentiment reigns in the kitchen and the ante-chamber as well as in the ship or the workshop, that none other reconciles the subordinate with subordination. Two circumstances concur in alleviating it. The servants retain their share of independence, and they cleave to it. In London many of them have a club, an association whereof the members agree not to continue longer than two consecutive years in the same house; this is in order to leave less power to the masters. Moreover, as their hours are regulated, they are their own masters during the intervals of their service. They [111] have their hall, a large room wherein they take their meals and sit. In the house of which I spoke, their dinner and their breakfast are served half an hour before those of their masters. They have a small library for their use, draughts, chess; after dinner they may go out; one only is kept to answer the bell. In order to obtain much, too much must not be demanded; he who commands must provide for the physical and moral welfare of his subordinates. If he desire the obedience of the heart, he must be their leader, a true chief, a general and responsible official, the accepted and authorised governor of their conduct. In this respect, on Sunday evening, he is their spiritual guide, their chaplain; they may be seen entering in a row, the women in front, the men behind, with seriousness, gravity, and taking their places in the drawing-room. The family and visitors are assembled. The master reads aloud a short sermon; next a prayer; then everyone kneels or bends forward, the face turned towards the wall; lastly, he repeats the Lord's Prayer, and, clause by clause, the worshippers respond. This done, the servants file off, returning in the same order, silently, meditatively. I have observed them several times—not a muscle of their countenance moved. By this community and direction of the moral sentiment, the master succeeds in filling his true place. In France he is very far from possessing in his house, amongst his servants, and even amongst his children, legitimate authority and entire authority. I note at once the inconvenience, the opposite side. In the habitual commerce of life the English are not easygoing; conditions among them are separated by a barrier, and in place of making a passage through it, they strew it with thorns. For example, Mr. N———, an [112] Englishman settled in France, chose a French tutor for his children. At the end of a month Mrs. N——— ceased to find him to her taste, spoke no more to him, communicated with him by letters only. One evening in the drawing-room, Mr. N——— went to sleep, and Mrs. N——— began to read. The young man not daring to take up a book, and not being able to converse with any one, ended, after many struggles, by going to sleep also. Next day she said to him, in a dry and arbitrary tone, "Sir, your conduct last evening was very improper; I hope that it will not be repeated." Some days afterwards a young lady being invited with whom he was acquainted, he went and seated himself next to her at table. Mrs. N——— said aloud to him, "Sir, that is not your place; come and sit beside your pupil." He refused, left the table, quitted the house, and demanded, according to agreement, a year's salary. This was refused. A lawsuit followed. Mr. N——— was defeated. This recalls an anecdote of the last century. Lord A——— having engaged a French tutor, advised him not to speak anything but French to his children. "I am charmed, my lord, to find that you lay such store on that tongue." "Sir, we despise it, but we wish that in France our children should know how to speak as well as the natives." One can picture the smiling, effusive air of the Frenchman in quest of a compliment, and the immovable features, the haughty tone of the Englishman, who returns him a slap in the face.

The post of governesses in England is not a pleasant one; witness on this head the novels of Charlotte Bronte. The majority of those I have seen, had assumed a wooden face; nothing is more surprising when such a face is youthful. The tone, the demeanour, [113] the whole is artificial and made to order; composed and maintained in such a way as never to give an opening; even after several days of familiarity, and out of the house in which they teach, they remain on the defensive; the habit of self-observation and of control is too strong; one might say they were soldiers on parade. As to the servants, their expression of humble and subdued respect greatly surpasses that of those whom we can have known; it is even unpleasant to observe this attitude of a man face to face with a man.

There is the same fund of stiffness in the intercourse of relations. A son when speaking familiarly of his father, says, my governor. In fact, by law and custom, he is the governor of his house, which is his castle, and of the garrison that lodges there. Except in the case of an entail, he can disinherit his children, and it has been seen that his wife is subject to him. Mr. W———, a rich landed proprietor, and a gentleman of the old school, has, among other children, a son in consumption. The poor young man, who returned from Nice and felt himself dying, stopped at Boulogne; he wished to end his days with his father, in the house wherein he was born; but he neither durst go thither without being invited, nor even ask permission. His mother, who is ill and wishes to embrace her son again, dare not take upon herself to rejoin him. At length, one of these days, he received a letter from his father, and set off on his journey. The inequality of positions is another cause of coldness. Between the eldest son, who will be a nobleman with an income of £8,000 a year, and the younger son, who will have £200 a year, who inhabits two furnished rooms, and spends the day in a machine shop in order to become an engineer, the distance is too great; real familiarity, fellowship, is [114] impossible. Even when similarly educated they feel their separation. Two brothers were mentioned to me who were both at the University of Oxford, but the elder brother had one hundred pounds sterling a year more than the younger. Final cause of division is the independence of the children: a son, a daughter, can mary without their parents' consent, and very often exercise this right; hence occur squabbles which last a lifetime. Meantime, the father knows that his child can leave him, run directly counter to his will in the most mortifying manner. Frequently he says: "Since you have the right, you must take the consequences." Reasoning thus, many, above all those who have a legion of children, do not trouble themselves about marrying their daughters; they leave that to them; it is their business, as it is the business of the sons to gain a livelihood. That differs greatly from our homes, where the parents give themselves up wholly and without restriction to their children, where the elder sons, the younger sons, the brothers and the sisters are so equal among each other, and almost on a footing of equality with their parents, the familiarity and the intimacy being so complete, where each one considers it natural to enter, every day and at every hour, by their questions and their counsels, into the thoughts, the sentiments, the actions of their relatives, where nothing is enclosed nor reserved, where every mind is disclosed, opened by an hundred thousand apertures to the curiosity and to the sympathy of his kindred.

The English are surprised at this; S——— greatly admires our sociability in this particular, our kindly character. He has often seen in France two or three families together under the same roof and at the same table, during six months in the country, sometimes [115] the entire year in the country, in town; at one time two married brothers, at another the parents with their son-in-law and their daughter, or with their son and their daughter-in-law. Nothing is rarer than this in England. Characters clash; each family requires to possess its independence as well as its abode. We coalesce, we hold everything in common; as for them, even when living together, they maintain distinctions, they draw lines of demarcation. Self is more powerful; each of them preserves a portion of his individuality, his own special and personal nook, a kind of forbidden field, enclosed, respected by every one, even by the brother and the father, even by the sister, even by the mother; to enter it would be an intrusion; no one gains admission, save perhaps the beloved person, the husband, the wife, to whom all one's life is pledged. This reserved circle is larger or smaller according to the personages. It includes at one time business matters, questions of money and of ambition, at another certain profound sentiments, a hope, a love disappointment, an old and protracted mourning, at another intimate and lofty ideas, for instance religious beliefs; sometimes it embraces them all; then the personage is tongue-tied, and does not like to be spoken to. But in every case the line he has traced around him remains intact; he does not overstep it when unreserved. If over-leapt by any one, it is owing to an indiscretion which cuts him to the quick; his relatives abstain from doing so as they would from housebreaking. Thus a father or mother is more imperfectly informed than among us as to the sentiments of their daughter, as to the business and the pleasures of their son.

[116] To make this obvious, would require too lengthened detail. I shall cite but one trait. In France a son tells his mother everything, even about his mistresses; the usage is ancient. Madame de Sevigné received from her son secrets which she related to her daughter—very improper and very distinct secrets—and which she was only able to express, owing to her verve, her gaiety, her wonderful lightness of touch. Even at the present day, without going so far back, very many young men make similar avowals to their mothers, or at least hint—allow them to suspect, an affair of gallantry. The mothers are not scandalised at this, they are too happy to be made confidants, almost companions. They scold a little, smile faintly, and, lifting the finger, send away the naughty fellow, telling him to take care. B——— is of opinion that this is impossible in England; the son would not dare do it, the

mother would be shocked or indignant. So in other matters; they have no acquaintance with these boundless conversations, these complete outpourings, where the differences in age compensate for the difference of sex, where the son entering the world finds in his mother separating herself from the world his most skilful guide and his most thorough friend.

These habits of reserve lead to a kind of stoicism. Even among their kindred they are not expansive, they are self-restrained. In a family which has lost a very near relative, a father, a son, there are never cries nor outbursts. From the morrow every one comes down, taking their places at table at the ordinary hour, and in the same manner; they merely talk rather less than their wont; it is all very well to feel sorrow, they have to do their work, whatever it be, as well and as [117] conscientiously as before. When the Queen, after Prince Albert's death, shut herself up alone and appeared to have given up the receptions and other occupations of her post, the newspapers, after allowing several months to elapse, began to blame her, and declared to her that a private loss did not absolve anyone from public obligations. A writer in the *National Review* praises Eugenie de Guérin,* so pure and so melancholy; but, according to him, she is wrong in giving expression to her sadness and even in being sad. "An Englishwoman of right and healthy mind would consider cheerfulness a duty in itself, and would refrain from expressing distaste for life." I have badly translated the word "cheerfulness" (*gaîeté*), being unable to render it; it means the opposite of dejection, a sort of smiling serenity. . . .

[118] . . . Amid all this, I think, two things are visible; the one is the native and acquired energy, the force of [119] character by which a man masters himself, always keeps himself in check, is self-sufficing, risks and resists misfortune, sorrow, and disappointment; the other is the institution of a hierarchy which, even in private life, upholds inequality, subordination, authority, and order. But there is the reverse of every medal. As far as I can judge this character and this system of rule produce many tyrants, louts, mutes, down-trodden and eccentric persons. A certain number of homes resemble that of the Harlowe family in Richardson; but on that head an observer's mouth is closed. I send the reader to the pictures of George Eliot, of Dickens, and of Thackeray; see in particular in Thackeray the portraits of Lord Steyne, of Barnes Newcome, of Lady Kew, of old Osborne, and of the step-mother of Clive Newcome.

* A woman author (1805-48) who mourned her brother's death and published his writings posthumously.

from

London Dinners

Thomson Hankey

THOMSON HANKEY (1805-1893) was an economist and member of Parliament who began his career by working in his father's import firm. He served as a director of the Bank of England for about fifteen years, and became its governor for a year before running for Parliament. During his active government career, Hankey wrote a number of lectures and papers on political and economic subjects. This gentle protest against the excesses of London dining customs is his only venture into other fields of writing.

From MACMILLAN'S MAGAZINE, vol. XXV, March, 1872, pp. 370-375.

. . . [371] In this country, where people do not converse freely with each other without an introduction, any foreigner should be specially introduced by host or hostess; and the only good reason which can be given for not doing the same to every guest, is that in our vast London society, those may be inadvertently asked together, who have been trying to avoid each other all their lives, and then an introduction becomes awkward. A little arrangement is of course necessary as to sending down the right ladies and gentlemen together, and also as to seating them properly at table, so that husbands and wives, brothers and sisters, &c., are not placed next to each other; and for want of this previous forethought the best assorted parties are sometimes quite spoiled. Having begun with the assumption that parties of fourteen or sixteen are best suited for the size of ordinary London dining-rooms, as well as for conversation, the number of attendants upon such a party must of course be regulated by the fortune of the entertainer; but to ensure perfect attendance, one servant to every three guests is about the necessary number. . . .

[374] I am told that at Buckingham Palace her Majesty's dinners are entirely concluded within the hour; but it must be remembered that the Queen's habits in this particular appear to have been formed without much reference to social requirements. Her Majesty partakes of a good luncheon and tea, and makes her dinner a short meal.

To return, however, to my subject of considering dinners as a means of promoting social intercourse in its most agreeable form. No one can deny the importance which is attached to this subject in London society, when it is remembered the infinite trouble taken by many in the arrangement of the company to be asked as well as in the decoration of the table, and other matters connected with the entertainment. Much pains are bestowed, and much money spent, in endeavouring to give agreeable dinners, and both are often thrown away by an attempt to do too much. Nothing is more true than the old saw of "enough is as good as a feast." More food than anyone can enjoy, more wit than anyone can listen to, are alike to be avoided. People are often so much exhausted by the heated atmosphere of a dining-room, and by long sitting during and after a protracted dinner, that conversation languishes when the adjournment to the drawing-room takes place, and the only anxiety is to get away either to some fresh scene of overcrowded amusement, or to bed, worn out instead of refreshed by the so-called evening's entertainment. It is to be hoped that hereafter the custom may be adopted, which obtains everywhere but amongst the Anglo-Saxon race, of ladies and gentlemen leaving the table together; so that conversation may go on without a break, and the grouping of gentlemen in one part of the room and ladies in another be avoided. It also enables those who wish to go elsewhere, to leave at an earlier hour—which is of more consequence, however, with foreign habits than with our own. Abroad people visit in the evening when they wish to find their friends at home, and thus avoid a great amount of card leaving and loss of time. I heard the present American Minister, General Schenck, observe that London visiting might be arranged more effectually and economically (as to time) by a system of visiting-clearing-houses, one for each district; boxes, like post-office letter-boxes, bearing the names of all one's acquaintance being arranged round a room, with a key belonging to the respective families, into which cards or invitations could be dropped, the boxes [375] to be emptied each day by some one sent from each family. Our Transatlantic brethren are certainly far ahead of us in practical suggestions, and might perhaps give us valuable hints upon the subject of the present article, as well as upon the art of visiting, or rather card leaving. In this country it is difficult to prevent politics from forming too large a portion of conversation; the addition of music or cards in the evening tends to prevent this, and to give a fair chance of amusement for all tastes.

A few words before I conclude, about the arrangements of the dinner-table. Although a dining-room should be well lighted throughout, the brightest spot, the high light of the picture, should be the table itself. Wax candles are the most perfectly unobjectionable mode of lighting, the most pleasing to the eyes, and without the distress to the organs of smell which may arise from lamps. Small shades upon the candles throw the light upon the cloth and table, and prevent any glare upon the eyes. Gas light is to many quite intolerable, at least as managed in England, for it frequently produces a feeling of weight on the head, and general discomfort, even if discomfort to the olfactory organs can be avoided. The present fashion of flower decoration is extremely pretty, and can be carried out without any great expense if bright colours and general effect are more considered than mere cost. All table ornaments should be kept low, so as not to intercept the view of any one by all the other guests. For the number of dishes for a party of twelve or sixteen, I recommend the Russian *menu* No. 3.

Having now gone through what seem to me the defects of the present system of London dinners, and pointed out some of the remedies, thinking that most people admit that some reform is desirable, I must leave the matter in the hands of those able and willing to head the great reform movement. A clever author who has written upon the art of "putting things," says that if you want to commend a subject to a Tory leader, you talk of it as a sovereign remedy; if to a Whig, you call it a radical improvement, so that in my wishing to please all parties I have been perhaps injudicious in calling a diminution of the hours and the quantity of food at dinners, a reform movement. A moderate constitutional change would best express what I want.

The question now is, who is to bell the cat, who is bold enough to reform the present system by shortening the hours and decreasing the quantity of food at our London dinners? Will the movement originate on the Liberal side? I remember hearing a remark made by a gentleman in the House of Commons, whose eyes were directed from the front bench on the Conservative to the Liberal side, "Is it possible that a ministry formed by those men can stand? I do not believe they have a cook amongst them who can dress a good dinner." If this be so, we must look elsewhere. Is there no lady of high rank, no Baring or no Rothschild, who with cooks about whose merits there can be no difference of opinion, will set an example of constitutional reform in this matter by—

1st. Limiting the number of guests to twelve or fourteen;

2nd. Keeping the dining-room cool and well-ventilated;

3rdly. Sitting down to dinner at 8.15 without waiting for guests who may be absent;

4th. Returning to the drawing-room by 9.30 to 9.45;

5th. Reducing the present number of dishes?

If this were done, London dinners might be, what they ought to be, from the materials to be collected in London society—the most agreeable reunions in the world; and much useless expense would be avoided, so that these entertainments might be within reach of even very moderate fortunes, and our nation be rescued from the reproach so often cast upon us by foreigners, of preferring quantity to quality, and a large party to a sociable and lively dinner. A French gentleman once said to me, "En Angleterre on se nourrit bien, mais on ne dîne pas." *

* "In England one is well nourished, but one does not *dine*."

SUGGESTED TOPICS FOR RESEARCH

Entertainment
Poverty and Social Reform
Transportation
Characteristics of the English
Crime, Crime Prevention and the Law
Industries and Occupations
Home Life and the Family
The Role of Women
Attitudes toward Courtship and Marriage
Clubs
Food and Dining Customs
Theaters
Parks
Street Life
Social Classes and Class Distinctions
Foreigners Evaluate English Customs
Appearance and Atmosphere of London

PRELIMINARY RESEARCH TOPICS

Before embarking on a full-length research paper, it is often useful to write a shorter paper of about 500 words, making use of information from research sources. Papers of this sort give the beginning student practice in finding information, fitting it together, and writing appropriate footnotes. The student should be asked to find material on such subjects as the following by consulting at least three of the different sources in the booklet, and to report on his findings in a fully-documented short paper.

What occupations could women pursue in earning a living? Give at least three.
What occupations could children pursue?

What functions did the men's clubs perform?
What were London policemen like?
What was the extent of alcoholism among Londoners?
Is there any evidence to show that criminality was common among children?
How active was London as a port?
How pleasant or efficient were the London cabs?
What was Covent Garden?
What visitors reported that Londoners were rude?
What visitors reported that they were exceptionally courteous?
What different types of theaters existed?
What methods of transportation were available?

BACKGROUND STUDIES

These topics suggest ways in which the material in the selections may be used to amplify some of the Dickens novels most likely to be read in English courses.

Oliver Twist
Learning to be a criminal.
The daily life and customs of Sikes and Nancy.
Great Expectations
The life of a London gentleman, such as Pip hoped to become.
The problems and methods of a criminal lawyer like Jaggers.
The Thames and its traffic.
Social differences between Joe Gargery and his former apprentice.
David Copperfield
The home life of the Murdstones.
The boy David discovers London.
The home life of the Micawbers.
David's courtship and marriage: a social diagnosis.
Bleak House
Law and justice in the London courts.
Jo as a representative figure.
Mr. Tulkinghorn as a representative middle-class Englishman.
The social problem represented by Tom-All-Alone's.
Inspector Bucket and his methods and problems.
The Dedlocks and their way of life.

BIBLIOGRAPHY

This book contains enough material for short research papers on the suggested topics, and students will undoubtedly be able to frame topics of their own on the basis of the texts that have been reprinted. However, this short bibliography is supplied for readers who want additional sources of information or general discussions of Dickens and his London.

1. FIRST-HAND MATERIAL.

Adams, Henry, *The Education of Henry Adams*
Besant, Walter, *Fifty Years Ago*, London, 1888
Carlyle, Thomas, *Past and Present*
Cobbett, William, *Rural Rides*
Hawthorne, Nathaniel, *English Note-Books*
Massingham, Hugh and Pauline, *The London Anthology*, London, 1950
Masson, David, *Memories of London in the Forties*, Edinburgh and London, 1908
Thackeray, William Makepeace, *Sketches and Travels*
Timbs, John, *Clubs and Club Life in London*, London, 1872

2. SECONDARY MATERIAL.

Addison, William, *In the Steps of Charles Dickens*, London, 1955
British Broadcasting Corporation, *Ideas and Beliefs of the Victorians*, London, n.d.
Besant, Walter, *London in the Nineteenth Century*, London, 1909
Cruikshank, R. J., *Charles Dickens and Early Victorian England*, London, 1949
Dodds, John W., *The Age of Paradox; a Biography of England, 1841-1851*, New York, 1952
Hobhouse, Christopher, *1851 and the Crystal Palace*, New York, 1937
Houghton, Walter E., *The Victorian Frame of Mind, 1830-1870*, New Haven, 1957
House, Humphry, *The Dickens World*, New York, London, Toronto, 1941
Johnson, Edgar, *Charles Dickens: His Tragedy and Triumph*, New York, 1952
Young, G. M., *Early Victorian England*, London, 1934